AF333487

Hermann Röchling:
The Factory of the Third Reich

Margaret Manale

Hermann Röchling: The Factory of the Third Reich

Max Milo

Max Milo, Paris, 2023
www.maxmilo.com
ISBN: 9782315012091

"This is not about hatred or politics, but simply about one who - without being forced to - took an active part in the direction of the greatest banditry enterprise of all times and, as in 1916 and 1917, took advantage of the war of aggression to enrich himself by looting the invaded countries."

Paul-Julien Doll, magistrate
Plea, "Röchling" trial, Rastatt, 1948

Note on translations

The Röchling trials in Rastatt were conducted in both languages, French and German, and all documents presented before the Tribunal were translated, and the translations were excellent. Consequently, we have used them whenever a document in German is involved. The documents collected in the archives but not used in the proceedings have been translated by the author, as have the newspaper articles of the time, the speeches of Hermann Röchling and the quotations from secondary literature, in English and German.

What history for what present?

Who was Hermann Röchling? His story, and that of the Röchling family, bears the imprint of a century of conflicting relations between France and Germany. This story takes us back even before the 1870 war: the Röchlings, owners since 1856 in Pont-à-Mousson, in Meurthe-et-Moselle, contributed to the development of the forges that were to be the pride of the French steel industry. After the annexation of Alsace-Lorraine, which became the *Reichsland Elsaß-Lothringen*, they settled in Thionville, *Diedenhofen*, in the heart of this now German Lorraine, and sold their shares in the Pont-à-Mousson steelworks to one of the partners, the French industrialist Xavier Rogé. However, in the Lorraine region that remained French, they managed to obtain iron ore concessions under the guise of a limited company. The Great War broke out, and Hermann Röchling went to the front lines, using his connections in the military to plunder French competitors for the benefit of the Thionville and Völklingen forges. The defeat and the Treaty of Versailles marked a pause: the Moselle assets were returned to France and, in 1919, Hermann Röchling was prosecuted for war crimes, which would be repeated after the Second World War. He was sentenced in absentia to ten years of imprisonment, a ten-year ban on entering French territory and a ten million franc fine. But, as a sign of the times that heralded the aftermath of another war, he avoided prison by being appointed by the German government as an expert to the armistice commission.

Henceforth, the desire for revenge did not leave him and he rallied to Hitler from the start and without reserve. However, he waited for the return of the Saar to the Reich to join the NSDAP, only officially taking out his card in February 1939. He thought that this movement, ready to do anything to erase the "stab in the back" of the Treaty of Versailles, had the future ahead of it, and that its triumph could bring revenge and make his own interests and those of his family business prosper. His dream was to become reality: he ranked among the notables of the Nazi party and became an intimate adviser to certain government dignitaries, in particular to his friend, the minister Albert Speer. An absolute master of the Lorraine steel industry until the collapse, he would stop at nothing to support the National Socialist war effort, and he exercised such power over the entire Reich and the occupied territories that the Americans saw him as the "tsar" of the German industrial machine. Thus, what was the smallest company in the iron and steel sector was destined for a grandiose destiny. However, the war would once again bring our captain of industry back to a less exciting reality!

Second defeat, second appearance before the war tribunals charged with prosecuting the leaders of Nazism! Hermann Röchling, who had done everything to ensure the Reich's victory and who could not have been unaware of the extermination policy implemented by the Nazis, found himself, in 1948, before an international tribunal in Rastatt. Sentenced to ten years in prison, he was released two years later: because of the Cold War, the Western governments granted amnesty to all the magnates of German industry, whom they expected to serve their cause in return.

One would think that the career of this character, emblematic of a certain industrial elite and who occupied a special place in the

National Socialist system, would not go unnoticed. And yet: in the imposing literature devoted to the history of the two world wars, the rise of Nazism and the trials of war criminals, Hermann Röchling is rarely mentioned!

***

It was through the Internet, during a visit to the Unesco website, that we learned of the existence of this dynasty of iron barons and of their forgotten, even obscured, history. What was initially far from our concerns ended up in the foreground, and it does not seem wrong to assume that all our research should lead us to the "Röchling affair" and at the same time to ask some questions about historiography in the digital age.

What had been the fate of the abandoned industrial sites in eastern Germany, in the lands of the former GDR plagued by unemployment and deserted by the younger generation? Given the importance of "brands" or "labels" for the promotion of tourism in cities, especially in de-industrialized regions, one was led to wonder whether any former East German industrial site was entitled to the prestigious status of "cultural heritage of humanity" awarded by UNESCO. None was listed, so we turned the question around: had any abandoned industrial complex, anywhere in Germany or elsewhere, ever been granted this status? Only one, from the golden age of modern industry: the former forges and steelworks in Völklingen, Saarland, listed in 1994. And we will learn later that, for almost a century, these factories were known under the name "Röchling'sche Eisen- und Stahlwerke" (RESW)!

Given the number of factories and plants in the East that have been shut down since the fall of the Wall to comply with the requirements

What history for what present?

of the market economy, it was surprising that the label was awarded to an industrial site in western Germany. The evaluation file, published by Unesco on its website, provides information on the criteria used by the experts: the "intrinsic value" - a term borrowed from stock market language! - The "intrinsic value" - a term borrowed from the language of the stock market - of this ensemble comes from its "uniqueness", that is to say that we have here an exceptional place, the only ironworks of the 19th and 20th centuries which, "in the whole of the Western European and North American world", would have remained intact after its recent closure. Clearly, this inscription of one of the jewels of modern technology as a "place of memory of humanity [*sic*]" implicitly excludes any legacy from the countries of the former "Soviet bloc" from consideration. The same fate is reserved for the social memory of these factories, and the name of Carl Röchling, founder of this dynasty of iron barons, who bought the first installations in 1881, is barely mentioned. The highlighting of this industrial complex, which has now been declared a "cultural heritage of humanity", is about the technique, not the technician.

Such a case of Western ethnocentrism - in the narrowest sense - is not without problems for the historian and ethnologist. Here, the universal has been manufactured from a well-defined territory. The lesson is hardly implied: such a model, which combines technology and democracy, is necessarily representative of the contributions, civilizing by essence, of the West, of Western Europe or North America, and it has value of reference for the whole of humanity. So let us not expect the industrial relics of Eastern Europe to pose as rivals in order to be erected as symbols of excellence and technical innovation!

But why such discretion around the name of Röchling, when Unesco celebrates in its own way this family of engineers whose degree of technicality and competence is a guarantee of progress in our world? A search for the keyword "Röchling" on the Internet leads us to the contents of a sub-file kept in the National Archives, whose title offers a clue to explain this discretion: "BB 36. The Röchling trial before the military tribunal of the French occupation zone in Germany in Rastatt." This short document briefly describes the set of files on the "Röchling case" from the holdings of the Ministry of Justice, i.e. a shelf of 23 linear meters covering a period dating back to the Great War! But as incriminating as the materials it lists may be, this inventory is a simple research tool, and it can hardly serve as a counterweight to the history of the Röchling dynasty, which is displayed elsewhere on the web as a glorious page dedicated to the Völklingen factories, a Unesco world heritage site.

Better still, all we know about Hermann Röchling is what his hagiographers have told us. No wonder: the "Röchling affair" is hushed up, so that nothing is known about the war criminal's achievements, and nothing about the relationship between economy and politics during the war. The story on the web allows self-interested managers to boast that they are in charge of a heritage that is presented as "one of the most fascinating places in the world".

***

Since Nuremberg, the so-called "primacy of politics" thesis has dominated the historiography of National Socialism. For the American government, the trials had sufficiently highlighted the responsibility of German industrial magnates in the crimes of the Third Reich. And thanks to the intervention of the same American authorities, the steel industrialists, Flick, Krupp, Röchling, were all pardoned in the early 1950s, and their property in western Germany was returned to them. As the new Federal Germany was to be at the center of the Western defense program against the Soviet bloc, the European construction promised Federal Germany the protection of its interests, its borders... and thus its companies. With the Franco-German reconciliation, the compromising traces of the past are being erased and academic research must accommodate this reserve. The role of Hermann Röchling in the centuries-old conflictual history of these two nations and peoples is forgotten. Similarly, the publication in 1982 of Matthias Schmidt's damning thesis, *The End of a Myth,* on the true role of Albert Speer, will go almost unnoticed.

Of course, today, posterity knows nothing of the executioners in their daily practices, but there remains a gap: the study of the "Final Solution" from the point of view of those who planned it, who organized the genocidal apparatus and ensured that the industry met the needs of the work of extermination. Since these great masters of industry did not have to intervene in the field, they never appear as those directly responsible, even though it was they who planned the organization of the genocide. If we want to shed light on the process of destruction, we must shed light on the development of a production mechanism that the Nazis had to use in order to be able to use it. This shift allows characters like Speer and Röchling to remain out of the limelight and to occupy a place that could be said to be in the background in the history of genocide.

The fall of the Wall and the new geopolitical situation made us fear for a moment that through the breach thus opened another worrying voice would be heard: the demand for reparations from former forced laborers from Eastern countries. The leaders of the major groups suddenly became aware of a danger: could revelations about the use of forced labor not have a negative effect on their "corporate image"? The reaction will not be long in coming, and by granting certain academics selective access to documents, the firms will take the lead in directing research. Thus, the works available to us have inevitably passed the role and conduct of these major economic actors through the filter of this academic research, and left in the shade what deserved to be brought to light.

Whether in books financed by companies or in "history pages" distributed on the Internet today, the stories of this programmed disaster are no longer aimed at a national community, but at public opinion, whose only borders are now those of the market, and the image of companies as well as that of the countries themselves must conform to the demand. The consultation of Internet sites reveals a trivialized vision of industrial progress and of European history, where, in order to better clear this guiding line and erase the rough edges, the age-old Franco-German dispute is relegated to the background. In the face of "globalized" history, which favors a rhetoric of rapprochement and sharing, paper documents, preserved in archives and in literature, bring back a memory closer to the ground. They take us back to the nature and origin of the relations of power and competition between France and Germany. The role of the Röchling industrialists comes to light in its truth.

From then on, our study was directed towards answering the question, with multiple ramifications that run through all this research and all these documents: since the economy occupied a central place in the policy of the Third Reich, did all military decisions depend on the good functioning of this apparatus, and thus on the exploitation of slave labor? And why is it that all the big names in industry, who led Germany and the world to an unprecedented disaster, were not held accountable, or were held accountable only to a limited extent?

It is this part of the shadow that we wanted to bring to light.

*Hermann Röchling, portrait by Heinrich Hoffmann,
official photographer of Hitler. The scars are the badge of honor
of a student brotherhood practicing Mensur - fencing with live weapons.
Source: National Archives*

Part I:
"The Nation-Economy":
The origins of the German model

Chapter 1. The iron barons

The economic power of the German Federal Republic has its roots in the territorial reorganization of Europe after the fall of Napoleon I. A new spatial order was created to the benefit of Prussia and at the expense of Austria, which lost its western territories on the Rhine, and France, which lost its possessions. A new spatial order was created to the benefit of Prussia and at the expense, in particular, of Austria, which lost its western territories on the Rhine, and of France, which lost its possessions in the Saar with its coal mines. And it was in these regions that a real "energy revolution" was underway, linked to the extraction of coal to develop metallurgy towards the techniques of steel production as we know them today. We owe it to the English, driven by the deforestation of their iron basins, to have discovered the manufacturing process that allows the use of coke, obtained from coal, instead of wood to refine iron. These innovations led to the rise of a new category of "ironmasters", of which the Röchlings are the very example: coal merchants who had capital to invest in geological explorations underground and in inexperienced industrial processes[1].

The Prussian rulers then took the full measure of the administrative and territorial reforms - the *Zollverein* - necessary for this

---

1. Jean-Marie MOINE, *The Iron Barons. Les Maîtres de forges en Lorraine.* Nancy, Presses Universitaires de Nancy, Éditions Serpenoise, 1989, p. 38.

industrialization. Bismarck, not coincidentally known as the "Iron Chancellor", succeeded in overcoming the age-old fragmentation of the German territories and establishing Prussian hegemony through a liberal economic policy pursued over time. Although the important coal fields of the Ruhr and the Saar now belonged to the Empire - part of the Saar remained attached to the Kingdom of Bavaria until 1871 - the full extent of the subsoil riches, which would soon form the basis of an unparalleled metallurgical industry and enable the German military to increase its capabilities, was still unknown. These extraordinary resources made the Saarland, and later Lorraine, the focus of Franco-German relations.

To begin with, Prussian and Bavarian engineers and geologists based their exploration of the Saarland on an atlas of the subsoil that had been drawn up shortly before by three French engineers, Duhamel, Beaunier and Calmelet. In Lorraine, where there was still hope of finding equivalent coal deposits, the initiatives taken by the French authorities and by entrepreneurs such as the de Wendel family, which had been involved in the development of the Lorraine metallurgy for more than a century, did not yield any significant results. And when the Franco-English free trade agreements negotiated by Napoleon III finally encouraged French metallurgists to modernize their facilities, they realized, not without bitterness, what the loss of the Saarland meant for their industry.

In the meantime, the Saarland's ironmasters had to cope not only with the deforestation of the land, but also with the growing shortage of iron ore. They had a vital need for "strong iron", which was spread out in the surface layers, especially in the northwestern part of Lorraine, and was easily accessible from the Moselle. The Stumm brothers, who had bought a foundry in Neunkirchen from the French in 1806, dominated the Saarland iron industry at that time. They sourced their iron mainly from the Moselle. From 1859 onwards, their foundry began to exploit more and more phosphorous ores with a low iron content, the "minette" from the Lorraine and Luxembourg basins. As long as the factories were supplied with charcoal, this produced a cast iron that was somewhat friable, but in large quantities. However, with the introduction of coke as a fuel, it was possible to produce a much better quality cast iron from minette. The minette was of interest to the Saar, Rhine and Ruhr metallurgists. The Stumm barons, in particular, were able to make enormous profits from the exploitation of minette because of its low cost and the ease of transport between the Lorraine mines and the Saarland factories. The proximity of these three basins, the Saar, the Moselle and the Ruhr, linked by a network of waterways, became a guarantee of success for Prussia as well as for its ironmasters[2].

The new raw materials called for new refining techniques. Soon, the demand for Saarland coal, which was less solid and more difficult to cokerate than the more abundant Westphalian coal, was limited to factories not far from where it was mined. In 1877, the discovery of the Thomas process triggered a veritable rush for "minette". Saarland coal and Lorraine minette brought wealth and industry to the whole region, but they were also the source of its misfortunes during the two world wars. Moselle and Saarland swung between France and Germany according to the victories and treaties, while Meurthe-et-Moselle, which remained French, was no less coveted by the German steelmakers.

---

2. The Rhine and Marne Canal was completed in 1853; the Saar Canal went into service in 1865.

The Röchling House

The Röchlings, a Westphalian family, had settled in the small principality of Nassau-Saarbrücken around 1730, where Johann Friedrich Röchling ran a foundry. In 1822, after the Napoleonic Wars, his grandson Frederick established a coal trading company in Saarbrücken, which was now a Prussian city, and obtained a virtual monopoly on trade with the Saarland coal mines, which were under the authority of the state. Ten years later, when Charles de Wendel, the French ironmaster, introduced the puddling technique to the region and built the first coking plant, the sales of the Röchling company soared. The Röchlings also began to take an interest in the Lorraine "minette" trade, a natural complement to Saarland coal. In 1854, Carl Röchling, the founder of the Röchling Forges, went into business with another coal merchant, the Haldy brothers, also from Saarbrücken, to apply for a concession to mine iron ore at Marbache, on the Moselle, north of Nancy. Thanks to the continuous technical progress in metallurgy, the production of coke was becoming a more profitable use for coal than selling it in its natural state. Röchling decided to invest in this area and in 1855 set up a coking plant at his company headquarters in Ludwigshafen on the Rhine in the Grand Duchy of Baden. Two years later he acquired through marriage - his wife, Alwine Vopelius, was the daughter of a prosperous Sulzbach industrialist - the ownership of a coal mine in Hostenbach, at that time the only privately owned mine in the Saarland, and added to his portfolio a minority interest in the coking plant of the company Haldy & Cie in Altenwald, a community on the outskirts of Sulzbach.

Like the more established metallurgists - the Thyssen, Krupp, Stinnes and Stumm brothers - Röchling and his partners at Haldy aimed to master the entire iron production cycle. The opportunity arose in 1856, when the Frenchman Frédéric Mansuy, himself a coal merchant and member of the Marbache mine, offered them a stake in a company that was going to build two blast furnaces in Pont-à-Mousson in Meurthe-et-Moselle. This was an ambitious project for the transformation of French ore, extracted from the Marbache deposit, with coal and coke from the Saarland. In 1862, after a difficult start, the company had to be restructured: majority control passed to Röchling and Haldy.

The role played by these two men, and especially by the ingenious technician Röchling, in the development of Pont-à-Mousson, has been deliberately concealed for more than a century, both in the historiographical literature and in the patrimonial speeches of its leaders[3]. In spite of the incomplete state of the archives, particularly on the German side, we owe it to the work of François Roth to have lifted a corner of the veil on the twenty-six years during which Carl Röchling struggled to decisively raise the business of this company, which would one day become a jewel of French industry[4]. Today, only one of the three blast furnaces in Pont-à-Mousson remains in operation, the last witness to a long steelmaking past in Lorraine.

In 1871, the German metallurgists were exultant. With the annexation of Alsace-Lorraine to the Empire, did they not get their hands on 55% of the cast iron production and 46% of the ore mined in Lorraine? Throughout the conflict, Carl Ferdinand Stumm, a forge master and parliamentarian to boot, never ceased to remind the government of the imperative of this annexation, the scope of which

---

3. Similarly, the Saint-Gobain website is silent about the origins of the Pont-à-Mousson factories: http://www.pamline.fr/saint-gobain-pam/historique (accessed on 2.02.2023)
4. François Roth, "Les Prussiens à Pont-à-Mousson, histoire d'une interpénétration d'intérêts, 1856-1914", *Annales de L'Est*, n°1, 1990. Reprinted in F. Roth, *Lorraine, France, Allemagne*, Metz, Éd. Serpenoise, 2002, p. 105-128.

he himself suggested. He was rewarded for his unwavering support of Bismarck's policy: the new border of the Reichsland Lothringen was drawn with the help of geological experts, taking into account all the mineral deposits that were supposed to be exploitable at the time, in such a way as to deprive France of them forever. At least we thought so! Indeed, this annexation, in response to a geo-military policy, was one of the objectives of the war since its beginning[5].

In the annexed Moselle, mining operations were quickly allocated, and on the eve of the First World War, 172 mines were leased to 28 concessionaires, including a single Frenchman, François de Wendel. However, it was not yet known that most of the deposit, the largest in Europe, was buried deep in the Lorraine region, which remained French, between Longwy and Nancy! Between 1882 and 1886, while preparing a geological map of France, mining engineers carried out a first series of drillings in this area to determine the extent of the deposit. Carl Röchling, who had held concessions since 1872 in the vicinity of Volmerange, Angevillers and Tressange, on the Aumetz plateau, was a man of the art and, for his part, asked for drillings in the Auboué subsoil. The indications gathered confirmed it and in 1884, the Röchling-Haldy company obtained the concession of three new deposits in Auboué - an acquisition that would later make the fortune of the Pont-à-Mousson steel mill. Röchling, in its time, contributed significantly to this success[6].

---

5. Heinz Wolter, "Das lothringische Erzgebiet als Kriegsziel des deutschen Großbour-geoisie im deutsche-französischen Krieg 1870-1871." Materialien über die sozialökono-mischen Hintergründe des Annexions Elsaß-Lothringen. *Zeitschrift für Geschichtswissenschaft*, 19th year, 1971/1, pp. 34-64.
6. F. Roth, *op. cit.* p. 119.

*First photograph of the Pont-à-Mousson foundries. It dates from the time
when the engineer Carl Röchling, founder of the iron barons dynasty and father
of Hermann, was a member of the company. Source: Saint-Gobain archives.*

In order to reduce costs, the steel industry tried to bring production and extraction sites as close as possible, hence the search for
sites in Alsace-Lorraine for the construction of forges. Carl Spaeter
founded the Rombas forge company in 1881, the Stumm brothers
established themselves in Uckange in 1882, and the Dillingen
company set up in Rédange in 1888. Carl Röchling, who had owned
a foundry in Völklingen, Saarland, since 1881, did not want to miss
out on a location for a subsidiary in Lorraine. He found a suitable
location on the Moselle in Thionville (Diedenhofen), not far from
Angevillers and eighty kilometers from Völklingen - the former
Gassion farmhouse. In the meantime, a conflict arose between the
partners of the Pont-à-Mousson factory, a conflict provoked on
both sides by patriotic feelings: their company, which the business
world knew to be predominantly in German hands, began to lose

27

business in France. At the beginning of 1889, Röchling, now elderly, decided to sell his shares. He made a large profit which was used to build the foundry in Thionville. His son Hermann returned from a study trip to the United States, where he had been able to familiarize himself with the most advanced metallurgical processes, and it was he who took charge of the new plant, which was named the "Carlshütte" after his father. The first of four blast furnaces went into operation in 1898[7]. Soon a 5-kilometer long private railroad line linked the production site to the two mining concessions, Tressange and Angevillers. Thanks to a network of underground tracks, it was even possible to distribute the ore either to Völklingen or to Thionville. The Carlshütte produced exclusively Thomas pig iron, which was then delivered to the Völklingen works for refining. This pig iron is transported directly to the Saarland via a second rail link to Völklingen and Saarbrücken.

The enmity that opposed the Röchling company to the Stumm iron barons was now over. Both of them became involved in annexed Lorraine with other German industrialists in order to counter the age-old influence of the Wendel dynasty, which resisted takeover offers. Initially, between 1904 and 1906, Hermann Röchling invested in raw materials, acquiring concessions for undeveloped coal fields in Alsace and Westphalia[8] and diversifying through the purchase of a glassworks in the Vosges. Together with the Frenchman Alexandre Dreux, he acquired a stake in the Internationale Kohlen-Bergwerks-Aktiengesellschaft, owner of the coal fields in Folschviller, near

---

7. Philippe Stachowski. *Usine de Thionville. Un siècle d'histoire sidérurgique 1880-1980*. Serge Domini Editeur, Thionville, 2005, p. 10 *sq.* Cf. André d'Andon and J. A. Douffiagues, *Les Mines domaniales de potasse d'Alsace*, Paris, Dunod, 1932. p. 11-14.
8. This estate located in Hamm was transferred to the city of Berlin in 1917 to supply the municipal services in time of war.

Saint-Avold, in the Moselle region[9]. Another partnership, the Hohenzollern/Röchling mining group, with its headquarters in Freden near Hanover, obtained two concessions in 1911 covering an area of around 3,200 ha, "Anna" and "Reichsland", in Wittenheim in the Alsatian potash basin. All exploitable potash deposits are now in the hands of four owners: de Wendel, Röchling and two other German companies.

Fuelled by the pace of industrial development in the Empire, German metallurgists were quick to demand more extensive exploitation of the resources available in Meurthe-et-Moselle, even if this meant circumventing the prohibition in principle imposed by the French state and acquiring concessions under the guise of a joint stock company. In 1892, Prussia was the first country to introduce this new form of joint-stock company, the "GmbH", into business law. The Röchling company was able to use it early on to avoid public control of its accounts and business. In France, where the legal form of "SARL" was not introduced until 1925, Röchling used the "classic" company form to obtain an iron ore concession in 1908, covering 216 hectares in Pulventeux, in the Longwy basin. Then Röchling negotiated a share exchange with his business partner, Alexandre Dreux, general manager of the Aciéries de Longwy Mont-Saint-Martin: the Röchlings gave up a quarter of the shares in the Carl Alexander coal mine in Baesweiler, in the Rhineland, in exchange for 50% of the shares in the limited company that controlled the Valleroy concession in the Briey basin. The two iron barons then set up two independent companies for the future management of the coal resources and iron deposits that remained to be prospected.

---

9. Richard Nutzinger, Hans Boehmer, Otto Johannsen, *50 Jahre Röchling Völklingen. Die Entwicklung eines rheinischen Industrie-Unternehmens*. Saarbrücken-Völklingen, Verlag Gebr. Hofen A.G., 1931, p. 48.

Around 1910: the "Carlshütte", a steel mill built by Hermann Röchling in Thionville (Diedenhofen), in operation since 1898. Source: Thionville municipal library.

Lorraine in the Great War

The beginning of hostilities in 1914 offered the German metallurgists the opportunity to reinforce their hegemony in the French territory, where they already held a large number of concessions. For the historian Gerald Feldman, their "profiteering mentality" was "not the outgrowth of a war economy, but rather its institutional basis[10]". As soon as Prussian troops took control of the region between Calais in the north and Montbéliard in the east, they gained access to the bulk of France's coal and iron ore resources. And in the heart of this

---

10. Gerald Feldman, "The Political and Social Foundations of Economic Mobilization in Germany (1914-1916)". *Annals*. Economies, Societies, Civilizations. 24th year, n° 1, 1969. pp. 102-127, here p. 126.

zone, the so-called "army zone", is the district of Briey - supplier on the eve of the war of 10% of the ore used in the German metallurgy.

Most of the protagonists were convinced that the conflict would be short-lived. From the outset, the Prussian authorities received memoranda, whether requested or not, from notables who sought to influence the peace negotiations that everyone imagined were imminent. The deputy Matthias Erzberger, who had been in charge of the Reich's foreign propaganda since the summer of 1914, the Freiherr von Rechenberg, a retired Prussian officer, as well as the industrialist August von Thyssen, were among those who questioned Chancellor Bethmann-Hollweg on the issue of territorial claims. Hermann Röchling, who had succeeded his father as head of the family business in 1898, addressed the governor of the Reichsland Lothringen, Johann von Dallwitz, to explain his conception of the new borders to be drawn:

> "August 31, 1914. Your Excellency, [...]
> I take the liberty of submitting to you hereafter the outline of a border shift north of Metz. In the event of a new peace with France, it would be important to repair the mistake made at the time of the Peace of Frankfurt with regard to the large ore basin of Briey. The importance of this possession is shown by the fact that a good number of ore concessions in this area are already in German hands to a large or significant extent. These are the following concessions or mines: in the south, 1. Conflans (Dillinger Hütte), 2. Jarny (Phönik, Hösch and Haspe), 3. Batilly and Jouaville (Thyssen); in the middle, 4. Valleroy (Röchling), 5. Bellevue (Burbacher Hütte), 6. St Pierremont (Gelsenkirchen), 7. Murville (Aumetz-Friede); in the north, near Longwy, 8.

Pulventeux (Röchling). This does not take into account the interests of the firm of Wendel and Pont-a-Mousson, the latter company having German shareholders. If one wants to move the border completely, in this case, here is my proposal: the new border: Longuyon - Étain - Fresnes-en-Woëvre - Pont-à-Mousson. The disadvantage is that there is a little too much French population in the area where there is no ore. The ore region is inhabited today almost exclusively by Italians, Alsatians-Lorrains, and Poles, people who must be expelled in favor of the Germans, as the development in German Lorraine has taught us. This territory includes the whole Minette basin except for the part near Nancy. I would be in favor of this solution if it can be carried out taking into account other general interests [...][11]."

Von Dallwitz hastened to transmit this letter to the Reich Chancellor Bethmann-Hollweg, adding to Röchling's remarks and suggesting that Germany's western border be pushed back to the Vosges. The Chancellor's immediate response was that Röchling's proposals were "admirable" and that they received his full support. And Bethmann-Hollweg immediately signed a document that posterity will call the "September 9 program": Röchling's proposals and those of von Dallwitz are listed at the top of the list of objectives for the "victorious war"[12]!

---

11. BArch R 5101/119305. Reichsamt des Innern. War memorandum from Hermann Röchling to Johann von Dallwitz, governor of Alsace-Lorraine, August 31, 1914.

12. In his book *Griff nach der Weltmacht*, published in 1961, Fritz Fischer reminds us that the "Septemberprogramm" was in no way a piece of paper of circumstance, but that it confirms the convergence between the socio-economic interests of most of the elites that the military offensive was to serve. With this thesis, Fischer triggered a real "storm" in the world of German historiography, which preferred, and still prefers, to emphasize the defensive character of the Great War.

At the end of October, Bethmann-Hollweg requested the creation of a "permanent industrial commission" to advise the military governor in Metz, General Adolf von Oven, on the administration of the Longwy-Briey basin. This commission was to be composed of representatives of large industrial capital, but also of a former senior army officer and members of the civilian administration: Peter Klöckner, owner of the firm of the same name; Lieutenant General a. D. Conrad von Schubert, a member of the Prussian Parliament since 1903 and a relative by marriage of the Stumm industrialists; Georg Frielinghaus, member of the board of directors of the Krupp joint-stock company; Friedrich Springorum, managing director of the Hoesch steelworks in Dortmund; Emil Kirdorf, managing director of the Gelsenkirchen mines; Karl Wilhelm von Oswald, chairman of the board of directors of the Rombach and Moselle steelworks; and finally... Louis Röchling, one of the fourteen Röchling children, commercial director of the Völklingen steelworks and, since 1911, member of the Rhineland provincial parliament[13].

To promote their interests, which were also those of the Empire, the Röchlings had an influential lobbyist in Berlin itself: Carl Röchling, the eldest of the family, had been a member of the Prussian parliament since 1904 as a National Liberal. A member of the leadership of a party that posed as a fervent defender of the interests of trade and heavy industry, this Röchling was also close to the Chief of General Staff Erich von Falkenhayn and Colonel Max Bauer, head of the "heavy artillery" division of the Military High Command[14]. And he made sure

---

13. *Vossische Zeitung*, October 31, 1914, p. 2. http://www.ag-friedensforschung.de/themen/1wk/ind.html (accessed on 7.02.2023)

14. Frank G. Becker *"Deutsch die Saar, immerdar" Die Saarpropaganda des Bundes der Saarvereine 1919-1935* (2004) *http://d-nb.info/996723196/34* (accessed 7.02.2023) A shortened paper version of this 900-page thesis was published in 2007 in Saarbrücken by the Kommission für Saarländische Landesgeschichte und Volksforschung (vol. 40).

Chapter 1. The iron barons

that the Lorraine iron basin was considered the "special domain" of the Röchling family and treated with care in view of its imminent incorporation into the Reich. The district of Briey was again placed under the civil administration of Karl Freiherr von Gemmingen-Hornberg, governor of the district of Metz and father of Hermann Röchling's future son-in-law[15]. A body called *Schutzverwaltung* (protectorate) managed all the mines and metallurgical plants in the region, with the exception of Pulventeux, owned by the Röchlings, and the mining company of R. Böcking, whose family was related to the Stumm family[16]! And in 1916, Louis Röchling was appointed Reich Commissioner for iron ore and manganese. His mission: to ensure the supply of raw materials to the steel industry so that it could meet military needs.

The occupier was forced, however, to reduce the exploitation of these mines because of the shortage of manpower. Even so, the extraction of phosphoric ore from Lorraine did not have priority, since most of the Rhine metallurgists now manufactured their cast iron with the Siemens-Martin process and used strong, non-phosphorous ore, imported primarily from Sweden. The ore from Lorraine was therefore given priority to the steelmakers of Saarland and Lorraine for the production of Thomas steel, and was only extracted sparingly, in line with the Allied blockade, which reduced Swedish iron imports.

---

15. The son, Hans-Lothar Freiherr von Gemmingen-Hornberg, who was a partner in the Röchling works in Völklingen, was indicted together with Hermann and Ernst Röchling in 1948 as a director of the Röchling firm.
16. Jean-François Eck, Pascal Raggi, "Une première expérience d'occupation allemande des mines françaises : les charbonnages du Nord et les mines de fer de Lorraine pendant la grande guerre", *Entreprises et histoire*, 2011/1 (n° 62), p. 66-94. See *below* the articles by Félix Leprince-Ringuet, appendix 1.

In any case, the large industrialists in the Rhineland were reluctant to sell their steel to the German armed forces, unless they wanted to ensure immoderate profit margins. They preferred to export it[17]. The authorities were reluctant to impose controls on them, so Röchling, who understood how a certain patriotism could be beneficial to the health of his young company, seized the opportunity to become a supplier to the armed forces himself. When, in the autumn of 1914, the shortage of materials and ammunition became alarming, the Röchling company received an order for the production of grenades. As a result, Hermann Röchling had the machine tools he needed "taken" from a factory in Valenciennes, and relied on the Ministry of Foreign Affairs to cover this operation[18]. From 1916 onwards, 80 to 90% of the cast iron used to manufacture the 7.5 million steel helmets worn by German soldiers came from the blast furnaces of the Völklingen factory!

As the mines and factories of Briey were idling, the agents of the protectorate began to strip them according to the instructions and requirements of the iron masters. They requisitioned stocks of ore, goods and equipment - machine tools, pneumatic hammers, copper wiring, *etc.* - and transferred them to the mines. - They were transferred to production sites in annexed Lorraine and beyond. During the first months of the war, the buildings themselves were left untouched, the intention being to be able to hand them over quickly to German buyers. But as the war continued, the first dismantling operations were orchestrated in 1915, and after the implementation of the Hindenburg program in the autumn of 1916, the systematic

---

17. Gerald Feldman, *op. cit.* p. 105.
18. AN BB 36/10 HR 68: note from Hermann Röchling of August 27, 1915. See also the memoirs of Count Schwerin von Krosigk, *Die große Zeit des Feuers*, Tübingen, 1959, vol. 2, p. 125.

ransacking of the blast furnaces and steelworks in the French department of Murten and Moselle began. Since the government banned all orders for non-military equipment from the mechanical engineering industries in order to equip themselves with new facilities, the metallurgists had to take money from the enemy, an approach that also had the advantage of weakening the latter in the long term.

The authorities of the "protectorate" were soon replaced by two management bodies that depended directly on the Minister of War: the "WuMBA", Office for the Requisition of Munitions and Armaments, and the "RoMBA", Office for the Distribution of Machinery and Raw Materials. The iron barons assigned their own technicians to these offices and had even more direct control over the economic policy of the army. The WuMBA and the RoMBA "sold" them the stolen material, so that, if necessary, they could later hide behind the argument of the legality of their acquisitions. A circular dated July 26, 1916 ordered the metallurgists of French Lorraine to provide the plans of their factories and other installations to facilitate their dismantling! New machines were liquidated, and anything old was scrapped or sold as scrap metal. The RoMBa appointed Robert Röchling - another member of the clan - to the post of general delegate of the Minister of War in Sedan, in the northern department. With the help of his colleagues in Longwy, he took raw materials and machine tools from the Röchling factories in Völklingen and Thionville[19]. This involved equipment from the factories at Chiers, Homécourt, Micheville, Mont-Saint-Martin, Moulaine, Réhon and Senelle-Maubeuge. The Réhon steelworks, at the time the most modern of the French and Belgian plants and one of the first to be powered by electricity, was dismantled and transferred to Thionville in April 1917, and everything

---

19. AN BB 36/115.

that was not taken away was demolished[20]. However, the Röchlings were only incidentally involved in the demolition of the Longwy steelworks, since the owner of the latter was their business partner, the Frenchman Alexandre Dreux: the booty taken from Longwy went mainly to the factories of Thyssen, Borsig, Mannesmann, Rothe Erde and others, scattered over the whole of the Zollverein[21]. In 1919, the mining engineer Félix Leprince-Ringuet drew a balance sheet of this "scorched earth" policy: "The German companies that robbed the region the most were, in decreasing order of culpability: Thyssen, Röchling, Rombas, Knutange[22].

For the demolition operations, the German authorities resorted to the forced labor of prisoners of war, especially Russians: since the beginning of hostilities, the mobilization of the Germans and the departure of most of the Italian miners were compensated with contingents of prisoners of war. As early as March 1915, some were sent to annexed Lorraine; some were deported to the Auboué factory in Briey. The municipal and departmental archives of Lorraine and Moselle contain a few scattered documents about the living and dying conditions and the number of these soldiers who were forced to contribute to the German war effort against their own country[23].

---

20. The Forges de la Providence had facilities in Belgium and France, in the Nord and in Meurthe-et-Moselle; their depot in Lille was heavily damaged by the Germans. Cf. *Reports and documents of investigation*. Third volume, tome I. Report on the measures taken by the Germans against Belgian industry during the occupation. Brussels, Liège, 1921, p. 154.
21. Auguste Pawlowski's book, published in 1919, is based on the diary of Alexandre Dreux to describe the devastation suffered by the industries of occupied Lorraine: *La Métallurgie lorraine sous le joug allemand. 51 months of looting and devastation*. Paris, H. Dunod, and E. Pinat.
22. Félix Leprince-Ringuet, "Rapport sur l'industrie minière en Meurthe-et-Moselle", in *Revue Industrielle de l'Est*, n° 1280, September 28, 1919, p. 767. See Appendix 1.
23. Gérald Arboit, "L'Utilisation de prisonniers de guerre russes dans l'industrie ferrifère de la Lorraine allemande pendant la Première Guerre mondiale". *Guerres mondiales et conflits contemporains. Civils et militaires dans les conflits du xxᵉ siècle*, n° 202/203, April-September 2001, pp. 65-79.

It is estimated that, for the two Lorraine regions, the number of Russian prisoners alone constituted between 30% and 40% of the workforce in the mines and factories, i.e. a total of approximately 17,000 people. These figures were confirmed by Hermann Röchling himself, in a conference held in Brussels in June 1915. Addressing the main personalities of the industrial and political world of the Reich, he estimated the percentage of Russian prisoners of war employed in the mines of annexed Lorraine at 40%. However, Röchling regretted that these Russians, who were not miners by trade, were unfit to work as drillers, hence his recommendation that Belgian miners be deported in their place[24]! This did not prevent him from asking the military authorities for a contingent of Russian prisoners for the factory in Völklingen, where production now extended to the manufacture of various types of ammunition (hand grenades). Most of these Russians came from rural areas and were not in good health, and their condition tended to aggravate the insecurity of the working conditions, which were in themselves difficult, while everything was done to intensify the pace of work. Deplorable hygienic conditions, malnutrition, cold and lack of clothing - not to mention mistreatment - also contribute to the exhaustion that will be fatal for an undetermined number of these slaves[25].

---

24. *Reports and Documents of Investigation. Third volume - volume II. Report on the measures taken by the Germans against the Belgian industry during the occupation.* Annexes and plates out of text. Appendix no. 8: "Minutes of the June 19 meeting of the German economic commission. 1st meeting of the economic committee for Belgium", Brussels, 19 June 1915. Brussels, Albert De Wit, Liège, Georges Thone, 1921, p. 43-117, here p. 83.
25. In 1935, Gerhard Walter published his thesis which contains some information about the exploitation of Russian prisoners during the Great War. Cf. *L'Évolution du problème de la main-d'œuvre dans la métallurgie de la Lorraine désannexée.* Mâcon, 1935, pp. 185-190. The studies of the engineer Leprince-Ringuet in *the Revue industrielle de l'Est* in 1919 also contain figures on the forced labor of prisoners of war. See Appendix 1.

When, in the autumn of 1918, the supreme military command of the German troops requested peace talks, Röchling began to fear the imminent fate of Alsace-Lorraine and the Saar. In this regard, he called on Colonel Wilhelm Heye, who, as head of the command's operative cell, was in constant contact with the highest authorities of the Prussian army in Berlin. In his letter of October 21, Röchling recognized that the destruction suffered by the Belgian and French iron industries would serve as "pretexts" to justify the attachment of Elsaß-Lothringen to France after the end of hostilities. He judged that the seizure of German property in this territory was more than likely. Foreseeing this, Röchling proposed as a "solution" to this dilemma, to obtain political neutrality for the region:

> "In short, this would be an ideal situation for the Alsatians and Lorraines and acceptable to us. Naturally, it will only work if in the next note we send to Wilson... we say that "we are willing to withdraw our troops and let Alsace-Lorraine manage its destiny independently under an appropriate regime, provided that no soldiers of the entente remain on its soil." But this must happen soon so that Wilson will be forced to decide whether or not he is in favor of this step. This seems to me the only possible outcome in the present situation[26]."

The Treaty of Versailles will confirm his fears.

---

26. BArch R/901/80941.

Chapter 2. After Versailles

Not only did the vanquished lose the Reichsland Elsaß-Lothringen, but, to compensate for the destruction of the coal mines in northern France, it was forced to cede, for fifteen years, full and absolute ownership, with exclusive right of exploitation, of all the coal deposits located in the Saar basin. As expected, Versailles led to the liquidation of German property in Luxembourg and in the territories that had become French again. The Röchlings were dispossessed of both their mines and their blast furnaces in Lorraine, and the Reich was required to compensate them under the terms of the treaty concerning the loss of private interests. The Thionville plant and the adjoining mines were taken over by the Société Lorraine Minière et Métallurgique, a group of industrialists from the Longwy basin. At the head of this company was Alexandre Dreux, a loyal business partner of Röchling, who continued to operate the Carl Alexander colliery in Baesweiler on behalf of his partner and for his own company.

In 1919, the two Röchling brothers, Hermann and Robert, were charged with war crimes by a French military court in Amiens: the court accused them of a series of aggravated thefts and looting without military motives during the unrest, acts of violence as well as the destruction of French factories in an organized gang. However, the charges did not include their involvement in the deportation of forced laborers, the use of prisoners of war for work related to military operations, or the mistreatment of these slaves. Their trial nevertheless constitutes a first attempt to punish a certain number of behaviors deemed contrary to the customary norms of international law established by the Hague Convention of 1907, namely the destruction or seizure of enemy property not ordered by the necessities of war and the confiscation of private property.

Although Hermann Röchling was the subject of an arrest warrant, he could only be tried in absentia. He and another of his brothers, Louis, who were held in high esteem by the German authorities, had been assigned as experts to the armistice commission in Versailles, and this appointment came at the right time to benefit from diplomatic immunity. Hermann Röchling was nevertheless sentenced to ten years' imprisonment for having premeditatedly pursued a plan to permanently weaken France's economic and military capabilities. Having escaped arrest, he found himself on an equal footing with the highest French authorities. His brother Robert, who was arrested at the Thionville factory, was sentenced to five years; both were also banned from French territory for ten years and fined 10 million francs for robbery and destruction of buildings.

On Thursday, December 25, 1919, the front page of *Le Figaro* read:

"German Crimes.

**Good Jurisprudence: ten years imprisonment,
ten million fine.**

[...] The prosecution has established that the Roeckling brothers [*sic*] during the war continued the systematic destruction of the French steel factories in the Briey basin, at Réhon, La Chiers, Micheville and Longwy, in order to eliminate their competition. It took them two years to transport eight million tons of material to the Karlsruhe factories [this is the Carlshütte, in Thionville].

Everything else was deteriorated on the spot in such a way as to make it impossible to operate the factories.

At Robert Roeckling's house, linen, furniture and art objects stolen in France were also found.

The accused claimed to have acted on the orders of the German government, but the proceedings showed that he had acted on his own initiative and that the government had only approved."

Robert Röchling was released in October 1920, having obtained in the second instance a dismissal of the case by the Court of Nancy on the grounds of a technicality. To understand the background to this early release, let us return to one of the conditions laid down by the Versailles peace treaty: the principle of foreign participation in Saarland's metal industry. In December 1919, in order to avoid any intrusion of French capital into his company in Völklingen, Hermann Röchling, with the help of his friend Alexandre Dreux, president of the Nancy Chamber of Commerce and head of a group of French metallurgists, devised a fool's bargain: the Société lorraine minière et métallurgique, of which Dreux was the representative, was offered the transfer of the majority of shares in the Völklingen company in exchange for the release of Robert Röchling[27]. However, once his brother was released, the Saarland patriarch did not keep his promise and remained master of his steelworks. We recall the reply of one of the magistrates at the Amiens trial, who noted the link between the

27. AA, Berlin. R 75941. Correspondence from the director of public safety of the Saar government to the Paris management.

two men - Dreux having shown himself to be a witness fully favorable to his friend and business accomplice:

> "These people need to stand up for themselves and get along. The golden calf is still standing! That is all we see. Today peace is made, everything is finished. 1870 was useless! 1914 will be of no use, because there will always be people for whom profit will be everything. Our plundered provinces, our dead, our victims and our mourners will be forgotten once again. Our suffering women and children will be forgotten! We will forget our losses, we will not forget to throw ourselves into the arms of Röchling because it is peace. Mr. Dreux, if I am not mistaken, was holding out his hand to him the other day. Because of the fault of Germany, I am a man without fortune today, I am ruined to the end. I am glad that I am not an industrialist, that I do not need the Röchling firm, because if I had to buy Mr. Röchling's fortune by shaking his hand, I would rather remain what I am, a penniless magistrate, an officer to whom the war has given nothing, than to stoop before Germany, even for money[28]."

During the entire duration of the international protectorate, Hermann Röchling was the official representative of German influence in the Saarland, "the enemy of France, while exploiting, with a view to various profits, the weakness or negligence of France, and the entanglement of the interests of large international industry[29]".

---

28. AN 0/36/115: 5th session, p. 255.

29. AN BB 36/32 SEF 1.005,3: minutes (pv) of Constant Adler, December 21, 1947, for the trial in Rastatt in 1948. Adler, an honorary special commissioner, was a member of the French association of the Saarland and director of the public security of the Saarland territory, 1930-1935.

Cancel the Treaty

For the Röchling family, the "sanctions" of Versailles became challenges. The fight for the German Saarland became a family vocation, as did the desire to retain full ownership of the parent company in Völklingen. Despite the constraints imposed by the peace treaty, the Röchling Group became one of the hundred largest German companies under the Weimar Republic. And it spread throughout the world: a network of banks in Germany and Switzerland, a holding company in Zurich, sales offices for fine steel in France, Spain, Poland, South America, and even China.

In the ranking of the German metallurgy industry, however, the Röchling factories only came last, far behind the *Vereinigte Stahlwerke* (VS or Vestag) group, then the largest company on the old continent. What is more, the special status of the Saarland, which was under international mandate, kept them out of the wave of standardization, mechanization and rationalization that swept through the steel industry in the 1920s. Their potential for expansion was considerably weakened. In exchange for the goodwill of the Reich government towards his company, Hermann Röchling will stop at nothing to defend the German Saarland. And he will be paid in return.

First of all, Berlin compensated the Röchlings for the loss of the Carlshütte in Lorraine, which had become French again, and supported the steelworks in Völklingen with credits for the duration of the League of Nations' mandate. In 1920, in order to compensate for the fact that the Saarland was no longer an integral part of the German customs territory, the Röchlings acquired a majority interest in the Maximilianshütte steelworks in Haidhof, Bavaria, which manufactured railway rails, and sold their coal mine in Mont-Cenis, in the Ruhr, which they had acquired in 1910. They also acquired a half share in the capital of the Buderus steelworks in Wetzlar, on a tributary of the Rhine, in order to found a new company, "Röchlingstahl", in the form of a limited liability company, to sell their products. The Buderus-Röchling AG steel mills were useful in many ways, especially as a base for the political and research and development activities of Hermann Röchling, which he carried out discreetly between the Reich and the Saarland.

Röchling prided himself on having kept the Völklingen steelworks in the exclusive hands of the family despite pressure from investors and the French government, while at the end of 1919 his Saarland competitor, the old Stumm Brothers of Neunkirchen, was forced to sell 60% of the capital of his metallurgical enterprise to the "S.A. des Forges et Aciéries de Nord et de Lorraine". Discreet but substantial loans and various aids granted to Röchling by the Reich Bank and the Prussian Staatsbank are the manifestation of a very special consideration for the good health of this industrial group. From the point of view of the Berlin authorities, this support was justified by the need to provide sufficient funds for unforeseen circumstances. The interest was paid into an account called "Röchling-Rücklage" (Röchling Reserve), to be used in case of need!

In a letter to the Bavarian Minister of Finance on May 23, 1925, Röchling boasts that he had managed to circumvent French supervision of state aid: the Röchling shipping company in Berlin had received 15 million gold marks the previous year, a sum explicitly intended to support the Röchling company in the Saarland without the knowledge of the French government. The intention was to prevent the French authorities from raising the price of coal delivered to the Völklingen factories when they learned of this funding[30]. In

---

30. BArch R-43I/241.

order to understand this perfidy, it should be pointed out that thanks to the constant pressure exerted by the French and Luxembourgers present in the Saarland metallurgy industry, all the Saarland factories, including the Röchling factories, benefited from a highly subsidized price for coke coming from the mines in the region, which were then under the control of the French government[31].

Röchling also knew how to take advantage of the complicity of French business partners, and of course of Alexandre Dreux, his life-long friend. The Saarland tycoon was to conduct business in France under the cover of the tricolour in order to take over parts of the French market, while at the same time being the fiercest opponent of French influence in Saarland. For the purposes of this double game, which lasted until the Saarland referendum of 1935, he made use of his French associates, straw men, and opened a Parisian sales office "Société française [*sic*] des Forges et Aciéries de la Sarre" (Saffas) in October 1921. And while Röchling was in fact the only Saarland steel company without any foreign participation, it was believed that the Völklingen plants were now in the hands of French industrialists.

In November 1922, a report from the public security authorities for the French government in Saarbrücken mentions the maneuvers of the "Saffas" which was trying to get a substantial part of a market for the reconstruction of territories devastated by... German troops[32]! And in 1924, the direction of the Sûreté générale in Paris and the General Staff of the army received a testimony from the commissioner Constant Adler, who provided this piquant revelation of the activity of Hermann Röchling and his accomplices:

---

31. Paul Zahlen, "La sidérurgie de la région Sar.-Lor.-Lux. et le problème de l'approvisionnement en charbon et en coke dans les années 1920", *in*: Wynants, Paul and Herrmann, Hans-Walter, eds. *Huit siècles de charbonnage*. Namur, Colloques Meuse-Moselle, 2002, p. 316 *ff*.
32. AAA R 75941.

"Thus, in the spring of 1924, visiting the Salon de l'Automobile and having bought the exhibitors' guidebook, I was struck by a bookmark: adhering to the volume, to which was attached a large tricolored billboard that could be used as an index, I was not a little surprised to find that this patriotic advertisement was made by the Aciéries de la Sarre, suppliers of the French Navy, etc.[33]"

According to Mr. Robert Herly, administrative inspector of mines under the mandate of the League of Nations, Hermann Röchling had in fact managed to enter into numerous French businesses - in addition to the coal mine of Saint-Avold, Herly cites the Compagnie générale charbonnière in Strasbourg, founded in 1928 - and, thanks to these holdings, to set up a lively industrial espionage activity[34]!

It was thus long before Hitler came to power that Hermann Röchling became the leader of the Pangermanist action in the Saarland. In a memorandum he submitted to Chancellor Wilhelm Cuno in July 1923, Röchling addressed the question of Germany's membership in the League of Nations from the perspective of the fight against "our enemies - that is, against France and Poland, in part also (but to a lesser extent) against Czechoslovakia. Rather than relying on the support of the League of Nations, Germany should rely on the international "moral forces" with idealistic and pacifist intentions, namely, first the Catholic Church, then social democracy, and thirdly:

---

33. AN BB 36/32 SEF 1.005,3: pv of Constant Adler, French association of the Saar, honorary special commissioner, formerly director of public security of the Saar territory, 1930-1935. The quoted report is dated November 26, 1924.
34. AN BB 36/9, SEF 1.005,1: pv of Robert Herly, administrative inspector of the mines of the Saarland from September 1919 to February 1935, document of July 24, 1947.

"[...] the Golden International, which must be considered essentially Jewish. It too is more or less pacifist, and its most prominent representatives probably also have ideals to a certain extent: freedom, humanity, *etc*. One should not underestimate this international, since, for example, in the council of the League of Nations 20% of the members are Jewish; Salandre is Jewish as is Hymans[35]."

Although he did not formally join the NSDAP until 1939, Röchling was nevertheless an early National Socialist activist. He attended the conferences and seminars of the Nazi elite and spoke out on National Socialism, the economy and, above all, on the "diktat" of Versailles. Long before Hitler came to power, and while the Saarland was still under international mandate, he did not hesitate to decorate his factories with the Nazi flag, or even to grant staff leave to encourage participation in NSDAP training courses or congresses[36]. And every year from 1929 onwards, he organized summer solstice celebrations in the Warndt Forest "in accordance with the new religion invented by the Hitlerites." Röchling even offered his good offices to popularize Hitler's peace speech. The conference on naval disarmament, which took place in London at the beginning of 1930, served as a pretext for an article that Röchling published in February in the *Kölnische Zeitung*, one of the most important newspapers of the interwar period and widely read abroad[37]. His words in favor of "the abolition of war in general" were even taken

---

35. BArch R 43 I/240a.
36. AN BB 36/9 SEF 600: report, signed Herlach, drawn up on August 2, 1946.
37. Excerpts from this article, entitled "Flottendämmerung" [The Twilight of the Fleets], appeared in the *Frankfurter Zeitung* on February 16 and 18, 1930.

up and commented on in another daily newspaper, the *Frankfurter Zeitung*, renowned for its literary pages.

Röchling also wrote for the party, notably in the magazine *Volk und Reich*, a monthly published by the publishing house of the same name. From its foundation in 1925 until the NSDAP came to power, this periodical lived largely on donations from industrialists like Röchling. From then on, its columns were open to them, and in 1928 the Saarland steelmaker published an article entitled "East-West Thoughts on European Politics and Economy". In it, Röchling spread his views on the peoples of Europe and the markets, and expressed the opinion that German culture was more appreciated in the East than in the West, and that the peoples of the East even preferred German culture to any other! The Locarno policy was certainly the beginning of an agreement with France, but Röchling predicted that it would not be followed up, as the Western neighbor was "not yet sufficiently developed from a psychological point of view to be able to understand the value of what the Reich could offer him[38]."

His Francophobia was much more than a reaction to the consequences of the Great War. In October 1931, during a conference entitled "National Socialism and the Economy" given by Dr Walther Funk, Hitler's personal economic advisor at the time, Röchling intervened to give free rein to his dissatisfaction with the speaker's mixed comments, emphasizing the financial burden on Germany due to the reparations[39]. And Röchling, staunchly in favor of the Aryan model, cast moral discredit on France because of its nationality policy. In another speech, before the People's Union (*Volksbund*)

---

38. Hermann Röchling, "West- und Ost-Gedanken zu europäischen Politik und Wirtschaft", *in*: *Volk und Reich*, no. 2/3, 1929, 4th year, pp. 100-105.
39. AN BB 36/107.

for Germanism abroad, his Francophobia was illuminated by his obsession with race:

> "Lasting success is never in store for a people who, like the French people, try by naturalizing men from the inferior peoples of North Africa [*unterwertige Völker Nordafrikas*] and even Negroes from Senegal and [...] Anamites from Siam, to obtain the vital force which the nation no longer possesses [...]. This mixture will precipitate the loss of the French race. A power policy that does not rest on the lasting strength of its own *Volkstum* is doomed to failure[40]."

On the initiative of the steel manufacturer von Krupp und Halbach, a fundraising campaign, officially entitled "Adolf Hitler Fund for the German Economy" [*Adolf Hitler-Spende der deutschen Wirtschaft*], was set up in June 1933. Industrialists, not only those of the Reich but also those from the Saarland, contributed to the fund by paying into one of the accounts opened for the NSDAP. Although the bank archives themselves were destroyed during the wartime bombings, documents from an account at the Cologne and Koblenz savings banks were found, confirming the participation of the Röchling company in this fund from the very beginning[41].

---

40. AN BB 36/31 HR 131,2: speech held in Trier on April 19, 1934. All the documents used for the Rastatt trials exist in translation, in French and in German, and are of excellent quality. We quote the translations, but not without having compared them with the original documents.

41. AN BB 36/36 document SEF 868, TG 75: letter of June 1st, 1934. The precursor of the "Adolf-Hitler Spende", the "Hindenburg Spende" collected funds during the 1920s to support the NSDAP. Röchling contributed to it as early as 1927. See also AN BB 36/6, letter from A. Spaniol, Minister of Economy and Labor, to Gauleiter Simon, June 1st, 1934, TG 74, SEF 868.

Le Journal de Paris — **TROISIÈME ÉDITION** — Le Journal de Paris

L'INTRANSIGEANT

Samedi 1er Décembre 1934 — TROISIÈME ÉDITION

Où va la Sarre ?

III. -- Un Allemand 100 %

« L'Allemagne aura 99 % des voix », déclare Hermann Rœchling...

« Pas un sou pour le rachat des mines »... ajoute le roi de l'acier

De notre envoyé spécial Guy de TRAVERSAY

DEUX GRANDS PROCÈS DEVANT LES ASSISES

Bonnet et Catherine connaîtront leur sort au début de l'après-midi

Ce soir sera rendu le verdict dans l'affaire Bonny-« Gringoire »

LE BUDGET DEVANT LA CHAMBRE

M. Laval fera un exposé de la politique extérieure

A la suite d'une intervention de M. Franklin-Bouillon sur l'état de nos relations avec l'Allemagne

AU FIL DES HEURES

Solidité anglaise

UN RÊVE RÉALISÉ

Un vol dans l'avion "sans pilote"

La machine remplace l'homme

December 1st, 1934: the daily newspaper L'Intransigeant (circulation about 200,000). Laval, on the front page with Röchling, was a convinced supporter of collaboration with Nazi Germany. Source: Bibliothèque publique d'Information, Paris.

Hermann Röchling: The Factory of the Third Reich

Saarland will be German

The return of the Saarland to Germany seemed to be only a matter of time, but the National Socialists, once in government, decided to make it an event of great international prestige. Röchling put his entrepreneurial ambitions on hold during the Saarland campaign in order to play a major role in the preparation of the January 1935 plebiscite.

By its symbolic scope, this campaign was to become a powerful propaganda tool to consecrate the rebirth of the German people and to show the world how a people liberated itself from its oppressors. Better still, in terms of domestic politics, the Saarland plebiscite served as a model for orchestrating the submission of the entire German population to Nazism. Its scenography required, however, a certain prudence to avoid creating real opposition, because the "Saar battle" was to take place against the backdrop of a vast reorganization of the Reich aimed at bringing the regions themselves into line. The Länder, like the political parties, the churches, the trade unions - in short, all the social organizations - were merged into the *Volksgemeinschaft*, a community now embodied by the Nazi party. A number of laws on the territorial restructuring of the Reich were passed during these pre-war years: on the pretext of unifying the Reich, "commissioners" and then "governors" were established in the Länder, but without seeking any real administrative simplification. On the contrary, the laws that increased the number of authorities aggravated the confusion desired by Hitler and helped to establish his domination and the pre-eminence of the party. But the two Hermanns, Göring and Röchling, knew how to use this administrative maze for their own interests: the first by using the vestiges of rump-Prussia to constitute a bastion of power within the Reich and between the factions of the

NSDAP[42], the second by putting the interests of the *Gemeinschaft* at the service of his personal and entrepreneurial ambitions...

Hitler's accession to the chancellorship had prompted many members of conservative parties to "migrate" to the Nazi party, so that in mid-April 1933 the party imposed a temporary halt on membership. The moratorium was intended to stop the potentially counterproductive disappearance of the small parties of the center and the right, which might scare off the undecided and deprive Hitler of a popular plebiscite tidal wave. Röchling was then a member of the *Deutsche-Saarländische Volkspartei*. However, he did not hide his passion for the new chancellor. The *Westdeutscher Beobachter*, a National Socialist daily known for its virulent anti-Semitism, published, in its October 11, 1934 edition, excerpts from a public conference that Röchling had just held in Cologne, in which he invoked the desire of his Saarland compatriots to return to the Reich:

> "[They too] want to help build this new future for Germany. No power can do anything to change this, not even the League of Nations. The Germany of 1935 will not be the Germany of 1922/23. The German Reich has a Fuehrer of great political stature and unequalled human virtues, a Fuehrer who never abandons those who give themselves entirely to him. This man has been sent to us by God, and each one of us must help him so that our Germany becomes once again the honored and respected Germany[43].

---

42. Alfred Kube, *For Merit and Hakenkreuz. Hermann Göring im Dritten Reich.* Munich, R. Oldenbourg Verlag, 1986.
43. BArch R 8034-III 377.

The Röchlings, with their political support in Berlin, became the bearers of a "united front" project between the NSDAP and the small Saarland parties of the center and the right. Herman Röchling was the contact man between these groups and Hitler. The proposal for a mass movement, "Front for Germany" (*Deutsche Front*), was the subject of a first meeting between Röchling and the new chancellor on March 31, 1933. The Saar Baron was again at Hitler's home on May 3, and we have an account of their conversation written by the intimate adviser Voigt, Hitler's secretary in the chancellery. Röchling argued that he would be of more use to the party until the date of the plebiscite if he was not an official member. This ploy met with the full approval of the Führer, who feared that the rise of National Socialism on the periphery of the Reich would pose a problem for him, because the actions demanded by his supporters would create "foreign policy difficulties." And Hitler confided to him that, if the Treaty of Versailles inspired him as much repugnance as Marxism, it was impossible for him to ignore it, "as long as Germany had not become truly stronger, which would require another 8 to 10 years[44]".

At the Chancellor's request, Röchling organized a meeting with the Saarland representatives of the NSDAP, the *Zentrumspartei,* the *Deutsch-Saarländische Volkspartei,* the *Deutsch-Nationale Volkspartei* and the *Wirtschaftspartei.* On the morning of this meeting, May 15, 1933, the Saarlanders met to draw up the agenda for this "joint work of all those with German feelings." Voigt, the secretary of the meeting, indicated that Röchling wanted to discuss the issue of the presence of 5,000 Jews in the Saarland and the waves of refugees who felt threatened by the Reich, but this did not elicit any response from the other participants. The discussion with Hitler was therefore

---

44. AN BB 36/6 TG 73, SEF 1099.

limited to party problems, including relations with the Marxists and the unions[45]. However, the question of the Jews in the Saarland bothered Röchling to such an extent that in July, he addressed Hitler directly so that the necessary measures could be taken:

> "Most Honored Reich Chancellor,
> In the Saar region, there were in 1927 about 4,200 Jews, of whom 2,800 were voters according to the most common estimates, out of a population of 850,000 souls and 520,000 voters. [...] According to § 39 of the Treaty of Versailles concerning the status of the Saarland, the Council of the League of Nations will determine the conditions for the transfer of the Saarland to Germany, i.e., because of other regulations, the Saarland will become a natural reserve for the Jews after 1935 in every case. However, it seems to me that appropriate measures must be put in place very soon to prevent the region from becoming a Jewish ghetto for the whole of Germany[46]."

The Saarland delegation was received at the chancellery on the afternoon of May 15 by Hitler, surrounded by a good number of government members - Konstantin von Neurath, Minister of Foreign Affairs, Franz von Papen, Vice-Chancellor, Hans Lammers, head of the chancellery, as well as Robert Ley, head of the NSDAP's organization for the Reich - which is proof, if any were needed, of the stakes involved in the future vote. The archives preserve two reports of this meeting, one written by Voigt, the other by Röchling.

---

45. AN BB 36/6 TG 73, SEF 1100.
46. AN BB 36/113: Letter from Hermann Röchling to Adolf Hitler, Bayreuth, July 21, 1933.

The protagonists of this new alliance, the *Deutsche Front*, also wanted to win the vote of the Marxists, who were only opposed to the return of the Saarland for fear of sanctions or disadvantages to which they would be exposed. To allay these fears, a proposal was made to reassure them: a general amnesty on the very day of annexation. As for the separatists, the majority of whom had already adopted French nationality, Röchling described them as "scum": "[they are] lost to us anyway," he said, "and the harm is not great." Hitler, for his part, insisted on the psychological aspect of the campaign and said he was convinced that a crushing victory would allow the NSDAP to win over even the members of the "Marxist parties" and definitively distance the free trade unions from the Social Democratic Party. In conclusion, the Führer reminded his followers that the "pillars of the temple" would always be the Christian trade unions and the NSDAP[47].

With the support, financial as well as technical and logistical, of the Saarland's business community and the NSDAP, the "Deutsche Front" carried out a real offensive, staged in such a way that the entire population of the Saarland, along with the members of the party, had to experience the exhilaration of belonging to a mythical people. For eighteen months, the Saarland question served as a pretext for this agitation, from which the Nazi regime gained a considerable advantage over its detractors. The first large-scale rally was held in the summer of 1933. Entitled "Heimkehr des Saarlandes" (Return of the Saar to its cradle), it took place in front of the Niederwalddenkmal, a monument commemorating the German unification of 1871. On the eve of the festivities, Röchling wrote to Karl Freiherr von Gemmingen-Hornberg, his son-in-law's

---

47. AN BB 36/6 TG 73, SEF 1101 and SEF 1102.

father, to tell him how he had succeeded in convincing the Führer to attend this highly symbolic day on August 27:

> "It was very difficult to get him to speak personally. I approached von Papen and Neurath and also Göring through Dr. Schneider of the Prussian Interior Ministry. Fortunately, the matter was successful, because we need to be galvanized[48]."

On the morning of this great day, Hitler was at Tannenberg, in East Prussia, with Paul von Hindenburg and Göring: the crowd gathered to commemorate the first great German victory of the 1914-1918 war; in the afternoon, he was at the foot of the Niederwalddenkmal, overlooking the Rhine and the town of Rüdesheim, in front of some 200,000 people. A double unitary celebration that was an opportunity to call for a communion of the people "above classes, parties, and professions[49]"; it was the Führer's desire to re-establish the integrity of a territory that had been unduly amputated from both its eastern and western provinces. But this day of national unity masked events of a different scale: the first discriminatory measures and prohibitions taken in the Reich against the "enemies of the people", the assassinations perpetrated by the SS or the SA, with the internment of thousands of communists and socialists in improvised concentration camps... Nothing worthwhile for Hermann Röchling to be alarmed about in any way!

---

48. AN BB 36/6, TG 86, HR 263.
49. AN BB 36/6 HR 265, TG 89.

Successive events were organized in Deux-Ponts (Zweibrücken) where, on May 6, 1934, a "German Saar Day" took place, with Goebbels, Minister of Propaganda, as the main speaker, and then, on August 26, 1934, in Ehrenbreitstein, near Coblence. It was in the latter place that a skilfully orchestrated ceremony took place, during which the crowd, intoxicated by the speeches of Hitler and Goebbels, swore loyalty to the nation. A little later, on the same day, the leaders of the Nazi party accompanied by Saarland notables, including Röchling, went to Cologne for the opening of a travelling exhibition, the "Deutsche Saar". The communist press saw the events of that day as the "parade of the Röchling front[50]"; the *Völkischer Beobachter*, the official press organ of the Nazi party, stated that the black-white-red flag of the old German Reich had always flown at Röchling's house, even in the most difficult times. Inside the gate of the Völklingen steelworks, a sign proudly displays the message: "The French will be expelled[51]". And in due course, the publisher Volk und Reich published *Wir halten die Saar!* [We keep the Saar!], a propaganda pamphlet signed by Hermann Röchling, which was full of resentment against France and the Treaty of Versailles:

> "The hideous grimace of French materialism and atheism sneers in each of the 1,349 pages of this treaty of shame. The spirit of Clemenceau and Poincaré has broken every article of the treaty of Versailles of solemn promises. All those who signed it were marked by this fact as people who would be avoided in everyday life because they were without honor and perjured. It is only fair and just that this corrupt and dishonest society of statesmen and the classes from which they come should be excluded from the leadership of the state. The fifteen years since the signing

---

50. *Arbeiterzeitung* of August 28, 1934.
51. AN BB 36/31 HR 250: "83 more days", *Völkischer Beobachter*, October 22, 1934.

of the Treaty are but the prelude to the consequences of this criminal infamy[52]."

On the Sunday before the plebiscite, a demonstration on the Wackenberg brought together no less than 350,000 participants, without even a single senior Reich official attending.

The results of the vote were announced on January 15: the turnout was almost 98%, and more than 90% voted for a German Saarland[53]. Without delay, the new unity was celebrated: in the Saarland and elsewhere in the Reich, streets and squares were renamed; a special stamp was issued and postcards of all kinds were printed. On March 1st, 1935, the day of the official reunification, the world's press carried pictures of the town hall square in Saarbrücken, where the jubilant NSDAP hierarchy gathered under a flood of National Socialist banners. Even the Central Union of German citizens of the Jewish faith expressed its congratulations to the Saarland co-religionists: they too had returned to their homeland...

52. H. Röchling, *Wir halten die Saar!* Berlin, Verlag Volk und Reich, 1934, p. 35. A second edition of this book was published in 1935.
53. In his book on *Pierre Laval* (Paris, Editions Tallandier, 2006, p. 147), Fred Kupfermann refers to Hermann Röchling in the context of the Saarland plebiscite and notes that: "The great industrialist Hermann Roechling, boss of the Deutsche Front, guaranteed the honesty of the consultation."

1935 : to celebrate the return of the Saar to the Reich

a) Public meeting with Röchling under the banner "We have remained faithful!"
Source : National Archives

b) Postcard from Saarbrücken published for the occasion. In the center in the official car:
Röchling. Source: National Archives

Hermann Röchling: The Factory of the Third Reich

Saarland, June 16, 1935: inauguration of the monument dedicated to the dead of 1914-1918 of the seven German communes of the Warndt, a wooded plateau that crosses the French-German border. Röchling, in the center, in the uniform of the Prussian army with a pointed helmet.
The stele, made by the Röchling factories, also commemorated the return of the people of Saarland to the Volksgemeinschaft, their attachment and their loyalty. Destroyed in 1947, it will be restored from 2021 thanks to a generous participation of the European Union, and its history will be rewritten to make it a monument against war and for Franco-German friendship. Source : National Archives

Chapter 3. Towards the war of revenge: issues and strategies

From a political point of view, Hermann Röchling can be very satisfied with the results of this election. To mark the event, he created a company newspaper, *Der Völklinger Hüttenmann*. On the front page of the first issue, on May 1st, 1935, there is a picture of the Führer with Röchling's ambiguously titled "Zum Geleit", which means both "foreword" and "vademecum". Now we know who is the guide for the road ahead! As soon as the Saarland was reintegrated, Röchling, the businessman, was quick to take advantage of the hunt for Jews in the Reich and the spoliation of their property. He was the only potential buyer approved by the government to take over the Saarglas AG factory in Fenne, owned by two Jewish entrepreneurs, Leo Hammel and Leo Hirsch, at a derisory price! The deal was concluded in 1937[54].

As a steel manufacturer, Röchling must nevertheless fear that the change in the status of the Saarland will cause problems in supplying its steelworks with raw materials, a situation that could put it in great difficulty in relation to its competitors on the Rhine and in the Ruhr. The end of the customs union with France changed the economic conditions for the Saarland's metallurgical industry, which had been covering 85% of its iron ore needs with Lorraine's "minette". As the

---

54. AN BB 36/35 doc. TG 99: letter of May 21, 1947. Declaration on honor of Mr. Jan Lovenbach, CEO of the "Verreries AG" of Trois Fontaines in Moselle.

French government had set a very advantageous price for Saarland coal delivered to the factories in the region under mandate, the Saarland iron and steel industry remained very competitive despite its low profitability and the delay in modernizing its facilities. It should be remembered that the Treaty of Versailles confronted the entire German metallurgy industry with the problem of supplying mining resources to satisfy its enormous iron and steel needs; and that on the eve of the Great War, more than three quarters of the ores used by the German iron and steel industry were extracted from German soil. With the retrocession of the Reichsland Alsace-Lorraine, this figure would rise to 10% to 15% until 1933. And the loss of the colonies deprived German industrialists of raw materials from overseas, whose potential they had only just begun to explore. To compensate, they now went in search of concessions far away, in Newfoundland and Brazil, and the German iron and steel industry remained dependent on purchases of foreign ores, above all Swedish, despite their high price.

This shortage prompted the iron barons to take a new look at the domestic reserves, which had been little exploited until then, namely the deposits near Salzgitter, in the foreland of the Harz Mountains, in Franconia and in Baden[55]. There are calls for their development in a kind of "public-private partnership[56]". The ore of the Harz region in central Germany is easily accessible for Rhinelanders and Westphalians, but it is very acidic and low in iron (30%), and therefore unsuitable for the production of cast iron even with the most innovative methods. It is also known that there are iron ore reserves

---

55. Matthias Riedel, "Die Entstehung der Salzgitter-Hütte," *Tradition: Zeitschrift für Firmengeschichte und Unternehmerbiographie*, 15/4 (July-August 1970), pp. 197-214.
56. Thus the director of the *Vereinigte Stahlwerke*, Dr. Hermann Wenzel, *in: Stahl und Eisen*, 1928, 48th year, no. 19, pp. 615-616. This periodical is available on the Internet via a Polish university website: http://delibra.bg.polsl.pl/dlibra

on the Baar plateau in Baden, which are perhaps the most valuable in Germany. However, this *Doggererz*, as it is called, contains only about 20% of the iron with a very high percentage of silicic acid, so that it is even more difficult to mine than the Salzgitter ore. Although the deposits in Baden have been known since the middle of the 16th century, they have never been continuously exploited, because the lack of waterways and coal mines in the vicinity has meant that the concessionaires have always been frustrated in their expectations.

In 1919, the Rhineland and Westphalian metallurgists were therefore aware that they had to try to use indigenous ores. They commissioned the geologist Johannes Weigelt to carry out a series of drillings in the Salzgitter basin. However, Weigelt, who waited until 1927 to submit his report, estimated the potential of this region to be equivalent to about half the iron resources of Lorraine. On the basis of this report, the main iron magnates decided to apply for concessions in the region, even if it meant waiting for the technical progress that would make their operations profitable. Some of them, supported by technical institutes, started to look for ways to extract iron from this ore, but the experiments were not very successful[57].

Of course, Röchling also anticipated the question of resource independence that would result from the new geopolitical situation. He began with a study of the state of the art in poor ore processing and at the end of 1933 took possession of a concession in Blumberg in the Baar region[58]. The success of the plebiscite encouraged him to count on financial aid from the Reich to carry out his technical trials

---

57. The manufacturing process is long and complicated, as the ore must first be "pre-re-duced" to reduce its volume and to be able to transport it more economically; then it must undergo treatment, known as "reduction", so that the factories, equipped with Siemens-Martin furnaces, can use it to produce pig iron.
58. Zimmermann, "Les Problèmes de la réadaptation économique de la Sarre," *Politique étrangère*, 1re année, n° 4, 1936, pp. 32-46, here p. 37.

and expand the mines. He believed that he would be a winner in the medium term and that he would be able to improve his competitive position: as the new iron resources would increase his production capacity, he would automatically obtain the right to a higher steel quota when the international cartel was renegotiated and the quotas recalculated in 1940.

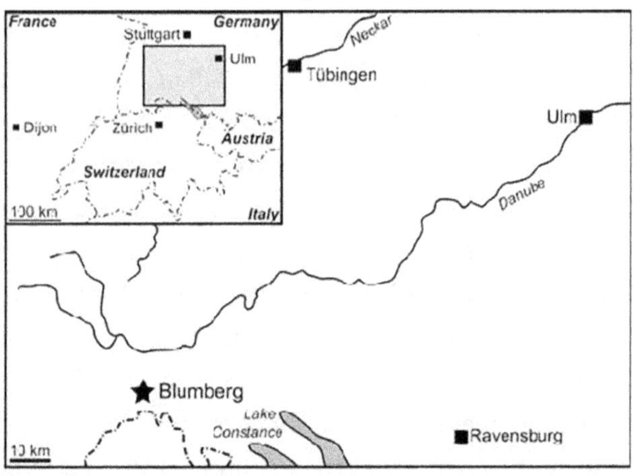

To the Rhine and Ruhr industrialists, who were looking to international trade, any attempt to experiment with the *Doggererz* on the remote Baar plateau seemed illusory because of the transport problems. And even when it came to the ore from the Salzgitter region, they continued to dither about the investments to be made, unwilling, in fact, to expose themselves to losses. The Saarlander took the opposite view: in his opinion, efficient roasting methods had to be developed at all costs in order to remove impurities from the indigenous ores and make them suitable for the production of quality steel. Röchling recognized an opportunity in this matter: as soon as Hitler came to power, he understood how the interdependence between

68

the arms industry and National Socialist politics could quickly turn to his advantage. His skill lay in the way he presented and implemented technical measures in the light of the economic and military interests of the new Germany, while at the same time satisfying his own entrepreneurial appetite.

And indeed, the National Socialist government was quick to intensify the pressure on the steel industry. Rearmament and autarky were the two pillars of the program to be implemented in order to increase the Reich's military potential without having to fear blockades and without depleting its foreign exchange reserves. To achieve this, industry in general, and the steel industry in particular, had to be as self-sufficient as possible in raw materials. However, during 1934, the shortage of foreign currency began to act as a brake on the import of raw materials, and the supply of heavy industry became very problematic[59]. In November, he decided to give his attaché Wilhelm Keppler a mission of primary importance: to steer the substitution of imports by domestic raw materials, regardless of cost. The steel industry was urged to take advantage of innovative technologies as quickly as possible. Keppler, himself the owner of a chemical factory, promises them a "basic bonus" for the opening of mines dedicated to the extraction of indigenous minerals. Now, within the government, two bodies were to compete for authority over raw materials: the mining engineer Paul Pleiger, who acted from the chancellery, alongside Keppler; and at the Ministry of Economics (RWM), the banker Hjalmar Schacht, assisted by Heinrich Schlattmann, an official from the Prussian senior mining administration. In this case, we are witnessing the establishment

---

59. Exchange controls had been introduced in the early 1930s under the Brüning regime. It was strengthened by the introduction in 1934 of a series of laws called the "New Plan", the work of the banker Hjalmar Schacht.

of this institutional overlap, which the Führer himself wanted and organized in order to consolidate his power. And Röchling knew how to use the rivalry between these two offices, and their confusion, taking up the cause of the autarky project.

In order to realize its military ambitions, the regime imposed a more concentrated reorganization of all professional sectors in 1934. The steel industry gave itself a new structure in the form of a cartel, the *Wirtschaftsgruppe Eisenschaffende Industrie*, in place of the professional associations. One of the first initiatives taken by the management of this grouping was to distribute to all members the text of a programmatic speech given by Hermann Röchling in August 1935 at the Leipzig Building Exhibition. In his five "Foundations of Industrial Change"[60], the Saarland industrialist once again emphasized the need to make better use of domestic resources, primarily domestic ore, in order to protect the various industrial sectors from the contingencies of foreign supply. Notwithstanding the publicity given to this appeal in the press, colleagues in the Rhineland and Westphalia remained sceptical about a programme of this kind, which called for massive investments.

In February 1935, Pleiger summoned the Rhineland and Westphalian industrialists to Berlin to appeal to them firmly: foreign exchange reserves were constantly melting away, and in view of the urgency of the situation, it was imperative to reduce the level of ore imports and to find a concrete project for the exploitation of indigenous ores. However, Schacht at the Ministry of Economics wanted

---

60. The *Baumesse-Tagung* (building trade fair convention) took place on August 26, 1935. Excerpts from the conference were published in an article entitled "Leipziger Tagungen" in the important daily newspaper *Kölnische Zeitung* on August 28, 1935. This document, which can be found under the AM, M 75.015 1 (Mannesmann Archives), is cited by Rainer Haus, *Lothringen und Salgitter in der Eisenerzpolitik der deutschen Schwerindustrie von 1871-1940*. Archiv der Stadt Salzgitter, Salzgitter 1991, p. 140 *ff*.

to act in the opposite direction: he was prepared to slow down the pace of armament rather than put the steelmakers in difficulty on the world market, knowing that the use of poor ores would be very expensive for them[61]. And Schacht made himself the spokesman for their arguments: isn't the export of finished and semi-finished steel products also an important source of foreign currency? At the end of February, Hitler's moneyman even managed to broaden his powers in the face of his opponents, having convinced the Führer to sign a decree law that took away the Länder's prerogatives in the management of raw materials and transferred to his ministry all authority over mines.

The Westphalian steelmakers therefore felt encouraged to stick to their guns. They said they could not afford the excessive costs that would result from the use of poor ores. On the other hand, Röchling and Erich Tgahrt - his partner in the Blumberg mines, who was also manager of the Neunkirchen steelworks in Saarland - were still optimistic. In August, Röchling tried to win over the Ruhr engineers and invited them to Völklingen to see a practical demonstration of the feasibility of smelting with acid ore. Tgahrt, for its part, presented a costed proposal for the expansion of the Blumberg site to the Ministry of Economics in Berlin: according to the two partners, the investment required for the whole project, including the construction of the ore extraction, beneficiation and sintering facilities, would amount to RM 70 million. Such a project, they say, would have the merit of finally freeing the Saarland industry from the yoke imposed by the French with their "minette[62]".

---

61. Matthias Riedel, "Die Entstehung der Salzgitter-Hütte," *Zeitschrift für Firmengeschichte und Unternehmerbiographie.* 15th year, issue 4 (July-August 1970), pp. 197-214.
62. Wolf-Ingo Seidelmann, "Die Eisenerze der Baar im Frühstadium der NS-Autarkie-politik (Schlattmann-Plan)", *Schriften des Vereins für Geschichte und Naturgeschichte der Baar*, vol. 40, 1997, pp. 61-88.

However, in order to carry out their ambitious project, the Saarlanders could not do without the support and, specifically, the financial aid of the Reich. Röchling tried to convince Göring, who was visiting Saarbrücken in November. Germany, he insisted, could stop importing iron ore altogether if his project to process domestic ore was supported. At the same time, and to make sure his message got through, he also sent Pleiger a copy of his memorandum entitled "Considerations on the aid to be given to the production of crude iron and steel from the acid and poor ores of the interior". Röchling wanted the government to impose a tax on steel and iron produced from conventional ores to encourage manufacturers to use poor ores. The collection and redistribution of this tax would be carried out by an association of all crude iron and steel producers, and Röchling proposes that Ernst Poensgen, CEO of the largest steel group, Vestag, should be in charge. Finally, he wanted the foreign currency saved by the reduction in imports to be used to finance the projects of industrialists seeking to equip themselves to exploit the indigenous ore[63].

Without waiting for the government's reaction to these initiatives, Röchling and Tgahrt started the first work in Zollhaus-Blumberg. In January 1934, Röchling had already seconded Wilhelm Peter Lillig, one of his engineers in Völklingen, to the project. Lillig was now in charge of hiring workers from the Saar and Ruhr regions for the extension of the mining tunnels and the construction of barracks. Lillig was even able to recruit a good number of Saarland miners from among those whom Gauleiter Bürckel had expelled from the new Reichsgau Saarland-Palatinate for having chosen the French camp during the plebiscite. However, as Lillig's mission did not go beyond

---

63. AN BB 36/6 TG 141, HR 269: letter from Röchling to Pleiger, memorandum with comments of 27 November 1935.

the technical aspects of development, and as the living conditions of the workers deteriorated rapidly, the Blumberg site acquired the reputation of a "penal colony". The misery in which the workers and miners of the Baar lived prefigured, to a certain extent, the fate that would be reserved for forced laborers, reduced to the condition of slaves to serve the Nazi war effort. However, since this was a German workforce with little supervision, the disgruntled did not hesitate to flee. The mayor of the commune, informed of their discomfort, tried in vain to intervene. Lillig was relieved of his duties at the end of 1935 and transferred to Pleiger's office in Berlin, where he proved much more useful to his boss Röchling.

In Blumberg, the chronic shortage of manpower prompted Tgahrt and Röchling to put off the expansion of the Baar mines until the government approved the construction of furnaces for processing ore on site. The expansion of the Baar mines was halted until the government would allow the construction of furnaces for the processing of the ore on site - and they were especially anxious to receive confirmation of public financing! The two partners want to involve the other three Saarland steel companies in their gigantic project, but the latter, which have stakes in foreign metallurgical companies, are completely uninterested in the question of energy self-sufficiency for the Reich! Nevertheless, time seems to be on Röchling's and partner's side, because the situation on the currency market continues to deteriorate and the steel industry is no longer able to meet the increased demand for iron and steel on which the increase in war potential - and their profits - depends.

1935/1939: Blumberg, energy autarky project in the Baar.

a)   *b)*

a) The engineer Wilhelm Peter Lillig, member of the Corps Montania and close associate
of Hermann Röchling.
Source : Corps Montania
b) Röchling, to the right of Walter Köhler, Minister President of Baden.
Source : National Archives

While the Westphalians and the Saarlanders were still in deep
disagreement, the foundation, in the summer of 1937, of an iron and
steel complex which was to be called the "Reichswerke Hermann

Göring", was to impose a decision which could only displease all the industrialists in the private sector. Initially intended to produce cast iron from domestic ore, this conglomerate did not in fact respond to a real economic necessity, but to a very precise political objective: to break the power of this old coterie, this interweaving of the public and the private that characterized heavy industry, and to allow Göring and his entourage, already under the control of the police and youth services, to establish their power over the most solid and least vulnerable of materials, money.

It was in the spring of 1936 that events began to unfold, to the great benefit of this new industrial strategy. On March 7, the Wehrmacht reoccupied the demilitarized zone of the Rhineland, and to mark the popular support for this operation, which flouted the Treaty of Versailles, elections to the Reichstag were scheduled for the 29th, a real plebiscite by acclamation. On the eve of the elections, when Goebbels wanted to issue a powerful and effective declaration of support to the entire press, to which of the government's external figures did he turn? Hermann Röchling, experienced in this exercise thanks to the Saar plebiscite, launched his "message of peace" to the world:

> "Just as the Führer restored peace within Germany, so, based on sound considerations, did he make an offer of peace to the whole of Europe. He offered all of Germany's neighbors non-aggression pacts for a period of 25 years. In this way, he demonstrated to the world that Germany is ready to make an enormous contribution to the maintenance of peace in Europe[64].

64. Hermann Röchling, "Innen und Aussen," *Hamburger Fremdenblatt*, March 23, 1936. See also AN BB 36/31, HR 23.

Chapter 3. Towards the war of revenge: issues and strategies

With this vote, the German people were called upon to express their gratitude to the Führer for all that he had just accomplished and for what he was undertaking "in the interest of peace on our blood-stained old continent." It is probably safe to assume that Röchling was not without expecting some positive spin-offs for his project at Blumberg, which was then at a standstill, in return for his good and loyal services.

December 4, 1935: Joseph Goebbels (front center) visiting the Röchling factory in Völklingen. To his right, a little behind him, Hermann Röchling.
Source : National Archives

Partisan economy and private interests: the Hermann Göring Reichswerke

April 1936: Göring received full powers to prepare for war, with the task of making up for the shortage of raw materials and restoring the balance of payments. He ordered Reinhard Heydrich, head of the NSDAP's security service and Himmler's right-hand man, to investigate all securities held abroad by German citizens. The powers of the Reichsmarschall thus began to encroach, on the one hand, on the prerogatives of Schacht, in the Economy, and on the other, on those of the men in the Chancellery, where Keppler and Pleiger were now under the authority of General Loeb of the Air Force. On May 26, the Marshall summoned the representatives of the most powerful heavy industry groups and the ministerial officials of iron and steel. He told them: from now on, it was no longer a question of what was profitable, nor of what was convenient, but of what would ease the country's position on the exchange market. In short, the parties must make it clear to what extent the poor ores in German soil can be used for steel production. For Schlattmann, the issue has already been settled, and now it is important to get past the cost considerations and finally proceed with the extraction[65].

During the summer, the Führer put on paper a "strategic memorandum" for the plan entrusted to Göring. He announced it publicly before the party congress in Nuremberg on September 9; however, the document itself, drawn up in four copies, remained confidential and was only distributed to his closest collaborators. Hitler ordered the planning of the economy in order to make the country totally independent of imports in the mechanical, chemical and extractive

---

65. Nuremberg Tribunal, NI-5380, Prosecution Document No. 400.

industries and to prepare it for the "war against world Jewry and Bolshevism." In four years' time, the German army should be operational and the German economy ready to fight! The Führer insisted that German talent - and technology - would make self-sufficiency possible in all these sectors[66]. Projects for the employment of domestically sourced ores in the steel industry should therefore be pursued without regard to costs. He also spread invective against the Jews and called for a law to make "the whole of Jewry responsible for an act committed by one of this criminal species against the German economy and thus against the German people.

Hitler held Röchling in high esteem, and it is therefore not unreasonable to compare the Führer's programmatic text with the memorandum that the Saarlander sent him in the summer of 1936. In his "Reflections on the Preparation and Conduct of the War," Röchling dwells on the technical nature of the coming conflict, proposing to the Führer a real protocol for the fighting army and a project for automatic armament for the infantry. War was almost inevitable, he wrote, a vital war against Bolshevism, but also against France, which was "sliding" more and more towards Bolshevism and where Freemasonry had allowed "the Jews to reach the highest levels of the state[67]". Like the Führer, his anti-Semitic hatred carried him to the point of delivering this passionate apology for the Nazi policy which made it increasingly difficult for Jews to live in Germany and which drove them out: if one makes "massive progress in

---

66. Laurent Murawiec, "Le mémorandum sur les taches d'un plan de quatre ans d'Adolf Hitler," *Vingtième Siècle. Revue d'histoire,* 1999, 62, pp. 85-105. Murawiec reveals that this memorandum was not published until 1955 by the historian Wilhelm Treue. Cf. *infra,* p. 145 ff.https://www.persee.fr/doc/xxs_02941759_1999_num_62_1_4528?q=Murawiec+Vingti%C3%A8me+si%C3%A8cle+1999 (consulté le 7.02.2023)
67. AN BB 36/6, document NI 299-I TG 125 of August 6, 1936. The document was sent on August 8, 1936 to the head of the chancellery Lammers for transmission to Hitler.

anti-Semitism wherever these refugees fail, one will touch the very life of the Jewish race."

In broad terms, the two writings share the essential: the expectation of a full-scale war against Bolshevism and world Jewry, and the same relentlessness with which they call for the total mobilization of the country's resources in preparation for this war[68].

In order to ensure that these grand declarations do not go unheeded, the fate of the Blumberg operation will be discussed at a meeting of all parties involved as early as September 2. For a few days now, Schlattmann has been in possession of the project drawn up by Röchling, i.e. the construction of four roasting furnaces, sintering furnaces, and warehouses for the storage of poor ore, to be financed by the participation of all the Saarland steelmakers. In order to secure his back, Röchling also sent a copy of the project to Colonel Georg Thomas, head of the War Economy Department at the Ministry of Economics, asking him to intervene with Schacht. The meeting resulted in a decision that satisfied Röchling completely. All metalworking groups in the Saarland were obliged to participate in the new company "Doggererz-Bergbau GmbH" (DBG) with an investment of over one million RM[69]. At first glance, Röchling seems to have been rewarded for his support, which flattered the pride and ambitions of the Nazi leaders. However, the basic problem - the scarcity of minerals to make steel - remains. Moreover, there is no guarantee that sufficient ore can be extracted from the Baar basin to increase the military potential and cover new needs in the event of

---

68. The historians George W. F. Hallgarten and J. Radkau have noted the similarity between the two writings. Cf. *Deutsche Industrie und Politik. Von Bismarck bis heute.* Frankfurt/Main, Cologne, Europäische Verlagsanstalt, 1974, p. 302 *ff.*

69. The companies Röchling, Neunkirchen and Burbach with 27%, the plants in Dillingen with 12.5% and Halberger Hütte with 6.5%.

Chapter 3. Towards the war of revenge: issues and strategies

war, not to mention the technical problems that are far from being solved, notwithstanding Röchling's claims and the Führer's orders.

As head of the "plan economy", Göring now played the strong man of the regime. As "Minister President of Prussia," he held the regular government meetings - Hitler did not even convene working sessions. In September, the field marshal unveiled the contents of the new plan to the ministerial cabinet. At the end of October, he announced it at a large mass rally in Berlin's Sportpalast, and two months later, in Berlin's Preußenhaus, the country's most important steelworkers received his instructions[70]. Despite all this eagerness, one essential question remained unanswered: "How far can we become independent of foreign iron ore supplies?"[71] Röchling was ready to answer this question and sent Göring a note with his plans for the construction of a large ironworks in the Baar basin - on a hillside to be safe from possible enemy attacks - comprising one or two blast furnaces, a Thomas steelworks, a coking plant and a rolling mill. The production capacity would be 600,000 to 700,000 tons of steel per year. This proposal, which is not very realistic if one takes into account the four-year deadline for arming the Reich for war, is coupled with an even more fanciful transport scheme for coal and steel: a canal is to be built along the Rhine from Basel to Waldshut (a distance of about 60 kilometers), with a ski lift to connect the port of Waldshut and the steelworks.

In defiance of the Führer's demands, the Rhine and Ruhr steel-makers persisted in sourcing foreign ores, primarily from Sweden. Worse still, those in charge of the Vereinigte Stahlwerke, the

---

70. IMT Doc N1 - 051, Prosecution Document No. 421 (NMT Trial Proceedings, Vol. VII, p. 853): meeting of December 17, 1936.
71. Memorandum of 27 October 1936. See Wolf-Ingo Seidelmann, "Die Eisenerze der Baar im Rahmen des Vierjahresplans von 1936," *op. cit.* p. 46.

Gutehoffnungshütte, the Mannesmannröhren-Werke, the Bayerische Staatswerke and the Ilseder Hütte, all of whom held concessions for mines in the Salzgitter region, shied away from the problem of poor ores. So much so that at the end of 1936, Pleiger sent Lillig, Röchling's man, to the recalcitrant miners with concrete proposals, accompanied by the threat of state intervention. In short: expropriation awaited them if they were not prepared to resolve the question of domestic ore supply on their own. The reaction of those involved? Röchling would be a "fantasist", Pleiger "an irresponsible storyteller"!

Both were convinced of the urgent need to produce steel from poor ore, but they differed on the choice of means to achieve this. Pleiger advocated a vast project for a steel complex in Salzgitter and, to flatter the Minister and Field Marshal, he even proposed to name these installations after Hermann Göring! However, doubts remain: what is the real quantity of domestic ore reserves? How could the steel mills be adapted to produce cast iron from this material? In order to clarify matters, Pleiger turned to Johannes Weigelt, the scientist who had conducted the drillings in Salzgitter after the Great War on behalf of the Rhineland-Westphalian steelmakers. Weigelt, a member of the party, the SS and vice-president of the prestigious German Academy of Natural Sciences "Leopoldina", was not involved in the affair, unlike Röchling. In January 1937, he therefore undertook, at Pleiger's request, a new series of drillings in the region which confirmed his initial estimates[72].

At the beginning of 1937, all eyes were on the poor ore, especially since in February the Reich government, anxious to reduce the trade

---

72. For a very thorough exposition of these events see the writings of Matthias Riedel, "Die Entstehung der Salzgitter-Hütte," *Zeitschrift für Firmengeschichte und Unternehmerbiographie*, 15th year, no. 4 (July/August 1970), pp. 197-21, and *Eisen und Kohle für das Dritte Reich*, Göttingen, Frankfurt/Main, Zurich, Musterschmidt Verlag, 1973, especially pp. 107-137.

Chapter 3. Towards the war of revenge: issues and strategies

deficit, decreed a quota for iron and steel. For Röchling, this was the moment to obtain financial assistance from the Reich for his construction project in Blumberg. Pleiger agreed and asked Lillig to draw up a preparatory note for a working meeting between Göring, Schacht, Loeb and representatives of the steel industry. The meeting was to take place on March 17, because time was short - the *Anschluss was a* year away. Also, the sentence that Göring uttered during this meeting was strangely premonitory: "Under no circumstances will Germany miss *Austrian* ore! And Röchling opportunely used his connections: he offered to act as an intermediary between the ministerial officials and Hermann Brassert, an Anglo-German engineer and inventor, known worldwide for his practical skills in the field of poor ores. Determined to outdo his Rhineland and Westphalian opponents and to sweep aside once and for all the authorities' remaining reservations about a technique for processing *Doggererz,* Röchling took Pleiger and Paul Rheinländer - a close associate in the minister's office - on his personal plane to meet Brassert in England itself. The small delegation visited Brassert's newly built smelter in Corby, a complex with several blast furnaces that operated smoothly on the basis of the processes he himself had developed for the treatment of acid ores. A note should be made here: on March 5, 1937, Röchling had concluded a "patent pool" for acid iron ore processing technology with Brassert and two other engineers from the German Iron and Steel Research Institute in Clausthal, Max Paschke and Eugen Peetz. The agreement stipulated that all of them would profit from the exploitation of one of the patents filed and pooled in the "pool". So they have nothing to lose from an agreement, and everything to gain!

Brassert became the providential man who had to resolve the conflict with the Rhine and Ruhr industrialists, satisfy Göring's despotic ambitions, and even respond to Röchling's particular designs. The field marshal quickly authorized Pleiger to secretly negotiate a contract with Brassert for the construction of several steel complexes in Salzgitter, in the Palatinate and in Baden. In mid-June, Göring warned the "steel kings" that if private industry did not rise to the challenge on its own, the state would take over a gigantic project of blast furnaces, steel mills and rolling mills with everything needed to process poor ores and produce steel. In reality, however, the die had already been cast and on July 23, Göring presented everyone with a fait accompli: they had been given four years to do what was necessary and nothing had been done! As a result, and without the slightest negotiation, the concessions in Salzgitter, owned by the largest steelmakers, were listed on the maps filed in the name of the new company "Reichswerke Hermann-Göring" and had to be transferred to it! From now on, the Reich will act by decree to obtain the transfer of these deposits and to seize the surrounding agricultural land for the construction of housing and ancillary buildings.

The outcome of this conflict marked the separation of Schacht and Schlattmann. With Göring at the effective helm of economic policy, the Ministry of Economics lost all autonomy, and its resources were henceforth under the authority of the Field Marshal. Schacht was replaced by Walther Funk, one of Hitler's most loyal collaborators, a talentless bureaucrat, in no way comparable to his predecessor Schacht. But who cares? To all intents and purposes, Röchling seized the opportunity to compliment the new minister, opportunely highlighting his own devotion to the Führer:

> "I add to my congratulations the hope that under your leadership the solution of the great tasks with which the Führer has entrusted us in the interest of the revival of the forces of our people will succeed and that it will thus

be possible to conquer for the German people the place it deserves under the sun and thereby the necessary living space[73]."

In Salzgitter, Brassert was responsible for the implementation of the project while Pleiger supervised operations. The project was very ambitious: to create a conglomerate of world dimensions by absorbing heavy industries throughout the Reich. All but one of the steelmakers - Hermann Röchling! - will have to divest themselves of mining concessions, and, depending on these divestments, their share in the financing of the new company will be reduced. They will be compensated for the buildings and other installations. The list is long: Hoesch, Krupp, Mannesmann, Gütehoffnungshütte (GHH) and Ilseder Hütte are to sell off estates in the Salzgitter region; GHH is also to sell off its mines in Baden; In the Palatinate, the Bayerische Berg-Hütten und Salzwerke AG, the Eisenwerk-Gesellschaft Maximilianshütte - which the Röchlings had sold to the Flick group in 1929 - and the Luitpold Hütte all had to give up their mines to the "Reichswerke Hermann Göring". A little longer and the RWHG will also be able to expand into the territories occupied by the German armies[74].

In order not to hinder this vast project by giving free rein to the ambitions of private industrialists, the authorities were quick to take a measure that could not please either Röchling or his competitors: from mid-September 1937, any construction of blast furnaces,

---

73. AN BB 36/6, HR 112, TG 93: letter from Röchling to Walther Funk of February 8, 1938.
74. In 1942, Franz Neumann, an immigrant to the United States in 1936, observed that this creation of a party economy "follows the well-known pattern of American gangsters, who, once they have accumulated wealth through blackmail and 'protection', realize their dream of respectability by entering legitimate business." *Behemoth. The Structure and Practice of National-Socialism*. 1933-1944. Oxford, Oxford University Press, 1942 and 1944. French translation by Payot, in the collection "Critique de la Politique", Paris, 1987.

coking plants, rolling mills, *etc.*, had to be submitted for prior approval to the Ministry of the Economy[75]. This being the case, the implementation of the plan required the involvement of these same industrialists, steelmakers who were affected by such measures, and in the absence of a central coordination body, the question of sharing resources between civilian and military production could only generate conflicts. The OKW had an "economic war council" (*Wehrwirtschaftsrat*), composed of company directors, Friedrich Flick, Otto Petersen, Fritz Thyssen, Alfons Wagner and Hermann Röchling[76], who became *Wehrwirtschaftsführer*. It was their task to arbitrate between the demands of the three military corps, to establish preferences and priorities and to adapt the capacities of private industry to them. They were entrusted with information missions for the military and they had a certain latitude in the execution of the decisions taken by the General Staff. But the structural problem that hindered the "proper" functioning of the Nazi hierarchy remained.

A "plan B" for the Röchling company

The launch of the *Reichswerke* program in Salzgitter did not mark the end of the project in the Baar. In February 1938, Röchling, who was still at a distance from the other Saarland industrialists, received a warning from them: tired of his opportunism, they accused him of jeopardizing all "fruitful cooperation in the service of the great tasks

---

75. Wolf-Ingo Seidelmann, "Die Eisenerze der Baar im Rahmen des Vierjahresplans von 1936," *op. cit*, p. 60.

76. To date, there is no specific study of the Wehrwirtschaftsführer and their role among the various authorities of the Nazi regime. Cf. Paul Fröhlich, "Der unterirdische Kampf. Das Wehrwirtschafts- und Rüstugsamt 1924-1943. Paderborn, Verlag Ferdinand Schoeningh, p. 280.

that the Führer has assigned to us[77]. His attempt to get his hands on the Baden mines of the GHH failed, but that did not matter: the state's commitment to finance the construction of a steelworks in Blumberg was of a different scale. Don't the political authorities call this extensive rural development program in Baden a "flagship project" of the four-year plan? In the National Socialist imagination, this village of 700 souls was to appear as a mining town with about 10,000 newcomers. The "Badische Heimstätte" GmbH, created in December 1936 to carry out these operations, cost the state nearly RM 8 million in infrastructure, public facilities and housing, built, for the most part, on agricultural land that was seized without a care in the world, and its owners received nothing in return.

However, military operations were launched even before the Hermann Göring factories in Salzgitter began to produce: on March 12, 1938, the Wehrmacht occupied Austria[78] and, as the Erzberg ("iron mountain") mines in Styria were now within reach of Göring and his cronies, the extraction of the *Doggererz* lost all its urgency. Not only was the ore in Styria richer in iron than that in Baar, Franconia or Salzgitter, but it was also cheaper to mine it almost entirely in the open. The owner of the Styrian mines, who was none other than Ernst Poensgen, director of the *Vestag*, was forced to sell the majority share of the capital to the RWHG. Göring then entrusted Brassert with the construction of a steelworks in Linz. The planned plants in the Palatinate and Baden were finished!

Despite the military situation, Röchling remained confident, because in order to meet the requirements of the plan, the Saarland

---

77. AN BB 36/110 HR 111-1: document of February 5, 1938.
78. On the same date, Röchling sent a personal note to Göring requesting permission to land his private plane at all of the Reich's airports: didn't his responsibilities within the framework of the four-year plan oblige him to make frequent trips throughout the country? AN BB 36/37: letter of March 12, 1938.

steelmakers had to increase the extraction of poor ore in the Baar region considerably, which required the Reich to finance a real steelworks in Blumberg[79]. He therefore contacted Major General Hermann von Hanneken, who wore two hats: as plenipotentiary for iron and steel to Göring and team leader at the Heereswaffenamt, he was the central office of the army for the development and production of weapons. Von Hanneken summoned all the protagonists to Berlin - it was the beginning of February 1939 - to challenge them to come up with an installation capable of transforming the raw ore into a concentrate containing at least 90% iron. He told them that only then would the Reich agree to participate financially.

Playing cleverly on the rivalries between the two steel factions, von Hanneken got the Westphalians to intervene for advice, and obtained their consent for a very large Reich participation in a new joint stock company. The "DoggerErz AG" (DAG), which was founded in August 1939, was intended to build the necessary facilities for the production of pre-reduced ore from Dogger ore. The amount to be invested was approximately RM 87.7 million. In short, the project was a success, not only for the people of Saarland, but also for the Reich government, which now had control over the supply of mineral resources throughout the country. Röchling himself was the head of the expert committee responsible for the technical aspects of the construction of the complex.

---

79. Here we take up the events according to Wolf-Ingo Seidelmann's meticulously documented account in his book *"Eisen schaffen für das kämpfende Heer!"* Die Doggererz AG - ein Beitrag der Otto-Wolf-Gruppe und der saarläischen Stahlindustrie zur nationalsozialistischen Autarkie- und Rüstungspolitik auf der badischen Baar (Konstanz, Munich, UVK Verlagsgesellschaft, 2016) as well as in the following articles: "Pläne zum Bau einer Eisenhütte auf der Baar (1938-1940)," *Schriften des Vereins für Geschichte und Naturgeschichte der Baar*, vol. 53, March 2010, pp. 35-58; "Die Baar verliert ihre Montanbetriebe (1940-1942)," *Schriften des Vereins für Geschichte und Naturgeschichte der Baar*, vol. 54 (2011), pp. 37- 60.

Chapter 3. Towards the war of revenge: issues and strategies

However, in anticipation of a "probable" war, the supply of iron is only one aspect of the much larger problem of the supply of all primary resources. On this subject, Röchling sent Funk a new memorandum in June, "Reflections on the present situation in Europe[80]": it was necessary to establish a "common economic front" between the Axis powers and the "friendly" countries in order to free themselves from dependence on England and to cover everyone's needs for coal, iron, oil, fuel and rubber. This was common sense advice, but it was to remain a dead letter, since the beginning of the "Polish campaign" in September 1939 upset all plans.

Along the borders and in the Saarland, the factories were shut down and Röchling himself retired to Baden, where he took up a job, with a comfortable fee, as project manager for the "DAG" in Neudingen, the new site near Blumberg, which had been chosen as the site of the facilities. But because the Ministry of Finance was slow to release the funds for the equipment and the Ministry of Economics delayed the delivery of the necessary iron quotas, even the clearing work could not begin until the end of April 1940. A month later, the Wehrmacht invaded the Netherlands, Belgium, Luxembourg and France. The industrialists once again turned to the West, where the ore from the Lorraine iron basin was waiting for them. It was cheaper and of better quality than German ore, consumed less coke and, moreover, was inexpensive in terms of transport costs! Of course, Röchling is immediately in Lorraine.

Although the domestic ore project ceased to preoccupy the steel magnates - and Röchling in particular - the Reich authorities did not abandon it. In December 1940, the state took a RM 20 million stake in the "DAG" and undertook to introduce a compulsory levy for all

---

80. AN BB 36/110 HR 121. At the beginning of July 1939, Funk, well aware of the Führer's respect for the Saar Baron, appointed the latter as advisor to the Reich Bank.

metallurgical plants equipped with Siemens-Martin furnaces that used iron-rich ores or scrap metal. This was a favourable measure for the Saarlanders, whose Thomas steelworks produced cast iron almost exclusively from minette or Dogger ore[81]. But the situation at the time demanded a response of a completely different urgency: how could one continue to exploit the mines and, at the same time, build the production site in Neudingen when military conscription was causing serious labor shortages in all industrial activities in the country? Moreover, the living conditions on the construction site are so harsh that the question of a stable workforce paralyzes the operations. At first, the activity was maintained by assigning Polish forced laborers, then French prisoners of war. As the Franco-German border was expected to move westward, the management of the "DAG" considered transferring the site to France, to a site in Auenheim in the Lower Rhine, and to build a complete steelworks there, capable of producing cast iron from all types of ore. The Saarland barons protested, of course, but after heated discussions, the members agreed that the work in the Baar would be completed and the buildings dismantled and transferred to the new site. On April 1st, 1941, two hundred French prisoners of war and a hundred Polish deportees were sent to Blumberg to raze the site and dismantle the barracks.

At that time, ore extraction at Blumberg reached up to 90,000 tons per month. The capital tied up in these mines exceeded RM 13 million; another four million were allocated for construction in Neudingen and Auenheim, plus the value of the stocks, estimated at about RM 2.8 million[82]. Eventually, the ministry realized that the project was too expensive. And since the use of quality ore would reduce the amount

---

81. Wolf-Ingo Seidelmann, "Die Baar verliert ihre Montanbetriebe (1940-1942)," *op. cit.* p. 52.
82. Wolf-Ingo Seidelmann, "Auf Messers Schneide..." *op. cit.* p. 68, note 15.

of coke consumed in the production of pig iron, they also recognized that it would make more sense for them to free up personnel by scaling back operations at Blumberg, so that they could employ this workforce in the Lorraine mines. The Ministry of Economics therefore proposed to reduce the tonnage mined at Blumberg by half. And now Röchling and his colleagues are demanding, without delay, that the site be shut down outright: the workers thus freed would be much more useful to them in the Saar coal mines!

However, it was not until February 1942 and the arrival of Albert Speer as "general delegate for armaments" that the two sites, Blumberg and Auenheim, were shut down. Röchling sent his recommendation to Speer on March 17, 1942, asking him to communicate it to Hitler "in the hope that he would take a decision along the same lines." The request for provisional closure that Speer sent to the RWM five days later was accompanied by two expert opinions, one from Paul Pleiger, the other from... Hermann Röchling[83]!

---

83. AN BB/36/6 doc. TG 154, HR 262.

Part Two:
Deciding for the big business
- the Millennium Reich

Chapter 4: Germanizing the economic space

An essential part of the "Germanization" of the occupied territories, the spoliation of companies had begun in the autumn of 1939, after the invasion of Poland. Göring was anxious to exploit the capacities of Silesian heavy industry in preparation for the war against France, which was already more than likely. Hermann Röchling and the other leaders of the large groups immediately entered into negotiations with the government to get what they considered to be their due. The large Silesian steel complex, the "Vereinigte Laura- und Königshütte" near Katowice, came under the control of Röchling. In December 1939, Hermann Röchling explained to his banker the "deep sense of benevolence" that the Reich government had shown him: because of his "special position" in the war economy, he was given the best location in Upper Silesia, leaving the less valuable enterprises to his competitors such as Krupp and Flick. Röchling, who also had his sights set on another Polish factory, the Baildenhütte, said he was convinced that he would obtain full ownership of these establishments, provided that he showed himself to be an "unwavering pillar of the Führer's policy", that he would demonstrate his adherence to the principles of National Socialism through his conduct and that he would promote a policy of Germanness to the end[84].

---

84. AN BB/36/31, TG 549, HR 56: letter from Hermann Röchling to Dr. C. A. Pastor, Dresdner Bank, Aachen, December 9, 1939.

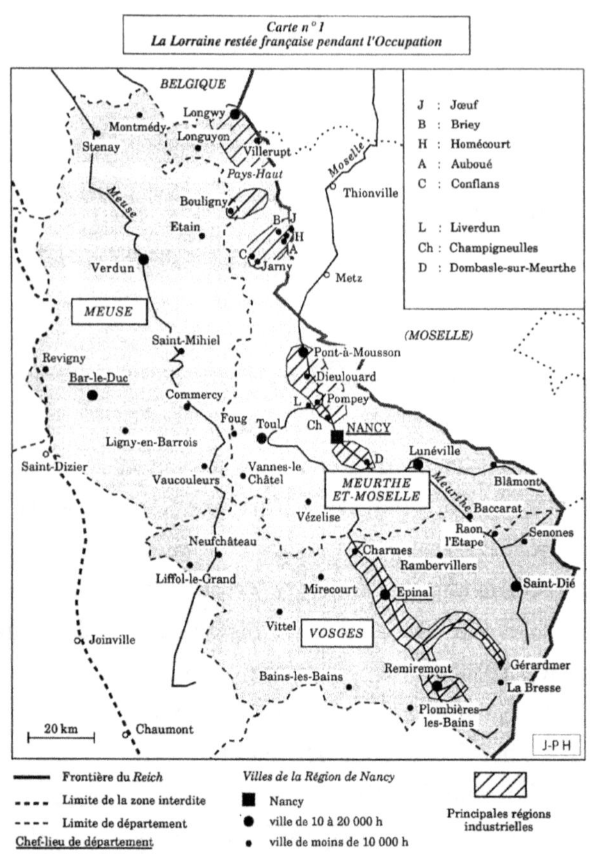

Lorraine remained French during the Occupation.

The Germanization process continued in the West after the military offensive of May-June 1940. Josef Bürckel, Gauleiter of the NSDAP in Saarland-Palatinate, was approached to take up the post of civil and political administrator in Moselle, which was *de facto* integrated into the Reich and attached to Saarland. Luxembourg was entrusted to the Gauleiter of Koblenz-Trier, Gustav Simon, and

Hermann Röchling: The Factory of the Third Reich

by a secret decree of August 2, 1940, directly subordinated to the Führer. Belgium, the north of France and three departments in the east, Meurthe-et-Moselle, Meuse and Vosges, were placed under military administration.

Without even waiting for the capitulation treaty to be signed in June 1940, Bürckel, the future governor of the Gau Westmark, sent Hitler his proposal for France, from the Moselle to Burgundy: he advocated "a kind of new Austrasia under German rule". The day after the "double armistice" came into effect, Bürckel anticipated an order that Göring would not sign until July 1st: he designated Hermann Röchling, his fellow fighter in the campaign for the German Saarland, as the person responsible for the metallurgy of the entire region.

The big iron industrialists expect the 1914 borders to be quickly re-established, and it is clear that they want to get their hands on their former steelworks and mines in Moselle and Luxembourg. In the Grand Duchy, which belonged to the Zollverein until 1919, Röchling itself had no old property titles to claim, unlike many of its competitors who wanted to recover their "lost" assets. Since the Great War, the Grand Duchy's metal industry had been restructured into joint-stock companies, with a strong Belgian and French participation, but, notwithstanding the absence of German capital, it remained heavily dependent on the market across the Rhine. The Luxembourg elites were therefore in no way opposed to the integration of their economy into Greater Germany, but this meant "cooperation" rather than "submission", which was incompatible with Berlin's intention to maintain the strictest control over the administration, operation and possible distribution of assets in all occupied territories. Hermann Röchling, who knew the terrain so well and could be counted on to act in accordance with the needs of the war industry, was therefore entrusted with the very first mission in the region. The Saarland

95

tycoon was given the task of taking stock of the workforce and the state of the facilities in Luxembourg and Lorraine, where they had been at a standstill since the flight of the French personnel, and of restarting everything that had been bombed or sabotaged during the withdrawal of the French troops.

However, the High Command of the Nazi regime was not unaware of the shortcomings of this early supporter. Bürckel and Röchling had certainly made common cause for the return of the Saarland to the Reich, but if the Gauleiter esteemed his industrial compatriot for his economic abilities, he did not appreciate his interventionism on the political scene, nor his quest for a position of command[85]. He, Göring and the other Reich dignitaries also knew about the long-standing business relationship between Röchling and the French steelmaker Alexandre Dreux, president and director of the Aciéries de Longwy, which is why they feared that a possible collusion between the two would cause problems. As a precautionary measure, Göring appointed Röchling as the Reich's representative for the metal industry in Moselle and Meurthe-et-Moselle, thereby removing the factories in the Longwy basin from his control. This sector was incorporated into the zone comprising the departments of northern France, Belgium and Luxembourg, and placed under the direction of Otto Steinbrinck, Friedrich Flick's associate. This measure could only complicate the management of affairs between the Reich and the occupied territories, aggravating the confusion of spheres of competence that was characteristic of the Hitlerian system; but Göring was anxious to assert his authority in the face of Röchling, whose claims and ambitions, both political and economic, were not unknown to him. The Abbé Jules Annéser would later use the expression "the

---

85. AN BB/36/107: Bürckel to Röchling, February 11, 1938.

match of the two Hermanns" to characterize the rivalry between these two megalomaniacs who were fighting for hegemony over industrial Lorraine[86]. In a letter to Karl Barth, the new head of the civil administration in annexed Lorraine, Röchling confided that, although officially the supervision of the iron mines was not part of his duties, he had every intention of exercising control himself as long as the government - Göring - had not appointed a specific administrator[87]. In practice, it was during the entire war that he ensured an increase in extraction in all the mines in the West and the supply of coal and minette to the steelworks.

Röchling addressed Hitler on June 24:

> "My Führer,
> Again, at incredible speed and with relatively minimal losses, considering the enormous scale of the success, the greatest that could be imagined has been achieved. France is overwhelmed. What no one thought possible and only a few insiders thought possible, that fortifications are useless, has become reality. Better than many others, I know how to appreciate what this success required in terms of gigantic preparation works, quality of engineering, psychological confidence and remarkable strategic power, but also in terms of absolute mutual trust between the leaders and the troops.
> You have awakened in the German people the absolute confidence that you will also bring England to her knees.

86. See *below*, p. 273 ff. Jules Annéser, *Vautours sur la Lorraine*. Metz, Éditions le Lorrain, 1948.
87. AD M, 1 W 3: Report from Hermann Röchling to Karl Barth, head of the civil administration (CdZ) for Westmark, July 3, 1940.

Chapter 4: Germanizing the economic space

After what has taken place before our eyes, no one doubts any longer that what has not been possible for more than 300 years will now succeed for you[88]."

As he had done in his 1914 memorandum to the governor of Lorraine, the steel magnate, who knew the lesson by heart, reminded the Führer of this "imperative duty": the annexation of the iron basins of Meurthe-et-Moselle in order to extend the German living space. In order to Germanize the region, Röchling advocated the relocation of "a pool of men who, because of their origin, would be able to provide this region with an appropriate backbone[89]", i.e. the Sarrois! The next day, he added this *pro domo* plea in a postscript to his letter:

> "We are also asking ourselves what we must do in order to achieve the task of truly winning the peace now. I need not assure you that wherever you can employ me in this matter, I am at your disposal. [...] also personal desires arise: I am still condemned to ten years of hard labor, to a fine of ten million francs and to a fifteen-year ban on residence. The judgment of the council of war of December 2, 1919, rendered by the council of war of Amiens, still stands.
>
> Greetings, mein Führer, your most devoted HR[90]."

A tireless zealot, Röchling obtained an amnesty, but he had to wait for the intervention of his friend Albert Speer, who became Minister of Armaments in early 1942.

---

88. AN BB/36/6 TG 101, HR 122: letter from Röchling to Adolf Hitler of June 24, 1940.
89. AN BB 36/4 SEF 1120, TG 179 bis.
90. AN BB/36/6 TG 102 ,HR 71 : letter of June 25, 1940.

Röchling made his first inspection visit at the end of June and beginning of July 1940. In his reports, written on the spot, he noted the state of the equipment and even outlined a plan for the reorganization of the territory and the Germanization of its steel industry. These documents were passed on to Bürckel, who used them verbatim to make his report to Göring. Like Bürckel, Röchling never ceased to make recommendations as to the political action to be taken in this border region. Back in Germany after this first visit, he commented on the near desertification of the Lorraine region since the defeat. Now, he says,

> "The most important problem is where to get the men from (...) Just as the Führer provided for the colonization of the East, this must also happen for the West. The claim to authority [*Herrschaftsanspruch*] implies that there are people to make it effective. A unified leadership would also provide the solution here[91]."

During the summer of 1940, he tried several times to convince the president of the economic association of the iron industries in Berlin, Jakob Wilhelm Reichert, that the Germanization of Lorraine, Alsace and Luxembourg was a prerequisite for economic expansion. In order to integrate this area into the Reich, Röchling considered it essential to erase the past and to draw new geopolitical borders. Only then could the steel industry be "Germanized", of course by replacing the French owners with Germans, and by dismantling the Wendel empire from top to bottom.

---

91. Minutes of discussion for gas by pipeline, July 22, 1940. Hauptstaatsarchiv Stuttgart - Landesarchiv Baden-Württemberg HStASt E 151/41-916. Quoted from Wolf-Ingo Seidelmann, *op. cit.* p. 278, note 30.

Chapter 4: Germanizing the economic space

"It should never be forgotten that just as my company served as the basis for Germanness [*Deutschtum*] during the fifteen years of the territorial separation of the Saarland, it was the firm of Wendel that served as a solid block to maintain a French tradition that was more than two centuries old during the 48 years of Germanness in Alsace-Lorraine[92]."

To put it plainly: to Germanize the region, Röchling wants to keep foreign capital out of heavy industry. His plan was to combine the factories in Lorraine, Saarland and Luxembourg into large production complexes, each with a capacity of one million tons of crude steel per year. Of course, the Saarland industrialists would be compensated for the losses they had suffered since the Great War by giving them a generous share of the Moselle factories.

Hitler himself merely asked Bürckel to remove the "French varnish" from the Moselle as a matter of urgency, and gave the heads of the civil administration considerable freedom. In Luxembourg, the first measure taken by Gauleiter Simon was to ban the French language. As for Bürckel, he only allowed the French "from the interior", French from North Africa, Jews of all nationalities, Asians and Africans, three days to leave annexed Lorraine. However, for Röchling, Bürckel, Simon and many other early Nazis, these were still only "half measures"; for them, "Germanization" meant the expulsion in the short term of all elements deemed incompatible from an "ethnic" point of view - i.e., French *and* Jews - or from an "ideological" point of view - the Communists.

---

92. AD M, 1 W 3: letter from Hermann Röchling to Dr. Reichert, Berlin, June 30, 1940. AN BB 36/4 doc. SEF 1120, TG 179 bis: letter of July 15 from Röchling to Reichert with copy to Gauleiter Josef Bürckel, Saarbrücken.

Röchling had clear ideas on how to reshape the geopolitical face of the region and how to manage the factories. His authority was such that he could initiate Germanization in the factories. He was formally opposed to leaving former French, Belgian or Luxembourg managers in place in the factories as sub-directors, under the pretext of using them as guarantors for trade with companies in the West[93]. And to protect his own interests, in June 1940 he appointed two people close to him as technical managers for the metal industry in Belgium and Luxembourg: the engineer Hans Hahl, who was his private secretary for eight years, and Erich Faust, who headed the stainless steel department at the Röchling works in Völklingen[94]. However, neither Röchling nor the political and military authorities were unaware that the expulsion and replacement of Francophiles and all those whose political or trade union activity seemed incompatible with National Socialism could in turn call into question the very functioning of the companies. If the civilian administration was careful to spare the foremen that the factories needed so badly, volunteers were quickly recruited from among the qualified personnel to be sent to the German factories.

By order of July 13 - the date was not chosen at random - the occupier decreed the spoliation of "enemy property" in the western territories incorporated into the Great Reich. On July 20, the synagogue in Thionville, Moselle, was burned down; in Luxembourg, the synagogue in Ettelbruck was ransacked at the beginning of September, and that in Esch was completely destroyed the following month. The deportation of all Luxembourg Jews was announced and the Aryanization of

---

93. Wendel fonds, AN 189 AQ/146: letter of August 6, 1940.
94. Ludwig Nestler, ed. in *Die faschistische Okkupationspolitik in Belgien, Luxemburg und den Niederlanden (1940-1945)*, Berlin, VEB Deutscher Verlag der Wissenschaften, 1990, p. 46.

businesses belonging to all Jewish residents, whether Luxembourg, Lorraine or foreign, began. Gustav Simon, the head of the civil administration, was free to expel Jews from their homes, take possession of their property and sell it as he saw fit. In the Moselle, Bürckel was also quick to drive out to the free zone, along with other undesirables, the Jews of all nationalities who had not been evacuated at the beginning of the war.

As soon as he returned to the Thionville factory, Röchling ordered the immediate dismissal of "250 workers of dubious political opinion[95]" and demanded that in all the Moselle factories the elements that were not compatible with Germanization be identified and replaced by Sarrois. In Moselle, this "Germanization" led to the exodus of approximately 100,000 Lorraine residents until the end of 1940 and prevented the return of undesirables. In practice, article 16 of the armistice agreement required Pétain's government to repatriate the evacuated population to the occupied territories - and for Moselle, this involved more than 300,000 people - but the results were largely negative. This "Umschichtung" - the transfer of Moselle workers considered undesirable and their replacement by "Reichsdeutsche" - began with the deportation of at least 2,910 people, entire families, workers, foremen, and employees, to the interior of the Reich, in Silesia for the most part, where they would have to work for the Reich. And the Röchling factories in Völklingen also benefited from the deportation of 210 workers from Lorraine[96].

The situation as described after the war by Henri Bornemann, office manager at the Rombas steelworks, is illuminating. This

---

95. Paul-Julien Doll fonds (la Contemporaine) F Δ 1724 (3), SEF 707.
96. Archives municipales de Thionville, letter from the Bureau pour le travail de Diedenhofen to the mayor, July 20, 1942. Cf. the indictment of Charles Gerthoffer at the Röchling trial in Rastatt, AN BB 36/10, p. 33.

employee recounts how, once the facilities came under the control of Röchling in June 1940, the management staff was expelled and most of those who had left the country in the face of the German advance were forbidden to return. In total, forty-eight Rombas managers were unable to work in Moselle. The deportations continued until the end of 1942, which meant the loss of approximately 260 people for the steel mills[97]. To compensate for these losses, the German authorities created an "air draught", attracting workers from Meurthe-et-Moselle to Moselle with salaries that were twice as high, thanks to the exclusive use of the Reichsmark, which was overvalued in relation to the franc, from March 1st, 1941.

On July 5, Göring appointed Paul Raabe, a member of the RWHG board, to manage and control the mines in the annexed regions. The reason for this appointment was that the ore needs of the state-owned factories had absolute priority. Naturally, Röchling and the other Saarland industrialists wanted to get their hands on the Alzette, Briey and Nancy ores for their Thomas steel at all costs, but Raabe had to follow the instructions of the political and military authorities to the letter. In the aftermath of the war, J. Chiffert, director of the Giraumont mines in Meurthe-et-Moselle, provided investigators from the Nancy judicial police with a report on the way in which the occupying forces had taken charge of mining activities: after the signing of the armistice, the directors, on their return from the interior of the country, found representatives of the new German administration already installed in the positions they themselves had previously held. Chiffert specifies that, on August 6, 1940, they were all summoned to Metz for a conference delivered in German by Mr. Raabe to inform them of the terms of the management to come: the monopoly of ore sales would

---

97. AN BB 36/35: pv of Henri Bornemann of February 10, 1947.

be attributed to an organization called *Liefergemeinschaft,* a sales office, and production would be placed under the technical direction of himself and his subordinates. Raabe tells them straight out that, if necessary, managers and engineers will go to Dachau to learn what National Socialism means. Chiffert's assessment of the situation in the past is very interesting:

> "It is not by chance that Marshal Göring appointed Mr. Hermann Röchling from Völklingen and Mr. Raabe from Neunkirchen to take over the factories and mines of Lorraine respectively. Personally, I was treated by the French like a pig and I have not forgotten it, although I want to behave like a gentleman[98] [...]."

The reference to the Saarland autocrat was not accidental: the Raabe organization was a replica of the system set up by Röchling in the early days of the occupation. Both had technical, administrative and commercial control over all the iron mines and factories. The *Liefergemeinschaft,* based in Metz and headed by a deputy of Raabe, served as a mandatory intermediary between the mines and the factories. In the Lorraine basin, one had to be a member of the Liefergemeinschaft in order to obtain permission from Raabe to extract and sell ore. The mines were required to deliver the ore according to the orders and formal instructions of his department, which decided on the allocation, destinations, shipment schedule, quantities to be delivered to each plant and selling prices. As a

---

98. AD MM WM 282. It should be noted that, despite the positions he held, Paul Raabe remains a complete unknown in the literature on the Second World War. In contrast to his brother Karl Raabe, general manager of the Maxhütte of the Flick Group, his name is not even mentioned in the voluminous *Neue Deutsche Biographie* online. Cf. *infra,* p. 322 ff.

result, the entire ore market escaped from the concessionaires and the French government. In the factories in the Longwy-Luxembourg region, which Göring had taken away from Röchling, Steinbrinck was content to place a controller to ensure that the German orders were carried out, without intervening in the particular management of the factories, or even in the distribution of the coal quota allocated to the whole. The three largest Luxembourg companies were even allowed to retain control over their mines. In an article in *Der deutsche Volkswirt* (a newspaper for politics and economics with a circulation of about 10,000), published at the end of 1941, Röchling directly attacked the Luxembourg steelmakers, accusing them of having led a "parasitic existence" at Germany's expense until the arrival of the Wehrmacht troops, taking advantage of preferential agreements for the purchase of coal and advantageous sales prices on the German market[99]. However, notwithstanding the admonitions of the most pangermanistic of the steelmakers, the presence of international capital ultimately slowed down the "Verreichlichung" of the steel economy in the Grand Duchy, so as not to jeopardize German investments abroad.

As for the division of the spoils of the two annexed regions, Berlin decreed that it would be necessary to wait until after the war before arbitrating between the various contenders. At present, the management of the Moselle factories was handed over to the trustees [*Treuhänder*][100]; and on March 1st, 1941, the boards of directors of the large Luxembourg companies were replaced by provisional German administrators. Röchling managed to exert his influence to have his

---

99. AN BB 36/110: Hermann Röchling, "Konkurrenz der Leistung", *Der Deutsche Volkswirt*, year 16, no. 12/13, December 19, 1941.
100. Émile Krier, "La Sidérurgie du Luxembourg pendant la Seconde Guerre mondiale", *les Cahiers Lorrains*, n° 1, March 1989, pp. 59-68.

Chapter 4: Germanizing the economic space

creatures, Faust and Hahl, entrusted with a Belgian-owned factory in Rodange[101]. An archival document attests that, at the end of 1943, the SD [Sicherheitsdienst of the RSHA] initiated an investigation to shed light on the excessive profits that the two trustees installed by Röchling had been able to make in just eighteen months. Although the outcome of this investigation is not known, in his post-war deposition, an accountant from the national iron and steel consortium in Luxembourg explains the circumstances of this lucrative lease: the two Röchling protégés had obtained the contract for the plant, which produced high-quality steel, at a "ridiculously low" price, the sale price of which allowed them to realize very high increases in value. And the expert concludes:

> "It can be said that Faust and Hahl had an annual net profit of about 3 million marks, while the shareholders of the Metallurgical and Mining Companies of the Red Lands [Arbed] became poorer every year. If Germany had won the war, it would have been possible for the lessees to compensate the former shareholders after two or three years and become the sole owners of the plant[102]."

The Moselle plants were divided between the RWHG and the main steelmakers of the Rhine-Ruhr region and the Saarland. Despite strong protests, Röchling could only take over "its" steelworks in Thionville. Although this meant a - momentary - reduction of its powers vis-à-vis its competitors, the fact remains that the authorities confirmed its right to control all the other production sites in

---

101. *Die faschistische Okkupationspolitik... op. cit.* p. 232ff.
102. AN BB 36/35: pv of Paul Wagner, accountant of the Arbed, on September 23, 1947 in Luxembourg. Investigation on the taking of possession of the factory of Rodange.

the name of the "collective interest": Rombas, which was assigned to Flick; Knutange, managed by Klöckner; Uckange, administered by the Stumm trustee; and even the Wendel factories in Hayange, which were integrated into the Hermann Göring Reichswerke. And this right of scrutiny was reinforced by his appointment, in May, to the presidency of the Metz Chamber of Commerce and Industry, the body responsible for monitoring the progress of all transactions of the Moselle metal industry with the Reich and other occupied territories.

In October 1941, Röchling sacrificed his operations in the East in order to concentrate on the spoils of war in the West. And because he was convinced that his special position in the organization of the war effort should result in profits for him and his company, he approached former Chancellor Franz von Papen, who was serving as ambassador to Turkey, to ask him to be supplied with chrome ore from the Daghardi mines. Röchling recounts how his company held a stake in this operation, one of the richest in the world, until the "struggle for the German Saar" forced him to sell to a Jew, Dr. Grünfeld, who was later deported to exile in England. And the Saarlander was not shy about claiming what he considered to be his due, and what was at the same time in the interest of the Reich[103].

Meurthe-et-Moselle, whose status as a "reserved zone" was tantamount to a quasi-annexation, was transformed into a personal fiefdom. Since the beginning of the occupation, the Saarlander had proceeded in such a way that the French owners were deprived of any right of control over their operations, the factories being managed by his trusted men. At the steelworks and blast furnaces of Neuves-Maisons, Pompey, Pont-à-Mousson, Homécourt, Auboué, Jœuf, Mont-Saint-Martin, Saulnes, Sevonces, Réhon, Micheville, Villerupt

---

103. AN BB 36/110 HR 122,1: letter from Hermann Röchling to Franz von Papen, October 13, 1941.

and Aubrives-Villerupt, he established an exclusive and despotic management. The factories in the Longwy sector, which Göring had attached to northern France and Belgium, fell back into Röchling's hands in the spring of 1942, after Steinbrinck resigned. As long as the occupation lasted, and even after the official return of the sites to their owners in February 1944, he exercised his dictatorship over "his" factories.

In annexed Lorraine, Gauleiter Bürckel announced the creation, on April 23, 1941, of a compulsory labor service for all Moselle residents of both sexes between the ages of 17 and 25. The *Reichsarbeitsdienst* [RAD] immediately aroused the resistance of young Moselle citizens. Entire families registered on lists to leave for French Lorraine and escape routes were organized. Bürckel, who was trying to stop this massive departure to France, announced that there would be no question of incorporating the Moselle into the Wehrmacht. Even Himmler and the high military commander were hardly in favor of this, given the failure of the voluntary service and the high number of deserters and rebels from the RAD. Hitler nevertheless decreed the mobilization of Alsatians, Lorrainers and Luxembourgers, and Bürckel had fourteen age groups called up, including four who had already served in the French army[104]! The decrees, published in August 1942, triggered a Germanization by force of the younger generation. The procedure provided for their enrolment in the Wehrmacht or the SS, with the granting of German nationality as a "reward". In Luxembourg, a strike movement broke out immediately, with work stoppages in metal factories and other companies, and protest actions in schools. Berlin responded by

---

104. Henri Hiegel, "L'enrôlement des Mosellans dans le R.A.D. et la Wehrmacht de 1940 à 1945", Mémoires de l'Académie nationale de Metz, 1982. http://documents.irevues. inist.fr/handle/2042/34366

declaring a state of emergency: a court was set up, some 20 people were put to the sword, and around 200 others were sent to concentration camps or labor camps.

Röchling tirelessly repeated the same antiphon about the preservation of "Aryanism" and, even in his personal letters, returned to the importance of the purity of the Germanic race. In thanking a young soldier for the good wishes he received at the end of 1942 on the occasion of his seventieth birthday, he reminds the new generation of the values of Germanism:

> "You, the soldiers on the front lines of the Second World War, must take care to preserve the meaning of this great struggle, namely that if the German people, healthy in body and spirit, united and united, ensure that the most capable are not only given every opportunity for social advancement but are also entrusted with, and retain, the political and economic leadership of the country, then we will take the lead in Europe. All assumptions are important: the German people must be healthy, they must produce healthy children in large numbers. Everything that is unhealthy must be eliminated from our offspring. But then healthy parents must have many children. If you think about the other principles yourself, you will understand that it takes a lot in order for all this to be achieved in the long run. But the top priority, today and forever, must be: love of the people and the fatherland! Heil Hitler, HR[105]."

---

105. AN BB 36/108, folder 263: letter to Jupp A. Hassdenteufel, December 5, 1942.

From 1943 onwards, a system of deportations succeeded that of expulsions, particularly to deal with acts of insubordination and desertion. In the technical language of the Third Reich, this new procedure was called "Umschichtung" or "Umsiedlung". Luxembourgers or Moselle citizens, "Volksdeutsche", who were deemed insufficiently "anchored in National Socialism", were transferred to the interior of the Reich, often to Silesia, to be replaced by "Reichsdeutsche". In simple terms: the Germanization policy meant a purge of the population and the banishment of about 4,200 Luxembourgers from 10,000 Moselle people. In the course of these operations, 327 employees and workers of the Rombas factory were deported to Germany - 174 of them did not return[106] - and 210 Moselle workers were sent to the Röchling factory in Völklingen[107].

This *Umschichtung* offered Röchling the opportunity to lecture his rival Josef Bürckel on the very importance of "Germanness. Addressing his former comrade in arms, with a copy to Speer, he spoke of the possible postponement of the transfer of 1,100 workers in the metal industry between the Moselle and Rhineland-Westphalia and urged him not to postpone it at the risk of "inadmissibly undermining his own authority" as a political leader[108]!

In order to ensure a "Germanic" future for Europe, not only the exchange of populations but also the purge actions to eliminate the Jews and the "scum" of the German people, the mentally ill, the handicapped, the unsocial, not to mention the Gypsies, were already well underway.

---

106. AN BB 36/35, pv of Henri Bornemann of February 10, 1947.
107. Archives municipales de Thionville, letter from the Bureau pour le travail de Diedenhofen to the mayor, July 20, 1942. Cf. the indictment of Charles Gerthoffer at the court in Rastatt, AN BB 36/10, p. 33.
108. AN BB 36/97, note to Gauleiter Josef Bürckel of January 12, 1943 with a copy to Minister Speer.

Spoliations

From his first assignment in Lorraine, between June 1940 and the end of February 1941, Röchling's functions in the war economy enabled him to make a profit on the credits granted for the rehabilitation of the factories and mines[109]. In practice, he financed the restoration of mines and metallurgical plants with loans from his in-house bank, the "Gebrüder Röchling Bank", but also from the Deutsche Industrie Bank, the Dresdner Bank and the Aero Bank, the latter, under French law, having been set up in Paris expressly to help German industrialists. He also made profits from the activity of these factories, taking 0.40 cents per ton of raw metal produced.

Notwithstanding his ambition to build a powerful kingdom in Lorraine on the "remains of the house of Wendel[110]", Röchling managed to recover only a small part of the French dynasty's property: a naval cannon factory belonging to the "Halles" of Ebange. The other half of this enterprise - a shell factory - was taken by the RWHG. In this establishment with its "secret and important character", the personnel was both German and foreign, mainly Slavs. German women, who had been deported for political reasons, were exploited and housed in a nearby camp[111]. Like the Carlshütte in Thionville, the Ébange factory was administratively incorporated into the operating accounts of the Völklingen forges and steelworks. A document drawn up by a Reich accountant in 1943 sheds light on the logic behind this stratagem: it made it possible to show a lower book value for the objects in question in order to facilitate their acquisition at an

---

109. Hans-Christian Herrmann, *Hermann Röchling in der deutschen Wirtschaftspolitik gegenüber Elsaß-Lothringen 1940-1944.* Unpublished diploma thesis, Saarland University, 1991, p. 65.
110. Jules Annéser, *op. cit.* p. 41.
111. AN BB 36/36/ SEF 1057,1.

advantageous price, which this clever industrialist would try to do well before the end of the war[112]!

All things considered, the Saarlander was hardly satisfied with his share of the spoils and the distribution of the Moselle steel companies imposed by Göring. Thus, as soon as he learned of the arrest of Baron de Dietrich in Alsace, he sent his emissaries to prospect the market in Reichshoffen, in the Lower Rhine: the De Dietrich factories "were up for grabs" and the management committee of the Röchling factories did not fail to note the "great interest" of such an acquisition for the machining of the steel produced in Völklingen[113]. The attempt failed, however, but Röchling managed to compensate itself with the seizure of another jewel of Alsatian industry: the S.A. Tréfileries et Câbleries Julien Wurth, also in Reichshoffen, a high-strength steel wire factory which filled a gap in the Röchling industrial group[114]. However, against all expectations, the managing director of the plant, Paul Moritz, had anticipated Germanization and, in good time, had taken care to evacuate part of the plant to a second manufacturing site in Beaugency, in the Loiret region[115]. It was Ernst Röchling who took action from Paris and, thanks to the support of Lieutenant-Colonel Caesar von Hofacker, who was responsible for iron and steel at the Military High Command in France, had this equipment reinstated

112. One example among many: the balance sheet shows that the Thionville company was responsible for loans used for work in the Völklingen factories. Document drawn up by Rodolphe Conrad, chartered accountant, Berlin, May 4, 1943. Archives of the cold rolling mills of Thionville, Centre des archives industrielles et techniques de Saint-Avold.
113. AN BB 36/35, Commission rogatoire established on July 3, 1947 by the delegated magistrate Paul-Julien Doll in Strasbourg with an extract of the pv of the meeting of the management committee of the Röchling factories in Völklingen, dated February 27, 1941.
114. AN BB 36/9 SEF 1000. Pv of Mr. Jean-Jacques Mathis, general secretary of the Ets De Dietrich in Niederbronn, July 9, 1947; AN BB 36/35, report of the police commissioner in Strasbourg, July 10, 1947.
115. AN BB 36/35, pv of January 16, 1947 of Paul Moritz in Strasbourg.

after threatening the members of the Moritz family management who had remained in Alsace with arrest[116]!

Under the name "Lorsar K", a subsidiary of the Röchling Group, Ernst Röchling had a good commercial organization base in the French capital to support the Reich's war effort. The "Lorsar" functioned as a purchasing office to manage relations between French suppliers and the German military services, in particular the Navy, the Air Force and the Todt organization. It obtained supplies from French manufacturers which it then sold to the German services. Its expenses were paid for by "clearing" or at least by the enormous occupation indemnity that France was obliged to pay. Röchling made a considerable profit on the basis of a 10% commission on the transactions. The accountants Socrate Bieuville and Gaston Bernard, commissioned in 1945 by the judiciary to investigate the business practices of the French companies that belonged to the Röchling group, noted this example: rails from the anti-tank works of the Maginot Line, a war booty, were sold by the "Lorsar" at a low price to the Röchling company in Cologne and then resold after processing at a high price to the German military authorities in France: This means that Röchling earned twice on the sale of material that had been taken from France during the war, and that France paid the bill again through the occupation indemnity that it had to pay[117]. A lucrative operation destined to be repeated during the war years!

---

116. After the war, when the Moritzes took over the factory in March 1945, a large number of machines had been removed. Victor Moritz went to Völklingen to find out more and found not only the missing equipment, but also, to his great surprise, the same Ernst Röchling, who claimed to be a member of the resistance and to have participated in the plot against Hitler. AN BB 36/6 TG 169, SEF 695, pv of May 21, 1947 of Victor Moritz in Paris.
117. AN BB/36/36/106, TG 196: Expert report of October 16, 1945 on SAFFAS and LORSAR, drawn up by Mr. Socrate Bieuville and Mr. Gaston Bernard, expert accountants.

Another governmental organization was responsible for the sale of raw materials: the "Roges", Rohstoff-Handelsgesellschaft mbH - the equivalent of the "RoMBA" and the "WuMBA" at the time of the Great War - which was set up by order of Göring in December 1940. From its headquarters in Berlin, it centralized information on loot taken from occupied countries in the West and on black market goods obtained in France and Belgium, and managed their distribution in conjunction with von Hofacker, head of the economic division of the Military High Command in Paris. Ernst Röchling became a privileged interlocutor, even a friend, of von Hofacker and of Jean Bichelonne, Secretary of State in charge of the distribution of industrial raw materials from March 1941 on. As a result, Röchling was in the front line to take full advantage of the various sources of supply used by the occupying forces. And from 1942 onwards, when Hermann Röchling was appointed Reich Director for Iron and Steel, his cousin became his delegate for France. Through his participation in the monthly meetings with the directors of the Lorraine metallurgical plants, in the presence of an officer of the Feldkommandatur in Nancy and von Hofacker[118], Ernst Röchling had unique sources of information to ensure certain advantages for his company. Although his precise functions are poorly documented on the basis of the sources, "there is nevertheless every reason to believe that he played a major role in exploiting France and in organizing collaboration with French companies[119].

After the war, the French magistrates at the Nuremberg tribunal were interested in the resales made to the companies Flick, Krupp,

---

118. AN BB 36/6, doc TG 174, deposition of Jean Raty, May 22, 1947.

119. Hans-Christian Herrmann, "Das Departement Meurthe-et-Moselle in der deutschen Kriegswirtschaft 1940-1944. Zur Organisationsstruktur: Das Janus-Gescht der NS-Kriegswirtschaft", in: *Lotharingia, archives lorraines de l'archéologie de l'art et d'histoire*, vol 5, 1993, pp. 433-450, here p. 450. The archivist H.-Ch. Hermann is one of the few German historians to shed light on the hidden past of the Röchling family.

I.G. Farben and Röchling and obtained a deposition from the former chief accountant of the Roges, Karl Sanders. The purchases of each of the four industrialists were quantified and the result was that the goods delivered to the Röchling works in Völklingen amounted to RM 558,112 in black market "purchases" and RM 175,800 in loot. These figures are certainly much lower than the 6 million in purchases and 5 million in loot acquired by Krupp alone, but they must be weighed against the fact that the Krupp factories had several times the production capacity of Völklingen. However, between 1939 and 1942, crude steel production at the Röchling works increased by 70%, while the tonnage of the Krupp company was 80% of its pre-war level in the same period.

While conducting these profitable acquisition and sales activities, Ernst Röchling became the business partner of the lawyer Alexander Kreuter with a view to acquisitions from which the family group could expect equally successful results. Since the Great War, Kreuter had served as a factotum for the German government and, in this capacity, participated in the Versailles Economic Commission, along with Hermann and Louis Röchling. In the interwar period, Kreuter was a partner of the American financier William Henry Draper, vice-president of the investment bank Dillon, Read & Co. and responsible for the market capitalization of the Thyssen and Vestag groups, two important financial supporters of the NSDAP. After 1945, Draper played a key role in the American military administration in Germany in order to build a new Germany on the basis of the business relations of the past.

In 1921, Kreuter set up a holding company in The Hague, called "Tredefina" (*Treuhandverwaltung für das deutsch-niederländische Finanz-abkommen*), to finance the German-Dutch trade proscribed by the Treaty of Versailles and, in practical terms, to circumvent the prohibition on building submarine warships. The Tredefina funds were frozen by Berlin in 1941, and Kreuter asked Ernst Röchling to intervene at the highest level, with Minister of Economics Funk, to free up RM 200 million[120]. Kreuter and Röchling used this money to found the "Société de Crédits et d'Investissements" (SCI) in July 1942, one of whose immediate objectives was to acquire "Aryanized" French companies. Kreuter's dual role as agent for the Ministry of Economics and the Military High Command in France for the sale of shares held by the Reich's "enemies" allowed him to be both a seller and a buyer. The "SCI" succeeded in acquiring stakes in the capital of various French companies: Galeries Lafayette; the "Société des schistes bitumineux d'Autun"; the "Société des Entreprises industrielles Charentaises-Rochefortaises", a manufacturer of railway equipment; the "Société des Travaux et Mines du Midi", which exploited bauxite deposits; the "Société des Moteurs René", which was used for the production of military vehicles; and finally the "Entreprise forestière de Provence", a front company for financing German orders. Kreuter also sought, unsuccessfully, to take control of a French company owned by an English Jew in order to build a chain of luxury hotels for the National Socialist government. Toward the end of the war, and in view of the advance of the Allied armies, Kreuter and Röchling also took over a Monegasque company, the "Société maritime et commerciale," with a view to transferring their rights in the "SCI" to it in order to protect them from possible seizure.

After the war, Kreuter married a German art historian who worked in Paris for the Rosenberg intervention team, "Einsatzstab Reichsleiter Rosenberg," which was responsible for the looting of art

---

120. John Gillingham, "Zur Vorgeschichte der Montanunion. Westeuropas Kohle und Stahl in Depression und Krieg." *Vierteljahreshefte für Zeitgeschichte*, no. 3/1986, pp. 381-405.

objects from Jews and Freemasons, and he never had to explain his role during the Third Reich. In the 1960s he worked as treasurer at the German Institute for Art History in Florence and was awarded the Grand Officer's Cross of the Order of Merit by the Federal Government for services to his country in the field of culture!

Ernst Röchling, no less than Kreuter and Hermann Röchling himself, had a good hand in the business he conducted on behalf of the Reich. The premises of the "Lorsar" on Avenue Victor-Hugo in Paris housed an official service called the "Arbeitseinsatz" (Employment Office), staffed by a delegate of the Ministry of Labor and by administrative personnel responsible for recruiting and distributing French skilled workers for the metal factories of the Saar, the Rhineland and the Ruhr. Recruitment progressed so well that Röchling rented another apartment on the Faubourg Saint-Honoré in the name of the "Lorsar" for the needs of this organization. The real functioning of the "Lorsar" was to be of great interest to the French magistrates who investigated the spoliation of the occupied countries after the war. Miss Kieper, secretary and translator at the "Lorsar" between June 1942 and the end of the war, made an enlightening statement about Ernst Röchling, its director. She noted that whenever she needed to obtain a favor from the economic departments of the military high command, Ernst Röchling was the one to intervene. However, he himself was only personally in charge of the Société métallurgique de l'Aisne, which Röchling had acquired following an Aryanization procedure. Its director, the Romanian-born engineer Lazare Finchelstein, was the soul of the company, and Ernst Röchling kept him at his post throughout the occupation, even providing him with false papers in the name of François Larre, born in Luneville. And Miss Kieper adds:

"Dr. Röchling was in charge of obtaining every 2-3 months from the SS Obersturmführer Röthke, 41 Avenue Foch, the renewal of a permit for a "Jew useful to the economy" (*wirtschaftlich wertvoller Jude*). Thus, this gentleman was exempted from wearing the yellow star, obtained permanent passes for the North, and even permits to travel at night[121]..."

The "Société métallurgique de l'Aisne" manufactured welded tubes with strip from the Röchling factories using a process invented and developed by Mr. Finchelstein. As the "Lorsar" only operated about half of the production, Mr. Larre-Finchelstein was free to negotiate the sale of the rest himself with the German authorities. Other depositions collected after the war confirm the chameleon-like character of the cousin who fulfilled the mission Hermann Röchling entrusted to him. "Our relations with Minister Bichelonne," he later wrote to Hitler, "were always excellent, and my cousin was truly the guarantor[122]."

---

121. AN BB/36/36/106, investigation of the "Lorsar K", hearing of 26 November 1947.
122. Cf. *infra*, annex 6: AN BB 36/6, TG 185 document HR 221, letter from Röchling to Hitler of October 24, 1944.

Chapter 5. A workforce that can be forced to work at mercy

As soon as the armistice was signed, the French evacuees from the iron-rich regions of Lorraine began to return, except in the Pays-Haut (Longwy), where in October 1940 the population was still more than 50% below its pre-war level. In Briey, the underground miners, mostly Italians, but also Poles, Czechs and Romanians, had stayed behind, but the return of the cadres was delayed by rumors of annexation. Due to sabotage or acts of war, only six of the twenty-eight mines in the basin were in working order when, on the night of 8 to 9 September, the first rail convoys began to run between Lorraine and the factories in Saarland - four trains each carrying 1,000 tons of minette. It is symptomatic of the skilfully organized disorder that characterized the institutions of the Third Reich that all the ore deposits and coal mines in the region had to be managed as a whole, while the metallurgical plants in this same territory were under the control of three rival authorities.

To make up for the shortfall in minette extraction compared to demand and to stop the depletion of stocks, the authorities felt it necessary to increase the number of people working in the mines to a level one-third higher than before the war[123]. This was a fantastic

___

123. Pascal Brenneur, "Les Prisonniers russes dans les mines de fer lorraines (1940-1944)", *Cahiers lorrains,* 1989, n° 1, March 1989, p. 39-57.

figure, because before the exodus, 16,760 people were employed in the mines out of a population of 150,000 in Briey alone. Röchling, who was in charge of dewatering and repairing the installations, and Raabe, who was responsible for their operation, wanted all the available manpower in the region to be sent to them[124]. However, the workforce in the mines of Meurthe-et-Moselle (the basins of Briey, Nancy and Longwy) never exceeded 15,000 people for the entire duration of the four-year occupation, even with the contribution of forced laborers, both deported and prisoners of war. However, detailed statistics are lacking: On the French side, the reports submitted by the Prefect of Nancy to the Feldkommandantur - the occupying forces' mobile command post - did not detail the composition of the workforce for the mines and metallurgy; On the German side, it was only in the spring of 1942, with Speer at the helm of the war economy and the beginning of the "Sauckel actions", that the occupying forces began to keep a more or less precise account of the number of workers and specialized workers - and to record all the requests for what, in the language of the Third Reich, is called "complementary labor".

The most telling sources on the daily work of the miners and metal workers are the individual files drawn up by the personnel office, as well as the daily reports provided by the mine directors to the representatives of the Delegate General with information on the performance of each category of personnel. These documents were largely destroyed or lost, some by the Germans when they left the territory, others, more recently, due to the closure of the sites and the dispersion of the operator's archives.

The local authorities, led by Röchling, kept asking for an extension of the working day in order to increase production. To force the

---

124. AN AJ/40/925. Report from the Feldkommandantur of Nancy, September 18, 1940.

extraction, the "Comité d'organisation des mines de fer" in Paris - the employers! - took the initiative for a directive that increased the workday to 9 hours, starting in the spring of 1941. The prefect of Nancy informed the occupying power that this measure raised a big wave of discontent among the workers, all of whom were underfed[125]. In principle, the factories operated 24 hours a day and, from May 1941, the teams had to work 56 hours a week in the mines of the Briey and Longwy basins, and the working day at the bottom was extended to 9 hours.

A report drawn up for the year 1941 by the chief engineer of the Meurthe-et-Moselle mines shows the number of accidents and serious incidents caused by the needs of production: 21 deaths and 182 permanent disabilities. The causes were multiple: maintenance work was reduced to a minimum and often unqualified personnel were assigned to the cutting work. To feed themselves, the workers had to keep a vegetable garden, and as they were asked to make an "exagge-rated effort, taking into account the authorized rests and the possible supplies", the result was "a state of physical and moral stupefaction of the worker such that the man is too disinterested in his own safety[126]".

The "Röchling plants" in Meurthe-et-Moselle are now considered a "privileged sector" and produce almost exclusively for Germany. However, since coal was in short supply and the minette reserves were used primarily to supply the sites in Germany, in particular at the RWHG in Salzgitter, very few of them were operating at full capacity. A report from November 1940 estimated the workforce in all mining and metallurgical companies at about 15% of the normal workforce[127]. Until 1942, unemployment continued to affect the

---

125. AD MM WM 391.
126. AD M W 1403.
127. AD MM WM 391: Economic situation of the Meurthe-et-Moselle department, Nov. 1940.

Lorraine metallurgy industry, and specialized workers allowed themselves to be hired in factories across the Rhine, where wages were much higher than in Meurthe-et-Moselle[128]. At the Micheville steelworks in Villerupt, a border town between the two Lorraine regions, the authorities had to grant workers residing in Moselle but working in Meurthe-et-Moselle the Moselle wages, which were about twice as high as those provided for by the French collective agreement[129]. However, the voluntary recruitment of workers for German companies did not produce the expected results and stopped in January 1941 with the agreement of the Labor Office in Metz.

In April 1941, the forges and factories of Pompey, which manufactured special steels that were much needed by the occupying forces, was the only site that came close to its pre-war production level[130]. As for the de Wendel family's plant in Jœuf, it was never even started up again. Röchling was content to use its workshops to carry out certain work, mainly for the steel mills of his group, and to send some of the inactive personnel to his factory in Völklingen. Mrs. Elise Troestler testified in 1946 about her husband Joseph, who was sent to Röchling in the Saarland with a contingent of workers from Jœuf. She recounts how, in order to force him to join the Wehrmacht, the farm managers mistreated and abused him. When he returned to Meurthe-et-Moselle on April 18, 1945, he was in such a weakened state that he could hardly tell anyone about his years in Völklingen. He died six days later[131].

---

128. AD MM WM 391: report to the Ministry of the Interior in Vichy on the unemployment situation from June 17 to November 2, 1940.
129. AD MM WM 391: report of the prefect to the Feldkommandantur, May 1941.
130. AD MM WM 391: report of the prefect of Nancy to the Feldkommandantur of April 1941; report of the mining engineer of Nancy, August 1941, AD MM WM 1343 art 69.
131. AN BB 36/32 SEF 1041 2, pv du 14 mars 1946.

April 17, 1941

"My Führer,

On the occasion of your birthday, it is not only the best army in the world that cheers you, but also the brave and capable German people, to express their deep gratitude. The Italian people, equally grateful and respectful, will think of you. Perhaps we will even hear the first voice of the great chorus of the other European peoples who realize that everything you do will ultimately serve the good of all of Europe.
I, too, am authorized to express to you, on this day, my humble wishes and hope that the Almighty will continue to guard and bless you.

Heil, my Führer, your faithful Hermann Röchling."

Birthday message from Röchling to Hitler in 1941. Source: AN BB 36/6 TG 105 HR 45

The labor shortage began to weigh heavily on iron mining and steel production. Röchling, who made great use of foreign labor - prisoners of war, common law and political prisoners, civilian deportees, STO - immediately turned to French prisoners of war from the surrounding Stalags. We will see how he tried to obtain the implementation of a real forced labor policy in the Reich and in the occupied territories. An internal memo from the administration of the Röchling iron and steelworks in Völklingen mentions the presence, as of September 3, 1940, of 235 French prisoners of war, detached from Stalag XII-D

---

in Trier[132]. A second contingent of French prisoners of war from Stalag XII B in Frankenthal in the Palatinate arrived in October. According to an agreement signed two months later between the Röchling establishments and the military command, 595 French prisoners were made available[133]. These forced laborers, parked in barracks surrounded by barbed wire and a palisade on the outskirts of the factory, were guarded inside the production site by agents of the factory police, the *Werkschutz*, outside by groups of six soldiers, a non-commissioned officer and a sergeant-major, and during the night by reinforced units of fourteen men.

Since 1939, the *Werkschutz* served as the Gestapo's right-hand - and armed - arm in German companies for the surveillance of foreign workers and, more generally, for the maintenance of discipline. Violations of work regulations, such as late arrival at the factory, refusal of overtime work, sabotage, escape or theft were to be reported to him by the head of the department. Food sanctions seem to have been used frequently, according to the saying: "If you don't want to work, you don't have to eat! Nevertheless, from the very first days, the management of the Röchling factories, which had to deplore a number of escapes due to the complicity or negligence of

---

132. The attention paid to Röchling's demands in the aftermath of the armistice contrasts sharply with the slow response to the needs of the Volkswagen factory, even though it was a flagship company of the regime. Hans Mommsen, author with Manfred Grieger of a 1,000-page book on the car manufacturer under the Third Reich, lists the steps taken in vain by Volkswagen as early as 1940 to obtain French workers, who were considered reliable workers. The first commando of 800 to 1,000 French prisoners did not arrive until the end of 1943 at the VW-Werke, which had been converted into an arms and munitions manufacturer. Cf. Hans Mommsen, "Der Arbeitseinsatz von Franzosen im Volkswagenwerke," *Frankreich und Deutschland im Kriege*, ed. Stefan Martens and Maurice Vaïsse. Bonn, Bouvier, 2000, p. 461 *ff.*
133. AN BB 36/99. The contract with the Röchling firm, dated September 11, 1940, concerns 328 French prisoners of war.

the German military, promised a reward of 10 RM to the guards who succeeded in preventing the departure of prisoners of war[134].

Polish civilians, who had been subject to compulsory labor since the end of 1939, were the first group of nationals to be deported to the territory of the Reich to serve the war economy. In October 1940, the South-Western Association of Iron and Steel Industries (RVE) in Metz, of which Hermann Röchling was president, distributed a four-page circular to all its members with legal texts on the treatment of Polish workers. In the preamble, the document explains that in order to guarantee the success of the four-year plan, the Reich government had assigned a "special function" to the Poles, a function that resembled slavery. It is made clear, however, that it would not be "reconcilable with the common sense of the people" (*mit dem gesundem Volksempfinden nicht vereinbar*) to allow them to participate without hindrance in the social progress of the new Germany[135]."

The following rules apply to them:

- the wearing of a "P" as a distinctive sign sewn onto their clothing,

- the curfew,

- prohibiting, unless authorized by the police, the use of public transportation or the ownership of a bicycle,

- the ban on participating in German demonstrations of any kind and on entering public establishments!

In June, Röchling had requested 2,170 Poles for construction work at Völklingen. Instead, the authorities sent him a contingent of Serbs

---

134. AN BB 36/10, indictment Paul-Julien Doll.
135.AN BB 36/10, circular of the Bezirksgruppe Südwest der Wirtschaftsgruppe Eisenschaffende Industrie, Metz, October 10, 1940. At the end of April 1941, Gauleiter Bürckel decreed the implementation of measures to isolate "Polish civilian workers" from the local population in the Westmark, which included the Moselle, the Saar and the Palatinate.

taken from the thousands deported from the Balkans to the Reich after the capitulation of Belgrade in April 1941 and the establishment of a German military administration. The first group of 1,208 arrived during the summer, but a good part of them were immediately sent back to the country because of their state of health; as for those who remained, Röchling found their performance so disastrous that he approached Albert Speer, then head of the construction staff, to obtain 1,259 Spanish workers instead[136]. He even alerted General von Hanneken, a key figure in the military and civilian bureaucracy, and told him about his more or less unsuccessful attempts to bring Belgian and French civilian workers to Völklingen. Röchling, who "rightly" demanded these arms, which he considered to be of decisive importance for the war[137], even anticipated the authorization to employ Russian civilians on the territory of the Reich[138].

When his "old comrade-in-arms", General Heinrich Danckelmann, was appointed commander of the military administration in Serbia, the Saar Baron congratulated him, giving free rein to his contempt for the Serbs. It is not so simple, he wrote, to overcome this "savage people, little disciplined and even less cultivated". It was difficult, given their state of health and their inability to work, to exploit this workforce. The solution? "Our men are gradually learning different methods to deal with such people. These free Serbs are not treated too gently[139]."

---

136. AN BB 36/106, letter from the Arbeitsamt Saarbrücken to the Minister of Labor Berlin, November 6, 1941.

137. AN BB 36/10, doc. HR 203 TG 287, letter from Hermann Röchling to General von Hanneken, October 7, 1941.

138. AN BB 36/106, note from the Arbeitsamt Saarbrücken, November 20, 1941.

139. AN BB/36/8 HR 99, letter of October 21, 1941. Röchling was unaware that at the time of writing to Danckelmann, the latter had just been dismissed after only three months in office due to his inability to put an end to the Serbian insurrection.

At the Völklingen plant, these "methods" included the deprivation of food, which led the starving to appeal to public charity. The local newspaper, the *Völklinger Volksfreund* ("Friend of the People of Völklingen"!), spoke on behalf of the steelworks management to warn the inhabitants against "sterile mercy with the Serbian workers":

> "The methods of educating these lazy elements must be employed in this sense, that is, such Serbs who, with bad intentions, refrain from working, will be deprived of supplies. One might think that any reasonable German (*vernünftig-denkend*) would approve of this position. Unfortunately not! Recently it has become clear that those elements who flee from work and prowl around the city begging are supported by the inhabitants who give them coupons for bread (*Brotmarken) so that* they can get bread in the bakeries. (...) We must demand that the citizens of the enemy states, who have volunteered for work in Germany, earn their bread by working. We would not know what to do in Germany with surplus eaters who flee from work. Therefore, in the future all misunderstood sentimentality must disappear[140]."

In April 1942, the head of the foreigners' department of the Röchling factories, the *Werkschutz* and the people in charge of the accommodation camps agreed to publicly announce that Serbs - and Spaniards - would only be fed if they brought daily written proof from their superiors that they had "worked properly[141]"!

---

140. AN BB 36/31, HR 179,1 and 179,2 "Falsches Mitleid mit serbischen Arbeitern", October 10, 1941.
141. AN BB 36/10, document HR 294. Report of Mr. Langwieler, head of the foreigners' services to Hermann Röchling.

***

Many of those at the helm of the Third Reich, led by Hitler, were not in favor of employing foreigners. On the contrary, Göring and the industrialists were looking for ways to use them, but the guardians of Germanness feared above all the arrival of Soviet communists on Reich territory. They were not only a potential threat to racial purity, but could also be a source of propaganda that would undermine the ideological integrity of the people. Although a great defender of Germanness, Röchling was nevertheless convinced that the solution lay in "compulsory labor service" for men and women in all occupied territories. The failures he encountered in obtaining slave labor for "his" factories in Meurthe-et-Moselle reinforced this conviction. He would return to this point again and again during his monthly conferences with the commissioners of the metallurgical industry.

August 1, 1941: L'Écho de Nancy, a major regional daily newspaper, was entirely in the hands of the occupying forces (circulation of more than 50,000 copies). Source : https://kiosque.limedia.fr/recherche/?uniform_title=L%27%C3%89cho%20de%20Nancy

Chapter 5. A workforce that can be forced to work at mercy

...RAVAIL COMMUN

Par M. Paul-Cavallier
MAÎTRE DE FORGES
...NOMIQUE DE L'EST

LA REGION DE L'EST

PLAQUE TOURNANTE DES ECHANGES FRANCE-CENTRE-EUROPE

La Collaboration franco-allemande

Par HERMANN RŒCHLING
MANDATAIRE GÉNÉRAL DU REICH POUR LES INDUSTRIES
DU FER ET DE L'ACIER EN MEURTHE-ET-MOSELLE

M. Jean POUYER, secrétaire général de la Chambre de Commerce de Nancy nous dit...

Les Marches de l'Ouest

PONT ENTRE DEUX PEUPLES

Par M. BŒSING, président de la Chambre de Commerce de Sarrebrück

It was precisely such a "lack of participation" by the French in the war effort that led the collaborationist newspaper *L'Écho de Nancy* to publish a special anniversary edition entitled "Towards a New Europe" on August 1st, 1941. French and German politicians were among the contributors - as well as Hermann Röchling! - to celebrate the potential benefits of "Franco-German collaboration". While the editorialist reminds us that Germany is able to "remake our continent without French help," Röchling is not afraid to insist on Germany's magnanimity: it "gave France the opportunity to take its rightful place" in order to "develop our continent into a domain for all" and to move forward on the path leading "both peoples to prosperity."[142]

Towards the end of August 1941, the offensive against the USSR became anything but a blitzkrieg, and the manpower shortage had to be addressed. Hitler took the measure of the problem and ordered the transfer to the Reich of half a million Soviet prisoners of war. The first convoys of prisoners of war quickly arrived in Moselle, at the Ban-Saint-Jean camp, attached to Stalag XII-F in Boulay, and were then sent to the factories and mines in the Briey basin, in Luxembourg and in the Saarland. Some of them were assigned for a time to work in the farms in the area, while 3,000 were sent to the mines in the Moselle. Those in charge made an initial selection of able-bodied men, who were sent mainly to the mines of Creutzwald and to the steelworks of Rombas, Brebach and the Lorraine fiefdom of Röchling. In 1947, the French magistrates initiated a judicial inquiry to determine the fate of the prisoners of war who had passed through the Ban-Saint-Jean camp. According to the witnesses, it must be admitted that there were about 22,000 of them interned

---

142. https://kiosque.limedia.fr/ark:/31124/dtj06sklkxhrld4v/p1.item.r=Roechling

there, almost all of them peasants, without any experience of the working world[143].

In November, the Nazi hierarchy finally found a compromise on the question of the employment of civilians. They began to requisition Soviet soldiers, at first only Ukrainians. Göring set the rules for their employment on November 7, 1941: as previously decreed for Poles, civilians had to wear the "Ost" insignia sewn onto their clothing; both civilians and prisoners of war had to wear clogs, which became the distinctive acoustic sign of the Soviet and helped to thwart any attempt to flee[144]. It was also stipulated that they were to be fed "below the German level" and that they were not to be "spoiled" by being allowed to become accustomed to German food: food that was *artgemäß*, "in accordance with the needs of their species", was provided. In return for their work, these "Ostarbeiter", so-called free workers, were to be paid "pocket money"[145]. To prevent this new category of slaves from coming into contact with the German civilian population, their employment was only authorized on the condition that they were deployed in "closed columns" and kept away from all other foreigners, deportees or prisoners of war. And when he saw the first Ukrainian deportees arrive in the Saarland at the beginning of February 1942, Röchling, an ardent supporter of forced labor, rejoiced that soon Frenchmen would join them[146]!

---

143. Pascal Brenneur, "Les Prisonniers russes dans les mines de fer lorraines (1941-1944)", *Les Cahiers lorrains*, n° 1, March 1989, p. 39-57, here p. 49.
144. Pavel Poljan, "Die Deportation der Ostarbeiter im Zweiten Weltkrieg", (translated from Russian). *Stuttgarter Beiträge zur historischen Migrationsforschung*, vol. 2, 1995. http://elib.uni-stuttgart.de/opus/volltexte/2007/3283/pdf/Poljan_Deportation_1995_Migartionsforschung.pdf (accessed on 7.02.2023)
145. Dietrich Eichholtz, *Geschichte der deutschen Kriegswirtschaft*, vol. 2, 1941-1943, Berlin (East), 1971, new edition Munich, K.G. Saur, 2003, p. 191. Document 1193-PS, IMT , vol. XXVII (1), pp. 56-59.
146. AN BB 36/10, TG 255: letter to engineer Jacobs in Berlin, February 5, 1942.

***

The working class, especially in the factories and mines, formed the basis of a resistance that was organized from the very first days of the occupation. The communist party went underground and was reconstituted in Meurthe-et-Moselle, while in annexed Lorraine, where expulsions decimated the ranks, groups were not set up until the end of 1941. Between the two Lorraine regions, passing through the Pays-Haut, the inhabitants set up, as events unfolded, networks of smugglers for escaped prisoners of war, for those who refused to perform compulsory service, for those who did not comply with the law; tracts were distributed and a system of false passports, food cards, and weapons caches and depots were organized. Immigrant workers and miners, Italians and Poles, were very present among the activists.

However, in Lorraine, there was no mass movement comparable to the general strike that occurred in May-June 1941 in Nord-Pas-de-Calais, where 100,000 miners sabotaged the extraction of coal, which was so vital to the enemy[147]. In Nancy, the prefect Jean Schmidt, a fierce opponent of the communists, opportunely took measures that went beyond the demands of the occupier to prevent social and political strife. In January 1941, at the time of the first actions taken by the miners in the North, Schmidt signed an order authorizing warrantless searches of suspected communists or sympathizers, and ordering the indefinite internment of those who participated in the

---

147. As part of his investigation for the Flick trial in Nuremberg, Magistrate Gerthoffer asked that an investigation be conducted to establish the role of Otto Steinbrinck, then Reich delegate for the northern mines, in the shooting of 300 to 400 miners, who had been taken hostage during these events.

distribution of leaflets[148]. Despite these efforts, the subversive activity in Nord-Pas-de-Calais was to have repercussions among the workers in the French department of meurthe-et-mosellans: strikes broke out at the Neuves-Maisons factory on January 20, and at Auboué and Bouligny on May 16. Unrest was particularly pronounced in the mines of the Briey basin after the arrival of a contingent of miners from the North, and the authorities responded with the most brutal repressive measures[149]. In October, the occupying forces asked factory managers, police commissioners and mayors to provide them with lists of communists, not just to intern them; this time it was a matter of "shooting them for example[150]".

And while the authorities thought they had control over the territory and its inhabitants, an event occurred that demonstrated the ability of workers to fight against this fate: on the night of 4 to 5 February, the first sabotage of an industrial site in France took place in Auboué, in Meurthe-et-Moselle, in the electrical transformer of one of the "Röchling factories". The occupying forces gave this act of resistance considerable publicity and ordered reprisals against the perpetrators, French and Italian communists. The blackout, which deprived the blast furnace, seventeen mines and the town itself of power, was in fact short-lived and did not cause any casualties. However, Hitler demanded the execution of twenty Communists as an example. The day after this sabotage, the authorities proceeded to arrest seventy inhabitants of the Briey basin, including about forty Communists from the mines in Auboué and the Pays-Haut, trade unionists and Jews, targeted not for their quality as Frenchmen but as

---

148. Jean Claude and Yves Magrinelli, *Anti-fascism and Communist Party in Meurthe-et-Moselle*, 1920-1945. Jarville, 1985, p. 201.
149. Nicolas Hobam, *4 years of clandestine struggle in Lorraine*, Nancy, 1946.
150. AD MM WM 391: letter from the sub-prefecture of Briey to the prefect of Nancy, October 3, 1941.

Communists or Jews. All of them were sent to the camp of Royallieu, in Compiègne[151].

The affair provoked interventions and requests from local authorities to the highest level: after the protest of the prefect of Nancy, Jean Schmidt, it was the turn of Jacques Barnaud, general delegate for Franco-German relations, and then of Jean Raty, director of the Chiers blast furnaces and the Gorcy forges and president of the French delegation to the Franco-German economic commission in Wiesbaden, to protest against these reprisals, judged to be disproportionate to the facts.

Meanwhile, in Berlin, the death of Fritz Todt, killed in a plane crash during the night of February 7/8, led to some changes in the highest command positions: Albert Speer immediately took over as Reich Minister of Armaments. On the 20th, General Carl-Heinrich von Stülpnagel replaced his cousin Otto von Stülpnagel at the High Military Command in Paris, and on the 24th, a new government of occupied France was formed under the aegis of François Darlan. That same day, the military command of Bezirk C in Dijon announced that the date of execution of the "twenty communists" chosen from among the Auboué hostages had been set for March 12... unless the perpetrators of the Auboué transformer attack were handed over to the authorities.

February 17, 1942

"On the occasion of the sudden death of your most intimate collaborator, Reich Minister Dr. Todt, I would like to express my deepest condolences. We all know what you have lost

---

151. Lieutenant Colonel von Gemmingen, who was attached to the political internment and hostage camp at Royallieu, was related to the Röchlings.

in this man, as we know what we have lost.
Each of us who worked with him feels his loss
cruelly. It only remains for me to say to you,
my Führer, - and all those who attended the
funeral have confirmed this to me - that we
will do everything in our power to ensure that
the task undertaken by Dr. Todt and which will
be continued by his successor, whom we will
support with all our strength, will be carried
out successfully.

Heil, mein Führer.
Hermann Röchling"

The Auboué hostage episode was brought before the commission in Wiesbaden by Jean Raty on March 6, 1942. During his interrogation at Nuremberg in 1947, Raty stated that he had stressed that such a mass execution, contrary to the law, would risk arousing "great discontent" in the French working population, with a consequent "decrease in output"[152]. Raty obtained from Paul Raabe, the Reich's plenipotentiary for the management of the mines, the promise to intervene, and, at first, the decision was taken to postpone the execution. However, Raty decided not to stop there and called Ernst Röchling in Paris. The matter seemed so serious that Marshal Pétain had to make a plea. On March 30, the head of the Vichy government submitted a request for clemency to Marshal Keitel. For his part,

---

152. Interrogation conducted by Charles Gerthoffer, magistrate in charge of the Röchling trial, May 22, 1947. AN BB 36/6, SEF 609 TG 174.

Hermann Röchling initiated a petition, including a commitment to the regime, which was signed by 20,000 employees of the Meurthe-et-Moselle mines and sent to the military High Command. Other interventions followed, including those of the Italian ambassador and Albert Speer, who was also concerned that such an act of repression would be counterproductive at a time when French workers were being requisitioned en masse for work in Germany. On April 2, Hitler announced that the twenty hostages would not be sentenced to death, but ordered that all those arrested be deported to Auschwitz. Of the convoy of seventy, which left on July 6, 1942, there were only seven survivors. During the trial in Rastatt in 1948, Röchling claimed to have been at the origin of this "gesture of humanity", a gesture whose effectiveness can however be questioned...

Despite threats and reprisals, "communist acts of terror" - as the occupiers called them - continued and multiplied. A railway telephone line near Lunéville was destroyed on March 25; 425 kg of explosive materials disappeared from an isolated warehouse belonging to a construction company in Ludres. During the night of April 3 to 4, the explosives were used to demolish the engine of a turbine in the steelworks of Neuves-Maisons, where Röchling himself controlled the production and had experimental metallurgy tests carried out. In the Vosges and Meurthe-et-Moselle regions, the prefects were obliged to keep a close watch on the most important industrial and energy production companies. Röchling took advantage of the circumstances to enforce strict disciplinary measures throughout industry in Saarland and Lorraine. The Feldkommandantur reported that on Röchling's initiative, and with the approval of the *Bezirkschef* (district chief of the military administration), "several waves of arrests were made in order to lock up all men known to be communists who were not yet under arrest and

the Italians and to send them to the east later on. Also on Röchling's initiative, the Feldkommandantur intervened with the prefect of Nancy to offer rewards for the discovery of the criminals. The prefect posted this threat to the population concerning collective responsibility for the sabotage:

> "It is obvious that in the event of new acts of this type, any intervention by the French authorities with the occupier will no longer make it possible to avoid heavy sanctions which will hit the entire population[153]."

On April 12, Röchling informed Speer of the arrest of some one hundred to two hundred people "previously known as communists and agitators", and of their transfer, along with their relatives, to a camp with the intention of keeping them in detention as long as possible[154]. He demanded the introduction of close surveillance of all war economy production sites: outside each enterprise, people's militias; and inside, a *Werkschutz* of at least 5% of the staff and provided with weapons "for exceptional circumstances[155]". With the help of the Vichy police, the occupying forces arrested and shot eleven communist militants at the Malpierre clearing not far from Nancy; forty others belonging to a clandestine network in the Pays-Haut region were tried at the end of a well-orchestrated show trial, which took place over four days in July. Fourteen of these "Muscovite terrorists" were put to the sword, again at Malpierre;

---

153. AN AJ/40/926: Feldkommandantur K 591 of Nancy. Report for the period from mid-March to mid-May 1942.
154. AN BB 36/TG 257.
155. In reality, this factory police force was set up as soon as the Germans arrived in the two Lorraine. It was neither more nor less than the continuation of the French "factory guards" that were then placed under the control of the Gestapo.

twenty-two were sentenced to heavy deportation; only one was acquitted[156]. One month later, another group of twenty-eight FTPF was destroyed. The Lorraine Resistance lost a total of sixty-seven partisans to the platoons at La Malpierre, but sabotage continued, mainly on communication routes, accompanied by passive resistance in the mines and factories.

156. AD MM 102 W 1: communication of Jean-Claude Magrinelli.

Chapter 6. Röchling, master of the war machine

In 1969, the historian Willi Boelcke published a book entitled *Germany's Armament during the Second World War. Interviews of Albert Speer with Hitler 1942-1945* [*Deutschlands Rüstung im Zweiten Weltkrieg. Hitlers Konferenzen mit Albert Speer 1942-1945*]. These are in fact the reports that Speer wrote of 91 conferences with his Führer[157]. Never translated, nor republished, this work gives us information on Speer's hold on the Reich's economic potential and opens a window on the major role of Hermann Röchling. It is also a lesson in history, for it reveals a revealing discrepancy: the academic world showed little interest in this collection of documents, but it did pay attention to Speer's own memoirs, the first volume of which, also published in 1969, was an impressive success.

Yet Wilhelm Treue, a specialist in German social and economic history, was quick to denounce Speer's mystification, calling Boelcke's book to the attention of the general public: *Speer is unmasked by his own writings.* Treue criticizes his skill in playing with figures, a skill "developed to perfection" to convince the Führer and other high political figures that everything was fine, and to "demonstrate his own

---

157. Willi Boelcke, *Deutschlands Rüstung im Zweiten Weltkrieg. Hitlers Konferenzen mit Albert Speer 1942-1945.* Frankfurt am Main, Akademische Verlagsgesellschaft, Athenaion, Bibliothek der Geschichte, 1969. Text conforms to the documents used in part in the Nuremberg trials.

irreplaceability." Hermann Röchling, his creature, played the role of "éminence grise" in this organization built by Speer.

Treue, who himself had to suffer from the deceitfulness of former Nazis after the war, was convinced that from now on the history of the Second World War would not be written without reference to the documents and data collected by Boelcke[158]. More than half a century later, we can see that this is far from being the case.

***

By appointing Speer as director of armaments and munitions, Hitler gave him a larger space and freed him from a dependence on Göring, which was the greatest obstacle to the concentration of functions in the conduct of the war. Speer not only sought to reorganize administrative competencies, but at the same time to integrate industrialists into the management of their sector of activity. With Hitler's support, he forced Göring to hand over to him the services of the Five-Year Plan, in charge of the military economy, and to appoint him as General Delegate for Armaments (*Generalbevollmächtigter für Rüstungsfragen*). This was done, and despite the obvious need to reduce confusion and conflicts between the ministries and to avoid any dispersion of effort, Hitler placed Fritz Sauckel, the new plenipotentiary for manpower employment (*Generalbeauftragter für den Arbeitseinsatz*), formally under the authority of Göring, and not Speer.

For the new Minister of Armaments, war production and manpower issues had to be planned and centralized. However, despite a desire to simplify and unify the management bodies, their

---

158. Wilhelm Treue, "Spiel mit falschen Zahlen," *Die Zeit*, October 31, 1969.

tangle accelerated during the first months of the Speer era. In order not to depend on military control and to clean up the existing structures, new ones had to be created. Negotiations already underway in the RWM were resumed with a view to forming a steel cartel along the lines of the "RVK" (*Reichsvereinigung Kohle*), which had been set up the previous year to restructure the coal industry. Speer wanted to overcome the rivalries and ambitions of the steel magnates and achieve the crowning and planning of the production chain, from the iron, coal and lime mines to the forges and steelworks and the recycling of scrap metal, an approach that would facilitate "self-management" by the manufacturers themselves.

In order to bring together senior military officers and the armaments industry, an "armaments council" (*Rüstungsrat*[159]) was set up as a first step towards negotiations for the establishment of a central management. The textile industrialist Hans Kehrl was appointed head of industry in the Speer Ministry and was given the task of reorganizing the entire system of raw material management and quotas. In his memoirs, published in 1973, Kehrl emphasizes the fundamental role played at that time by Hermann Röchling, an "imposing personality" whose inventiveness and vitality "were comparable to no other [...] despite his advanced age[160]".

Speer placed another of his deputies, the chemist Walther Schieber, in the Directorate of Armaments Procurement [*Rüstungslieferungsamt*] and, in the autumn, gave him the

---

159. The Rüstungsrat included five high-ranking Wehrmacht officers - Milch, Fromm and Leeb, Witzell and Thomas - as well as eight industrialists from the armaments sector, Bücher, Keßler, Pleiger, Poensgen, Röchling, Röhnert, Vögler and Zangen. Alfried Krupp, Hans Malzacher and William Werner joined them in July 1942.
160. Hans Kehrl, *Krisenmanager im Dritten Reich. 6 Jahre Frieden - 6 Jahre Krieg. Erinnerungen.* Critical notes and afterword by Erwin Viefhaus. Düsseldorf, Droste Verlag, 1973, p. 263.

Chapter 6. Röchling, master of the war machine

supervision of a network of "armaments commissions". In practice, this meant that at the regional level, the heavyweights of private industry would be able to appoint people to act as "arms supervisors" [*Rüstungsobmann*]. In the summer, Speer finally succeeded in ousting von Hanneken, a military officer close to Göring and notoriously inefficient: he was relieved of his duties for the distribution of iron and steel, and the Marshal also made some tactical concessions, delegating the distribution of coal and iron for France and Belgium to a reserve officer, Caesar von Hofacker, a friend of Ernst Röchling. Better still, Hermann Röchling's cousin became the RVE representative to the military high command in France, and thus the pivot in the negotiations between von Hofacker, Pierre Cathala and Jean Bichelonne at the Ministry of Industrial Production for the Vichy government. He had a double mission: to help achieve the objectives set by Speer... and to negotiate, if necessary, advantages for Röchling.

***

Even before his official appointment as President of the RVE and Reich Commissioner for Iron and Steel in the occupied territories, the exchanges between Speer and Röchling followed the course of affairs that marked the stages of this reorganization of the war machine, consolidating the powers of the new minister and his protégé. Without specific skills in the fields concerned, Speer had to surround himself with expert collaborators, technicians and engineers, to gather opinions and studies. As rivalries at all levels of the Nazi hierarchy made trust and collaboration difficult, the working and friendly relationship he cultivated with Hermann Röchling was all the more valuable. This industrialist of the older generation was not only an experienced arms specialist and fervent Nazi, but also a personality that Hitler greatly appreciated.

Long before the beginning of the Speer era, the Saar Baron, always on the lookout for a more efficient organization, had taken care to send a series of memoranda on the subject to the right person. In the autumn of 1941, he advised Fritz Todt to use "some of our Russian prisoners of war" to increase the extraction of raw materials. And in January 1942, he sent Göring his memorandum entitled "Steel in the War", in which he spoke of concentrating skills in the steel industry. For the time being, he was "powerless" to witness the lack of coordination between the business of the mines and the needs of the steelworks in Lorraine, Luxembourg and Meurthe-et-Moselle, which led him to say that, for the proper conduct of the war, it was necessary to put an end to the current division between "forge people" on the one hand, and "mine people" on the other. This implies, of course, that his powers allow him to "explain to the people of the mines what they have to do[161]".

Concerned about the low production of steel in the western territories, Speer spoke with the Führer on 19 March, who made the following proposal: to continue negotiations with French and Belgian bosses with a view to improving output, relying "particularly" on Röchling, whose merits as an expert are not in doubt[162]. Finally, Speer asked Röchling to communicate his proposals to him[163]. This was done on April 12: a workforce of 5,000 managers and 55,000 workers would be needed to improve the performance of the iron industry in

<hr>

161. BDIC FΔ 1724/II. Document of January 20, 1942, HR 84, TG 205.
162. Willi Boelcke, *op. cit.* p. 76.
163. AN BB 36/6 doc HR 20, TG 207.

the protectorate (Bohemia-Moravia), in Poland, and in the occupied territories of the West[164].

On April 20, Hitler's birthday, Röchling explained to his Führer the problems already inventoried in his January memorandum "Steel in the War"[165]; he addressed to Speer five pages of comments on the reorganization of the war economy, which must break with the unfortunate "democratic spirit" of the Schacht era:

> "We must get out of this economic democracy in which individual egoism is always considered good even when it goes against the general interest. For at present there is no authority to compel the individual to do what is necessary for the welfare of the people and the state. But what should be done? One can imagine - to start with the simplest - that in economic and scientific associations everyone is required to share his experiences in all important fields without reservation[166]."

And Röchling concludes on the need to establish in industry, as in any military organization, a *Befehlsgewalt*, absolute authority of superiors to ensure perfect obedience to orders!

On the 22nd, he submitted a memorandum to his minister on two projects that he believed would solve the problems of electricity supply: the first, validated by Swiss engineers, consisted of a series of dams on

---

164. AN BB 36/9, NI 2522.

165. AN BB 36/10, TG 110 HR 32. Röchling gave him a bust of the late Fritz Todt, modeled by the sculptor Fritz Berberich and cast at the Völklingen plant. At Röchling's request, Beberich had sculpted a bust of Hitler in 1941 as a birthday present for the Baden State Minister Schmitthenner. Finally, in 1943, Berberich made a bust of Generalfeldmarschall Rommel.

166. AN BB 36/107: letter from Röchling to Speer, April 20, 1942.

the Rhine to facilitate river transport between Basel and Lake Constance. This project, which was to be carried out entirely by Swiss firms, was to be supported at all costs, as it would allow the production of energy in quantity as well as alleviate the burden on the Reich's railroads. The second was a project to expand a power plant in Kembs on the Upper Rhine, which had already been initiated by the French on the eve of hostilities[167]. On the 29th, he expressed his dissatisfaction, because mobilization affected a higher percentage of men in the Saarland factories than elsewhere and this had to be remedied[168]. And the next day, when Speer asked him how to increase iron and steel production in the western Saarland, his answer was clear: to achieve economies of scale, i.e. by reducing the number of sites operated[169]. An increase of 3 to 4% can be achieved, perhaps more in Belgium, he believes, even if the 7,000 miners he is calling for are still lacking. He insists, however, that the *sine qua non* for an improvement is this *Befehlsgewalt*, which allows for "brutal and ruthless" repressive action "with impunity" (*bei schärfstem rücksichtlosen Durchgreifen*). Röchling knew only too well the expectations of the Nazi leadership not to exceed them.

This total control of iron and steel production was to be matched by an association that would oversee the entire sector. Speer discussed with the Führer the delicate question of choosing a president for this cartel, the nerve of the war and the key to the new central planning. The following is Speer's account of their talks:

> "April 19-20, 1942: The Führer also considered it necessary to commission someone within the framework of the four-year plan to increase iron production. He has been

---

167. AN BB 36/107: letter from Röchling to Speer, April 22, 1942.
168. AN BB 36/107: letter from Röchling to Speer, April 29, 1942.
169. AN BB 36/6 TG 209, HR 88-2.

reminded that this task is now the responsibility of General von Hanneken, but he also thinks that it would be better to have someone from the economy in this position. He considered my proposal to give this task to Vögler acceptable, but nevertheless thought that Röchling could do a better job. He leaves it to us to decide.

May 6-7, 1942: I briefly reported to the Führer the establishment of the 'Reichsvereinigung Eisen' and the proposal to give the presidency to Röchling. The Führer seemed to have great faith in Röchling's appointment. I informed him of Röchling's memorandum of April 30, in which it appears to be quite possible to increase iron production by 5% over the previous level without additional coal and without the need for additional means of transport. At the same time I pointed out to the Führer that it would not be desirable for the gentlemen of the Ruhr to be entrusted with the leadership of the iron association.

May 18, 1942, Führerhauptquartier, Berlin: The Führer notes that the Reich Marshal, Reich Minister Funk, and I want to entrust the management of steel production to Röchling, but that the statutes drawn up by the Ministry of Economics are excessively democratic (*durchaus parlamentarisch*) and too soft.

He approved my proposal to strengthen and clarify these provisions, also my proposal to have Herr Röchling appointed, following the example of Gauleiter Sauckel, by a Führererlaß[170]."

---

170. Willi Boelcke, *op. cit.* pp. 106 *ff*, and p. 122. The *Fühererlass* was a special decree of the Führer.

At the end of April, Röchling and Speer were received in the Führerhauptquartier. Röchling gave his version of this meeting during an interrogation conducted by the American authorities in 1947: he explained to Hitler that during the First World War, Germany, including Austria, had not produced enough iron and steel, and that even to reach this totally insufficient level, it would have been necessary to destroy a good part of the factories under German control in Belgium and France in order to have scrap metal available to feed the blast furnaces.

"Hitler replied: "You don't want to start this nonsense again. (...) He then asked me if I would be willing to direct the iron industry in Germany and the occupied countries, I declared that I would be willing on the condition that I had enough authority[171]."

June 1942: Röchling, with his son-in-law Hans-Lothar Freiherr von Gemmingen-Hornberg, visiting Hitler at his Werwolf headquarters near Vinnytsia, Ukraine.
Source: National Archives

---

171. Interrogation conducted by Mr. Eric Kaufmann on November 9, 1946. French translation AN BB 35/93 SEF 1013. See also AN BB 36/9 SEF 1013,9, interrogation 264 d.

And the Führer immediately ordered Speer to transfer these powers to Röchling. The *Reichsvereinigung Eisen*, "RVE," an association under private law with state powers, was created on May 28, and the next day Röchling was appointed its president. His appointment, however, was not made by the supreme authority, the *Führererlaß*, but simply by order of the Minister of Economics Funk, who at the same time appointed two deputies, Walter Rohland and Alfried Krupp von Bohlen und Halbach. From then on, Röchling's control extended to the decision-making process of the entire steel industry. He replaced Reichert and Poensgen, who had moved away from the circles of power, and he combined this first mandate with the management of the Confederation of Iron Production (*Hauptring Eisenerzeugung*), a subsidiary grouping of iron-producing industries. Then, on June 18, Göring appointed him "Reich Delegate for Iron and Steel in the occupied regions", i.e. in the West, including Alsace-Lorraine and Luxembourg, in Norway, Northern Styria and Southern Carinthia (Austria), Bialystok (Poland), in the Sudetenland and Bohemia-Moravia, as well as for the Reich Commissariats of Eastland, Ukraine and Serbia. Röchling delegated a region to each of his competitors: to Rohland (Vestag) the Ruhr, to Pott (Ballestrem Konzern) Upper Silesia, to Flick the center, and to the Austrian Schmid von Schmidsfelden the southeast region. Röchling himself kept control of Western Europe and, thanks to this system of rivalries instituted within the Third Reich, he was now the superior of Paul Raabe, the Reich delegate for iron mines in the occupied territories in the West, and of Otto Steinbrinck, responsible for iron and steel in the northern zone[172].

---

172. In June, Steinbrinck resigned in haste, tired of the perennial conflicts with Röchling, to join the "Reichsvereinigung Kohle" (RVK). Steinbrinck was also the trustee of Fritz Thyssen's shares in the Vereinigte Stahlwerke, after the latter had left Nazi Germany.

On June 10, in Knutange, Moselle, Röchling announced his finally acquired authority to the steelmakers of the south-western grouping. He outlined a number of objectives that had to be achieved if the private industry was to prove its worth, namely to strengthen the locomotive and wagon construction programs and to start building the Eastern Wall - which Hitler did not decree until August 11, 1943. Röchling was also very clear about the powers he had been given: "Dictatorial powers are necessary to carry out operations more quickly[173]." The fact remains that the "military obedience" and "disinterestedness" expected of his subordinates remain pious words, because in the end everything will depend on the goodwill of those who, like himself, will never stop looking for future markets and financial advantages for their own companies.

***

As chairman of the RVE and Reich delegate for the occupied territories, Röchling centralized the labor demands for the entire iron industry and communicated them to Speer, who decided on the basic policy for the allocation of raw materials and workers, German and foreign, deported and prisoners of war. He demanded that on the 1st and 16th of each month all factories provide him with their raw steel production figures. In Meurthe-et-Moselle, a monthly meeting was held with the directors of "his" factories to dictate his orders, i.e. to demand a precise output. In August 1942, for good cause, he dismissed the first German director of the Neuves-Maisons steelworks for having been too complacent with the French workers.

---

173. AN BB 36/30, NI 060, tg 215.

Every month, the technical directors of all the sites, in Germany as well as in the occupied territories, informed him of their growing needs for manpower, men and women, prisoners of war or civilians, lists that were transmitted to Fritz Sauckel, at the end of the chain of command, which meant deportation for hundreds of thousands of people. At Nuremberg, Sauckel paid with his life for having been the zealous executioner of a program ordered by Speer and Röchling. Some of the RVE reports, signed by Hermann Röchling, were filed in 1947 by the prosecution in the Flick trial at Nuremberg[174]. One of these documents, from July 1942, mentions the request transmitted by Röchling to Sauckel for 6,000 prisoners of war to be assigned to the iron mines of Meurthe-et-Moselle, in addition to the 5,000 prisoners of war and 45,000 Russian civilians that Röchling expected to transfer before the end of August. His remonstrances speak for themselves:

"... The 5,000 prisoners of war have arrived, but the Russian civilian workers did not meet our expectations either in number or in ability. Many more women have arrived than the factories can employ at the moment. It is all the more unpleasant that the hopes we could have entertained of soon being allocated, after the RVK, other Russian prisoners of war, have considerably weakened[175]."

174. The Nuremberg trials have left an impressive number of documents of primary importance. However, everything that relates to the mechanisms of the war economy and that explains to a large extent the functioning of the National Socialist system has hardly been exploited in the literature. In 1965, two historians of the German Democratic Republic attempted to fill this gap, publishing documents from the "Flick case," one of twelve "successive trials" that took place in the Bavarian city between 1946 and 1949. This volume, entitled *Case No. 5. Anklageplädoyer, ausgewählte Dokumente, Urteil des Flick-Prozeßes*], has never been translated or even republished.
175. AN BB 36/36 NI 2523: 7 September 1942.

In his "central plan" adopted in July, Speer reported on the situation in the presence of the Führer from August 10 to 12. None of the various industrial leaders had any qualms about implementing a forced labor policy, but not all had the same decision-making power. It was Röchling's turn to present and comment on the fourth-quarter program to produce 2,650,000 tons of steel per month, which could only be achieved if sufficient coal and manpower were available. However, Pleiger, who was responsible for coal, admitted that he had difficulties with the work of the prisoners of war, their low output and the shortcomings caused by the air raids. Sauckel, for his part, promised to provide one million Russian "workers" before the end of October 1942. Speer then reported that the Führer had authorized Sauckel to take all necessary measures to "settle" this manpower issue. Clearly, if this could not be done on a voluntary basis, then "any measure of force would be lawful, not only in the East but also in the occupied regions in the West." The meeting concluded with the following statement: if the output was achieved, the industrialists would obtain in return an increase in the price of coal and iron from January 1st, 1943!

The problems were not solved for all that. In October, Röchling sent Speer a new memorandum on the need for manpower: in the coal mines, between 100 and 200,000 men were needed[176]! For the iron ore mines, a contingent of 150,000 Soviet prisoners of war was planned, which seemed to him to be cruelly insufficient, even to maintain the level of production, as most of these prisoners were physically ill-prepared for this hard work. An RVE report records the result of these requests: "We have received only 9,000 workers out of the 60,000 requested for the 4th quarter of 1942, for the iron and

---

176. AN BB 36/6 doc. HR 187, 2 TG 219: memorandum of October 5, 1942.

Chapter 6. Röchling, master of the war machine

steel industry, including the iron mines, which leaves a deficit of 51,000 workers [...][177]."

Röchling was particularly inventive in obtaining labor for the factories under his direct control. As an example, let's take the case of the quarries and lime kilns of the Meuse (Billemont, Dompcevrin, Dugny-sur-Meuse, Haudainville, Saint-Germain, Montgrignon, Sorcy, Vaucouleurs), suppliers of the "Röchling factories" and thus exempt from providing quotas of workers to be sent to Germany. In May 1942 - a few months before the negotiations for the "relief" and even before his official appointment as grand master of steel for the whole of Germany and the occupied territories - Röchling had intervened with the Oberkommando of the Wehrmacht: 250 prisoners of war, former employees of the lime kilns of the Meuse, would be put back to work while waiting to obtain Ukrainian deportees as exchange labor[178]. When questioned by the judicial police in 1947, an engineer from the Haudainville lime kilns explained the real interest of this exceptional measure: Röchling simply wanted to be able to produce 100,000 more tons of steel per month in the autumn in the Lorraine basin. Thus, in exchange for the repatriation of their comrades, all the personnel of the furnaces had to promise to increase the output to supply the steelworks. For each repatriated prisoner, the additional production should reach 50 tons per month. If the proxy - a man from Röchling who was in charge of supervising the operations on the site - judged their output to be insufficient, the repatriates were sent back to Germany immediately.

In order to keep "his" companies under control, "so that they carry out my orders at all times", Röchling had to be on the spot

---

177. AN BB 36/9 doc. 294, NI-2522; doc. 295, NI-4526.
178. AD MM 102 W n°1801: file Röchling, pv of Mr. Henri Wolters, engineer of arts and manufactures of Verdun, director of the lime kilns of Haudinville during the Occupation.

as often as possible, which obliged him to travel a lot - between Luxembourg, Lorraine, Belgium and his own factories in Saarland and Wetzlar, Hesse, to say nothing of his regular trips to meetings in Berlin, Düsseldorf or Paris[179]. But his private plane, which he said was not very functional, was too slow and lacked a radio. He asked Speer for "help" to be able to fly at discretion, and with a more suitable machine, enclosing with his letter a list of the routes he had flown since taking office. His request is clear:

> "It was your desire that I should be head of the RVE. You certainly took into account in this that the great reserves of capacity that we will have to exhaust in the long run are in the West. You also took into account that I am best qualified to deal with the French, Belgians and Luxembourgers, etc., because of my own background and that of my family, a fact which I have seen even now very often[180]."

Speer immediately forwarded the request to the Ministry of Aviation, which authorized Röchling to purchase two "Siebel 104" aircraft.

***

The "levies" of civilian manpower in France, known as "Sauckel actions", which began in June 1942, were dependent on the "Röchling actions" defined beforehand and recorded in the "central plan". These

---

179. During his travels, Röchling noticed that there were often too many personnel in the small airfields. And writes, on this subject, to Speer to make him notice that these personnel would be better employed in factory! AN BB 36/107, letter of September 30, 1942.
180. AN BB 36/6, HR 49, TG 217, letter of August 1st, 1942.

actions brought to light a new contradiction, a new rivalry, in the highest circles of Nazi power, namely the opposition between Sauckel and Speer on the question of French labor: informed almost daily by Röchling about the reality on the ground, Speer wanted to try to exploit the French workers on the spot, knowing that the imposition of requisitions was swelling the ranks of the resistance fighters and that acts of sabotage were going to increase.

The Vichy government's response to these "actions" was "relief". In order to obtain the 250,000 men, including 150,000 specialized workers, to be sent to Germany by the end of July, the occupying forces said they were ready to authorize the return of one prisoner of war for every three departures, a ratio that was in reality only one to seven. "Mixed" Franco-German commissions established quotas and lists of departures by name for each company. Those who worked directly for the German armament industry were protected from these requisitions, but they were forced to work a 54-hour week, which was increased to 62 hours in the mines, and as a general rule, they had to work every other Sunday, and even every Sunday in some jobs. These "protected" workers in the factories classified as "Rüstung" or in the Lorraine metallurgical industry under the control of Röchling, including the ancillary industries, made up more than two thirds of the workforce in the three non-annexed Lorraine departments! For 1942, the net balance of the "Röchling factories" was neutral: the 300 skilled workers sent to Germany at the end of 1942 were replaced by 300 laborers.

There was another obstacle to the smooth running of the "Sauckel actions": at the same time, people were being recruited for the Todt organization, which was carrying out the construction of the Atlantic Wall in France and other work in the construction sector to repair the damage caused by the bombing of German cities. As a result, many French workers preferred to join the Todt organization, hoping to stay in France[181]. And since the Baron of Saarland was tirelessly seeking to provide the steel industry in the western regions with additional contingents of foreign workers and specialists, the burden of requisitions in this area quickly became intolerable for the "unprotected" industries. From the end of October, in view of the initial disappointing results, the German authorities took matters into their own hands, not without brutality, to "comb" each factory and each workshop in search of "human material".

In Belgium, on October 6, the occupying forces decided on compulsory labor service for all. Röchling, who was immediately apprehensive about the poor results of this recruitment because of the "anti-German attitude" that "stiffened" the Belgian population, took the initiative of writing a new memorandum to Speer with his advice on how to tame the rebels: he proposed enlisting 100 to 200,000 young people between the ages of 18 and 25 in closed battalions under German command and using them as hostages in order to guarantee the good conduct of their parents in the country[182]! Held "firmly in our hands", these units could then be sent to the Eastern Front so that the young Belgians "learn to defend their skin"! "Besides," he adds, "the women at least will have a strong diversion to their thoughts. That too is something." The situation in Belgium is such that Röchling will even complain about it to his Führer on the occasion of his New Year's greetings:

> "I have, of course, still to overcome many difficulties which arise mainly from the fact that, in Belgium especially, the

---

181. Rémy Desquesnes, "L'Organisation Todt en France (1940-1944)", *Histoire, économie et société*, 1992, vol. 11, n° 3, pp. 535-550.
182. AN BB 36/8, HR 97,2, TG 275, memorandum of December 5, 1942.

industrialists still do not believe and do not want us to win the war. ... This has not resulted in attempts at opposition, but cooperation has given way here and there to a wait-and-see attitude. Perhaps in the long run it will be necessary to take severe measures against one of the leading personalities who have in their hands the threads leading to all societies. In itself, it is ridiculous that these people think they can resist us. I always tell them at my monthly meetings that they have no hope of avoiding collaboration with us. When I told them recently that the Reichsmarschall had told us some time ago that this war could last 30 years and that they should organize for such an eventuality, their surprise was incredibly painful[183]."

However, the political authorities did not listen to the steel czar's warnings.

***

November 11, 1942: the whole of France came under the control of the Wehrmacht. Röchling now had direct authority over the steel industry in the southern zone, and he thought he could finally improve the productivity of his sector in the interests of the war. His technicians were sent to the mines in the Pyrenees in search of personnel to transfer to Lorraine, where, according to him, the level of output was particularly low[184]. And to counterbalance the departure of the Germans for the front, it was necessary to track down the last reserves of labor in the occupied countries in the West. The policy of "voluntary work" hardly

---

183. AN BB 36/36, TG 220, HR 100: letter of December 24, 1942.
184. AN BB 36/97: letter from Röchling to Speer of December 30, 1942.

paid off, and so, in a memorandum to Speer dated December 5, he returned, once again, to the importance of a forced labor regime:

> "As in the year 1916, it has generally been increasingly recognized that the growing needs in all areas of war conduct cannot be met without calling upon the able but not fully utilized inhabitants of the occupied areas. But the results of the voluntary work do not correspond to the needs. That is why, despite much hesitation, compulsory labor had to be resorted to[185]."

... And he took advantage of his New Year's greetings to the Führer to slip in this recommendation for more firmness in relations with the French:

> "In France, the collaboration with the industrialists is better. The occupation of the whole of France and the momentary loss of North Africa have naturally caused a strong emotion. If we take advantage of the circumstances to have a more energetic attitude in France, this can only have good results[186]."

As if to echo these words, on January 4, 1943, Sauckel sent an internal memo to his staff, which mentioned a telephone conversation with Speer. By decision of the Führer, "it is no longer necessary to have special consideration for the French." The use of more "consequential" methods to enlist the workforce in France was henceforth legal, and this at all levels of qualification[187]. So act!

---

185. AN BB 36/35 HR 97,2,: memorandum of December 5, 1942.
186. AN BB 36/36, TG 220, HR 100: letter of December 24, 1942.
187. ITM, vol XV, 556-PS.

***

November 12, 1942: for his 70th birthday, Röchling received the *Adlerschild,* the highest civilian award of the Reich, an event that was widely covered by the newspapers. It was not only a great "boss" and "technician" who was honored, but also a "politician", a "friend of the fatherland", an unconditional defender of Germanness[188]. In front of a phalanx of high-level officials from the metal industry, the armed forces and politics, Minister Funk saluted this personality who had always known how to "unreservedly subordinate his personal interests and those of his company to the interests of the nation[189]".

Indeed, Röchling was soon given new opportunities to serve the Third Reich - as a propagandist. His article "Eisen im Krieg" (Eisen in the War) - a plea for a man with exceptional powers to manage the war economy - appeared in the business periodical *Der Vierjahresplan* on December 15, 1942, and was reprinted in several Reich newspapers in early 1943[190]. And while the soldiers of the Sixth Army were starving and surrounded in Stalingrad under minus 30-40 °, how to maintain the illusion of victory in the population? For the New Year of 1943, he addressed a "message of hope" to the German people, which was published on the front page of the daily *Deutsche Allgemeine Zeitung.* Among the reminders of the National Socialist doctrine was the leitmotiv, the fight against the "Jewish plot", a fight which, for the Saarland's Iron Baron, gave the war its full meaning:

---

188. *Deutsche Allgemeine Zeitung,* November 11, 1942. The NSDAP newspaper, the *Völkischer Beobachter,* devoted two articles to him, on November 10 and 14, 1942.
189. *Völkischer Beobachter,* November 14, 1942; *Deutsche Bergwerkszeitung* (Düsseldorf), November 13, 1942; *Neues Wiener Tagblatt,* November 8 and 13, 1942.
190. See, among others, the *Neues Wiener Tagblatt* of February 14, 1943.

"On both sides, the interface is the Jew. In Russia, Stalin relies heavily on his Jewish henchmen [...], in England, the Jewish aristocracy always leads the people. In the United States, Roosevelt's entourage is full of Jews. Judaism is the link between Bolshevism and capitalism. In both cases, it exploits the people... in these three countries, the Jews and all that it implies have succeeded in making the people naively accept this fundamental doctrine in order to ensure the perpetuation of their domination, which is seen as inextricably linked to this doctrine."

Then, to conclude, this mock prayer: "May we serve the Führer and the people and provide our inimitable soldiers with everything they need for the war. May we be successful from then on. Amen[191]!"

Hermann Röchling at the podium of an NSDAP rally.
Source : National Archives

---

191. BArch R 8034/III 377, "Der Zweite Weltkrieg," *Deutsche Allgemeine Zeitung,* December 31, 1942.

Part Three:
Human Material and Raw Materials

Chapter 7. The "total war"

January 13, 1943: In a Führererlaß that would remain secret, Hitler called for "total mobilization" for the final victory: all men from 16 to 65, all women from 17 to 45, were concerned. The fervor of the civilian population had to be awakened and sacrifices had to be made, even though it had become impossible to hide the fate of the armies in Stalingrad from them.

January 30, 1943: Reich Marshal Hermann Göring speaks live on the radio. His mission: to prepare the population for the announcement of the surrender of the forces under the command of General Paulus, a crucial turning point in the Second World War.

Three days of national mourning were declared, during which only solemn music was played. But it was on February 4, 1943, that Hermann Röchling, responsible for the metallurgical industry in all the territories under German domination and president of the *Reichsvereinigung Eisen*, was called upon to praise the war effort accomplished so far and celebrated the "quite considerable results" obtained, not without evoking the "extraordinary feat" of the soldiers at Stalingrad. The whole people "should be remobilized for the great tasks" to come, and it is up to the women to devote themselves to the work in companies! The speech of the steel baron ends with these words of anthology: "It is a question of multiplying the successes already obtained", and "united by an iron will, to give to our Führer, to our Wehrmacht, what they need. Long live the Führer!"

February 6, 1943: In a one-hour program entitled *Believing in Germany: Testimonies from the daily life of the workers*[192], Röchling's speech from the day before was rebroadcast, slightly shortened. Among the speakers were the industrialist Willy Messerschmidt, artists such as Arno Breker, Wilhelm Furtwängler and Gustaf Gründgens, as well as the physicist Max Planck and the physician Gustav von Bergmann.

March 19, 1943: *Reichsrundfunk* broadcast a brief interview with *Wehrwirtschaftsführer* Hermann Röchling. The journalist states that Röchling, although more than 70 years old, is a hard worker, "known far beyond the borders of Europe, and also among our enemies" and that the entire European iron industry, and thus all weapons of war, depends on him. Röchling in turn took the floor to explain that his particular aptitude for these functions came from 16 years of fighting against the French and Belgians for the return of the Saar to Germany:

> "The struggle of the past was not in vain, since it made me win the consideration of our former enemies, who know that I never want what is in my personal interest, but that before anything else I always try to achieve what is in the general interest. And I think I have done well in this, because I have found many friends in those countries with which we

---

192. "Glaube an Deutschland. Berichte aus dem schaffenden Alltag". Program prepared by Friedrich Richter. See Appendix 2. These one-hour interviews were rebroadcast on the Reich program on March 28, 1943.

were only recently at war. This makes it easier for all of us to achieve what is in the interest of both sides. Our former enemies have a responsibility to look after their people, to provide them with bread and work, and so the circle closes perfectly. On the whole, I am deeply grateful to have been entrusted with this mission for which I feel I have a number of assets because of that background."

Röchling's repeated interventions mark the history of the Third Reich. His articles in the press and his radio speeches are certainly less spectacular than the public demonstrations of a Goebbels who now poses as a man of the situation, but no less significant.

If the grandiose propaganda campaign launched by Goebbels staged the call for "total war" with, to close the show at the Berlin Sportpalast, the question and answer "do you want total war?" and a huge banner unfurled above the stage with the message "total war - the shortest war", it was not this hand-picked audience that decided. The real propagandist was actually Albert Speer the architect, with strong support in the field, especially his friend, the engineer Hermann Röchling, who proved to be the master of this "total war".

Speer took over the Ministry of Armaments at a time when the Vichy government committed itself to delivering 150,000 specialized workers to Germany as part of the relief effort. For Hitler, it was now a matter of combing through all the Wehrmacht services in the rear to find soldiers to send to the front. In May 1942, he appointed Lieutenant General Walter von Unruh to head a team responsible for assessing the effectiveness of the deployment of personnel in the two *Reichskommissariate in the* east, Ostland and the Ukraine, and, if necessary, to close down anything that seemed unnecessary. Gradually, the scope of this commission was expanded to include also the NSDAP authorities and the civil administration. In January 1943, in order to meet the needs of "total war", Hitler set up a "tripartite commission" (Lammers, Bormann and Keitel). However, caught up in the rivalries between the different ministries, and even within the same administration, both bodies proved to be completely ineffective.

The measures were finally taken, and they made Speer the big winner in terms of powers: in May 1943, his tasks included the production of naval equipment, and, by order of 2 September, he took control of civilian munitions production, a sector that had previously been the responsibility of the Wehrmacht and the Ministry of Economics. Renamed *Reichsministerium für Rüstung und Kriegsproduktion* to reflect its expanded mission, the new Speer Ministry now included functions previously performed by the RWM and all sectors of the armaments industry except aviation. In an internal reshuffle in the fall of 1943, Hans Kehrl became one of its key figures, its secretary general, as it were, heading the planning and raw materials offices.

The Speer-Röchling miracle weapon

On the dreaded eve of the military defeat at Stalingrad, Speer and Röchling had presented the Führer with a program for the development of one of these "miracle weapons" (*Wunderwaffen*), secret weapons projects that promised to reverse the already very unfavorable balance of power. The initiative did not come from Nazi leaders, but from Röchling, whom Speer had joined as soon as he took office as Minister of Armaments, both of them being fond of technology. Called sometimes "high pressure pump" (*Hochdruckpumpe*), sometimes "V3" (*Vergeltungswaffe* - weapon of vengeance), this multi-chambered gun was supposed to reach targets 300 kilometers away and thus fulfill one of Hitler's dearest wishes: to put London under ruins, by bombing it from the north of France[193].

In 1936, Röchling had received the Führer's approval for the production of a shell capable of piercing tank armor. The first experiments took place in the Völklingen factory[194]. The occupation of France in 1940 was a real miracle for Röchling: he managed to get his hands on technical studies conducted by French engineers for a gun with multiple combustion chambers, in response to the German weapons used to fire on Paris in 1914-1918, and entrusted the further development of this model to August Coenders, chief engineer of the Buderus-Röchling factories in Wetzlar. As the site of Völklingen was then considered too easy to access, because it was too close to the borders, and as the use of French prisoners of war would have made the project vulnerable to industrial espionage, the research was transferred to the Wetzlar factory. Röchling will be there almost every Sunday to talk with his engineer.

Hitler, enthusiastic, was not averse to calling on secret financing to bypass the military authorities, which was all the easier since Speer had already received a mandate to reorganize and concentrate the war effort. In August 1943, after the British bombing of the secret V1 and V2 weapons research site in Peenemünde, the contracts were clear: they put forward production for the cannon and projectiles of the V3 without even waiting for the results of the first firing tests[195]. The following month, the Todt organization began the construction of immense underground galleries on the Opal coast, at Mimoyecques,

---

193. The idea of such a machine goes back to the thirties, when Röchling and his engineer Coenders engaged in clandestine research to improve the high impact shells ("Röchling-Geschöße") experimented during the First World War.
194. AN BB 36/107, letter from Röchling to Josef Bürckel, February 16, 1938.
195. Olaf Groehler, "Die 'Hochdruckpumpe' (V3) - Entwicklung und Misere einer Wunderwaffe", *Militärgeschichte,* 16/1977, n° 4, pp. 738- 745.

which were to house the launch pads. About 5,000 forced laborers, prisoners of war, civilian deportees, concentration camp prisoners and "volunteers" from the Todt organization were permanently employed there.

"Röchling shares" and "Sauckel shares"

While in the west of Germany, the allied bombings of cities and inhabitants were becoming more and more frequent - phosphorus and fragmentation bombs, incendiary bombs and those called "blockbuster" for their capacity to devastate an entire block of buildings - what was the question in the various ministries: what measures were to be taken behind the front to draw from the reservoir of mobilizable men? How can we ask even more of German women, at the risk of damaging the "biological health" of the people[196]? Is it really necessary to close down the small and medium-sized enterprises in the consumer sector in order to be able to employ this workforce in the armaments industry and the other sectors of the war economy?

In his argument before the Tribunal at the "Röchling trial" in 1948, Paul-Julien Doll, the deputy government commissioner, highlighted the central role played by the accused in the planning of the "total war" effort in the occupied territories, particularly in France. His recommendations concerning foreign labor had already been brought to the attention of the highest authorities of the Reich and the Vichy government, well before the adoption of the STO laws. In practice, the proposals contained in a report with the appropriate title "Use of human reserves in the occupied territories", sent to

---

196. Secret report by Fritz Sauckel, February 5-6, 1943, document PS-1739, IMT Nuremberg, vol. 27, p. 611.

Sauckel on February 8, 1943, with a copy to Keitel, were included in the STO law on February 16, 1943 in the form of directives. On the 24th, a labor commissioner's office was created and Sauckel demanded that another 250,000 workers and specialists be supplied by mid-March 1943.

The impact of this second "Sauckel action" on the "Rüstung" and the "Röchling factories" was only marginal. Ernst Röchling obtained from Bichelonne that the quota of 650 skilled workers to be taken from the "Röchling factories" would be compensated by the arrival of a contingent of 1,210 laborers, 20% of whom were women. Hermann Röchling was confident that the female staff could even be recruited from among the wives and daughters of "his" workers[197]! To meet their labor needs, the "Röchling factories" recruited directly in Lorraine - and in this way 1,430 people were hired in the first half of 1943. If these workers escaped the requisition to Germany, the factories did not have to provide them with accommodation.

During 1943, the number of "protected" factories increased significantly: not only was it easier to get French people to work at home, but Allied air raids on the Reich's industrial centers intensified, making it necessary to transfer as many contracts as possible to France, in the factories of the northern zone and Meurthe-et-Moselle in particular. Of the monthly tonnage of semi-finished metal products, 80% went to meet German needs (60% was sent directly to Germany, 20% was used by factories manufacturing for the occupying forces in France). The Pont-à-Mousson factory sent its entire daily production of 900 shells to the Wehrmacht. The Longwy steelworks in Micheville, with their adjoining iron mines,

---

197. AD MM Cab. Art 184. FK to the prefect of Nancy, February 10, 1943. Conference with Dr. Munzinger, OKVR (*Oberkriegsverwaltungsrat*), responsible for economic services at the FK, February 17, 1943.

sent steel across the Rhine to the Röchling-Buderus company in Wetzlar, which was involved in the manufacture of materials for aeronautical structures[198].

But the quotas of the "Sauckel actions" require that the "unprotected" Lorraine companies are doubly put to contribution, "levies", which, conducted directly in the companies and businesses, and without method, by the German services, exceed the "limits of the reasonable and even the possible":

> "In the face of this failure, and pressed by the March 15 deadline, the German authorities intensified their action and even proceeded to round up 448 men aged between 17 and 80 years old, belonging to the most diverse professions, in Nancy on March 9[199]."

In the meantime, Röchling is working tirelessly to quantify these "human reserves", which are "sorted" to eliminate the "waste", such as stocks of coal or iron ore:

> "... there are, in Belgium, 200,000 men and women, in Holland, 100,000 per age group. If I submit to this choice 8 classes, there are thus, in both countries, 1.2 million men who would be enlisted and properly sorted. If I assume that there is 20% waste, then there are 950,000. If I assume that 30 percent are unusable, or cannot be relieved from duty, or who, through corruption, escape our net, there are 840,000

---

198. AN F/1a/3945: note from the intelligence services of March 3, 1944.
199. AD MM, W 1343 bis 45: reports of the inspector general of industrial production of February 16 and June 11, 1943.

left. Certainly a sizeable number from which a good deal could already be derived[200]."

In view of the results of the first two "Sauckel" actions, he wanted compulsory work in France to be extended to the age of 60 "as soon as possible". In April, during a routine meeting with the commissioners of the metal industry, he invited the military to designate trusted doctors in communities of a certain size in order to flush out the malingerers who feigned illness to avoid deportation[201]. This was the third "Sauckel action" and it imposed new quotas on France: 120,000 men for the month of May, 100,000 during June. On June 1st, Speer reorganized the administrative procedures in France to facilitate the exploitation of the workforce and, more generally, of all production capacities useful to the war industry:

> "It is in the interest of the European armament potential to obtain from France a maximum industrial output by equipping it with the most rational working methods, thanks to the use of German professional skills and the commitment of efficient personalities, and also by the disciplined collaboration between the German services and between the latter and the French[202]."

---

200. AN BB 35/92, SEF 002, letter from Hermann Röchling of February 8, 1943. Keitel's return of the letter was handwritten with two anonymous remarks, both mocking and insightful, before being archived, the first calling the reply "the latest 'joke' on Mr. Röchling. Next to his name, this epithet: "the new Minister of Defense?" AN BB 36/35 SEF 602, document from Keitel to Röchling of February 16, 1943.
201. AN BB/36/31 and BB 36/8, HR 102. Pv of the 74th conference of acting commissioners (in the presence of Ernst Röchling), Nancy, April 5, 1943.
202. AN AJ/40/1353/A.

Similar directives were promulgated a few days later for Belgium. In order to "centralize" the recruitment operations in France and Belgium, an employment office was opened in Paris, in the offices of the delegate for iron and steel, who was none other than... Ernst Röchling[203]. In the Gau Westmark, where one of Bürckel's men held this position, it was through Röchling that the applications for Luxembourg miners went through - 1,000 in October[204]!

If "total war" meant sacrifices for all, then women had to pay their share! Röchling tirelessly raised the subject with those in charge of the metallurgical sector, in his memoirs and in his letters. As a witness at the Rastatt trial, the mining engineer Guy Delacôte reported that Röchling had asked the steel industry to employ 20 percent women, as he himself had done at the Völklingen works: "For those who know the hard work of this industry, there is reason to appreciate how little consideration was given to human beings[205].

During 1943, the percentage of women more than doubled in annexed Lorraine, where Polish and Ukrainian civilian deportees from the East were already at work. At the Rombas factory, 1,152 Ukrainian women and only 697 men arrived in 1943[206]. Whether German or foreign, these women could be assigned to jobs that required considerable physical effort: they were made to drive the overhead cranes, except for the casting cranes, the turbine and the

---

203. AN BB 36/31 SEF 731, June 25, 1943.
204. AN BB 36/35: letter from Paul Raabe to Max Paul Meier of the Arbed, Metz, October 30, 1943. In July 1944, on the eve of the rout, a new contingent of 600 was requested. Röchling intervened in Saarbrücken on the 23rd at a meeting with the two Gauleiter of the Moselle and Luxembourg and the head of the military command of the region. However, as the size of these levies threatened to close most of the mines, a compromise was reached to limit the number to 120. AN BB 36/110. Letter from the directorate for the extraction and distribution of iron ore to the director of the Arbed, July 29, 1944.
205. AN BB 36/35: letter to Charles Gerthoffer from Guy Delacôte, director of the state potassium mines of Alsace, March 12, 1948.
206. AN BB 36/35: pv of Mr. Henri Bornemann, February 10, 1947.

power plant; they were found cutting scrap metal with a blowtorch and doing electric welding. The working hours for certain categories of workers, including women, could be as long as 72 hours a week. In Meurthe-et-Moselle, during the monthly conference in March 1943 with the metal industry commissioners and the occupation authorities, Röchling added:

> "Women's employment must be planned for a long period. Training workshops for women should be organized everywhere. The heads of department must personally take care of the women's education [...]. If compulsory work for women is not yet legal in France, women can be hired by force. The proportion of women in the steelworks must be increased[207]."

At the beginning of July, he announced that it was no longer possible to delay the reinforcement of women's work in the occupied territories of the West, where women could be "mobilized[208]". When it was pointed out to him that the compulsory work of women would require strong action on the German side to break the resistance of the French head of state, Röchling declared himself ready to take charge of it personally with Speer and General von Stülpnagel.

***

In March, Berlin had been hit by the worst Allied bombing since the beginning of the conflict, with hundreds of deaths and tens of

---

207. AN BB 36/31 HR 101. Pv of the 73rd meeting of the acting commissioners of the iron industry in Meurthe-et-Moselle, March 6, 1943.
208. AN BB 36/31 HR 109: July 5, 1943.

thousands of homeless people. The entire population began to doubt the effectiveness of the "total mobilization" that was supposed to shorten the war. To counter this bad fate, the authorities orchestrated a new mass demonstration for June 5 at the Sportpalast in Berlin in front of thousands of workers from the arms industry: two speeches to convince the people that victory was more than certain. The first speaker was Albert Speer; using impassive and scientific rhetoric, he stressed the inevitability of the German triumph. The minister pronounced his thanks in advance to a few notables of the war industry, engineers, technicians, producers, who had been granted "dictatorial powers" (*diktatorische Völlmächte*) to ensure this victory: Paul Pleiger, who directed the entire coal economy; Carl Krauch, for the chemical sector; Walter Rohland ["Panzer Rohland"] responsible for the production of military equipment; Ferdinand Porsche, head of research and development of tanks; and... Hermann Röchling "who brought the metallurgical production to a record level thanks to his immense experience and energy[209]" Speer was followed on the podium by Goebbels, and, with the pathos and verbal violence that we know about him, this master in the art of brainwashing proclaimed revenge against the British and made the imminence of a definitive solution to the Jewish question seem imminent: "the radical extermination of Judaism in Europe." The texts of the two speeches were published on the front page of the major daily newspapers and included in a booklet with a circulation of 500,000 copies[210].

On July 10, with the landing of the Allied forces in Sicily, this propaganda optimism came to an end. Röchling, constantly preoccupied with the organization of the war economy, attacked the members of

---

209. Albert Speer, *Rede auf der Großkundgebung im Sportpalast Berlin*, s.l., June 1943.
210. *Völkischer Beobachter* and *Neues Wiener Tageblatt*, June 6, 1943; *Agrarische Post*, June 12, 1943.

the Belgian steel union, "Sybelac", industrialists who were notoriously resistant to German orders. On July 20, 1943, he threatened them in a thinly veiled manner:

> "I give you explicit orders, even written orders if you like, to execute the steel grades for which you are ordered. What is necessary during a war must be done. I want to spare you the inconvenience, but the laws of war are stronger than all of us. [...] If I try to work with you, you must know that if I meet real resistance, I will not back down. If your conscience forbids you to follow my orders, then I will not do without your factories, but I will have to do without your services. I see the future in a different light than you do.
> I believe that the future we can offer you is better than the one you hope for from the other side. [...] Believe me, I will do everything I can to see that my country wins the war[211]."

For the umpteenth time, he recalled the urgency of employing female workers and took the example of the Norwegian factories, with 28% female workers, and those of the annexed Lorraine, which had 23%. According to a Luxembourg witness, Röchling, proud of the 2,000 Russian and Ukrainian women he had put at the disposal of the Völklingen steelworks, repeated the same speech to the directors of the Grand Duchy's metallurgy industry[212].

The metallurgists of the "Sybelac" will testify against Röchling at the trial in Rastatt, portraying a man who is always threatening, ready

---

211. AN BB 36/6 TG 229, SEF 1112: report of July 21, 1943,
212. AN BB 36/6 TG 229, SEF 1116: pv of Gilles Perot, engineer, general manager of the Société Ougrée-Marihaye, November 5, 1947. According to the statistics collected by the inspectorate in charge of workers in the East, in March 1943 there were already 946 Russian and Ukrainian men and 1,145 women at the RESW.

to use all kinds of blackmail to force illegal production, contrary to the laws of war - deportation of workers, placing under the control of a German administrator - but whose methods will prove to be of little use compared to Steinbrinck, his predecessor in the administrative region of northern France-Belgium:

> "We evaded his threats by starting, while sabotaging them, certain insignificant manufactures [...] In short, Röchling behaved like a complete Nazi who did not hesitate, in the pursuit of war aims, to violate our consciences[213]."

For the engineer Émile Hobaer, Röchling, "a technician of great stature", was the model of an "accomplished Nazi" for whom there were no feelings or scruples. And for Paul Joseph Henrard, factory manager in Liège, Röchling was simply... a megalomaniac:

> "[...] who told us that he had taken over the production of steel in the whole of Europe and who, in fact, by trying to be everywhere and to take care of everything, gave us the impression that he was getting tangled up and ended up having to rely on sub-orders[214]."

While in Belgium the factory managers gave him a hard time, in the annexed regions of the Gau Westmark - Luxembourg and Moselle - the passive resistance of the workers made it impossible to achieve the planned objectives, an inadequacy that was due, in his opinion, to the presence in management positions of people who, not being

---

213. AN BB 36/6 SEF 1111: deposition of Paul Léon (Sybelac) on October 27, 1947 in Liege.
214. AN BB/36/6 TG 229, SEF 1113: deposition of Mr. Bihet; TG 229, SEF 1114 Mr. Hobaer; TG 229, SEF 1115, Mr. Henrard.

"Reichsdeutsche", did not have a sufficiently clear awareness of life's priorities, in other words, were incapable of waging the necessary battle. He therefore asked Goebbels for permission to convene some 200 of these Gau leaders for a propaganda meeting in Metz on May 9, 1943. Three lectures were to show how to link the Nazi cause with technical progress: "The fight for progress and its lessons", "Acid and basic ore reserves in Lorraine, Luxembourg and Meurthe-et-Moselle" and "The tasks of the steel worker in time of war[215]"!

In France, however, Röchling was not satisfied with going through Speer to solve these labor problems; on occasion, he addressed himself directly to the High Command of the Wehrmacht, which endorsed his requests. He also asked General von Grävenitz, head of the prisoner-of-war service, to take a census of all prisoners specializing in metallurgy who could be employed in his factories[216]. And Röchling, who knew how to win Hitler's favor, wrote to Keitel, who - let us remember - was none other than the supreme commander of the German armed forces, to inform him on how to combat the "lax attitude" of the "overly benevolent" military personnel stationed far from the battlefields in the western territories. These officers "fall over themselves," he wrote, "when asked something that is in complete contradiction to their sweet dreams of how to make these people happy or to their ideas about the most elegant way to exploit people and countries for war." And Röchling suggests transferring them to a place where they can learn the "realities of war"[217]!

In view of the problems raised, Sauckel himself had to come to Paris in August 1943 in order to obtain a commitment from Laval: a third contingent of 500,000 workers before the end of the year, not to

---

215. AN BB 36/97.
216. AN BB 36/8, SEF 735 a and b.
217. AN BB 36/107: Röchling to Keitel, March 20, 1943.

Chapter 7. The "total war"

mention a million men to be supplied for the Todt organization's work sites. In reality, however, there were no more than 350,000 departures for the entire year of 1943! For his part, Speer tried to unblock the situation by entering into talks with Jean Bichelonne, now *acting* Minister of Labor. There was talk of extending production orders in France beyond the arms industry: working for Germany while remaining in France was the way to turn the French into true collaborators! In September, Bichelonne was in Berlin and, to Sauckel's great displeasure, agreed with Speer, who had meanwhile been crowned "Minister of Armaments and War Production", on a new status for privileged factories, the "S-Betriebe[218]". By agreeing to produce at least 75% for the Reich, the French companies gained in return the exemption (or quasi-exemption) from compulsory labor for their personnel. During the autumn, the so-called *Patenfirmen* system was also put in place: German "supervisory" firms were appointed to supervise the production of the most important French companies, in other words, to ensure that the arms contracts were properly executed. Bichelonne, who was close to Ernst Röchling, thus became the relay for the policy that Hermann Röchling had been conducting in Lorraine for three years. And the results are not to be despised: in order to obtain the support of the French industrial elite for the war effort, the Röchlings succeeded in involving them in innovative projects, emphasizing the medium-term perspective of added value for both the installations and the production.

In spite of these arrangements, the failures in the organization of the metallurgy increased. Since the end of the summer of 1943, supply

---

218. The category of "S-Betriebe" was officially created on October 8, 1943. The letter "S" would indicate the "Sperr" [blocked] status of these companies, but they were also called "Speer-Betriebe" because of the homonymy and the fact that the minister himself was the inspiration. The label was supposed to cover all "Rüstung" [*Rü-Betriebe*] as well as "V-Betreibe" [*Vorzugsbetriebe* or preferential enterprises].

problems, due in part to acts of sabotage, caused the intermittent stoppage of the blast furnaces; coal, coke and lime ran out. To save coal, Röchling sought to improve the recovery and recycling of scrap metal, an essential supply for the Siemens-Martin furnaces, and, with the agreement of the Ministry of the Economy, placed the scrap metal unions under the control of a central management body[219]. However, the technical and logistical improvements that he tried to make were not enough to limit the slowdown in production. The temporary closure of blast furnaces and the shutting down of coking plants caused technical unemployment and exposed the workforce to immediate deportation to the Reich, which had the opposite effect to that intended. For its own interests, the French employers tried to intervene to negotiate with the Resistance so that the destruction of material would cease[220]. During a meeting with the steel industry commissioners, Röchling, anxious to protect his interests as well as those of the Reich, issued this warning:

> "Röchling particularly emphasized that there should be no doubt in the minds of the Frenchmen employed in the guarding of the works of art that in case of hostile actions on their part they would be punished with death without mercy (*gnadenlos mit dem Tod bestraft*)[221]."

The situation continues to worsen, however, and in November, the Industrial Production Department for Meurthe-et-Moselle notes:

---

219. AN AJ /40/327, letter from Bergassessor Sohl, RVE, July 30, 1943.
220. Jean-Claude Magrinelli, Yves Magrinelli, *Anti-fascism and Communist Party in Meurthe-et-Moselle*, 1920-1945, 1985, p. 303.
221. AN BB 36/31 HR 105: 80th session of the iron industry commissioners in Meurthe-et-Moselle, October 11, 1943.

"As in the case of the iron mines, the social situation in the steel industry, the physical deficiency of the workers, which reached its peak in July as in the previous year, was not significantly worse than in 1942. Absenteeism remains considerable, the wage readjustment promised by the head of the government has not yet been realized in the two branches of industry due to the refusal of the occupying authorities to authorize it. The discontent is very strong among the working population, who compare the situation of the workers in the mechanical industry and the workers in the steel industry in the same locality and sometimes even in the same factory. If this state of affairs is not remedied in the short term, the consequences may be serious[222]."

The fourth Sauckel action was not launched until February 1944. By then, the "S-Betriebe" system had already "drained" a large part of the people who could be deported to Germany[223]. Sauckel wanted 91,000 applicants per month, including able-bodied foreigners who were on French soil. In total, there would be only 50,000 departures! For his part, Röchling was convinced of the uselessness of these demands and continued to militate for compulsory labor to be extended to the categories of the population not yet enlisted, not forgetting women.

To encourage greater involvement of the people of Lorraine in the war effort, the Baron of Saarland saw fit to return, on paper,

---

222. AD MM W 1343 bis art.45: *Report of the general inspection of the industrial production*, Nancy, 3rd quarter 1943, November 11, 1943.
223. Of course, while employed in the service of the Nazi war economy, the 1,300,000 personnel of the 5,000 "S-Betriebe" in France were not formally considered as *Fremdarbeiter*.

the factories of Meurthe-et-Moselle to their owners, while retaining authority over their management. The operation took place against the background of a financial affair engineered by his cousin Ernst Röchling to enable him to make up for the largely loss-making management of "his factories". Indeed, Hermann Röchling had taken out two loans from Alexandre Kreuter's SCI amounting to 180 million francs, a liability that the head offices of the factories in the French department of Murten and Moselle were hardly willing to take over. Thanks to the diplomacy of his cousin and his relations with the ministers Bichelonne and Cathala, Hermann Röchling obtained a guarantee from Vichy for the repayment of the principal and the payment of the accrued interest to the SCI. At the same time, as the Reich's representative in the western territories, Ernst Röchling negotiated for his cousin a commission of 0.6% on all invoices from the steelworks in Meurthe-et-Moselle, central, western and northern France, to be paid from February 29, 1944[224]! However, the investigators at the courts in Nuremberg and Rastatt were unable to determine whether or not these commissions had been paid. The only thing that was found was a voucher for the month of March 1944, which shows that Ernst Röchling claimed to have paid this commission on a total of 200 million francs, or 1,200,000 francs...

A ceremony was held on 21 February at the Neuves-Maisons factories to mark the return of the six companies in Meurthe-et-Moselle Sud to their owners. The press widely reported on this event, in which Bichelonne himself participated. The French minister and Röchling, in turn, emphasized the need to promote both the production of French companies and the collaboration between French and German engineers to support the war effort: the handover of these

---

224. AN BB 36/35 SEF 683.

production units, a "gesture of moral value", was supposed to help not only to fulfill the industrial program underway and to "avoid the victory of communism", but, for the future, to "build a new Europe, more humane and broader[225]".

---

225. AD MM WM 284, 21 February 1944.

Chapter 8: "Fortress Europe", prison for the defeated

During the years of Nazism, the philologist Viktor Klemperer follows the way in which the "Language of the Third Reich (LTI)" is enriched with expressions that serve to "camouflage" or "veil" the intended object - Klemperer speaks of *Tarnbegriffe* or Schleierworte[226]. The adjective "total" was, for example, both a fundamental requirement of Nazi ideology and a keyword of the LTI. Another of these terms was *Fremdarbeiter*, foreign worker, a word that modestly encompassed all prisoners of war, IMIs, deportees from the East and STOs, who were forced to perform *Einsatz*, i.e. unnamed forced labor, to support the war effort of the Third Reich.

With the defeat at Stalingrad and the beginning of a withdrawal of the Wehrmacht troops, the term *Festung Europa was* added, symbolizing a continental space, liberated from Bolshevism, opposed to the English enemy and defended from its center by Hitler's "organizing power." All the so-called *Fremdarbeiter* - deportees, prisoners of war, but also those whom the occupier exploited at home, in the territories under its control - were summoned to contribute to the economy of this fortress[227], a space that was the precursor of the "new Europe" that would come about with the Reich's victory.

---

226. Viktor Klemperer, *LTI*, Leipzig, Verlag Philipp Reclam Jun. 1978, p. 231.
227. *Ibid.* at 172-174.

Statistics, admittedly crude, indicate that in 1944 more than 7.5 million foreign civilians and more than 2 million prisoners of war supplied the German war economy with their labor force. In the Saarland, 30,000 prisoners of war and deportees were used as slaves at the end of 1942, and this figure rose to 70,000 in April 1944 (some estimates put the number almost double), crammed into about 370 camps. Out of a total of more than 50,000 men, the Saarland mines were operating at that time with 12,792 Soviets[228]. Stalag XII in Forbach in Moselle alone provided 7,000 prisoners of war - French, Serbian and Russian - for the Saarland mines and factories. At the Röchling factories in Völklingen, out of a total of 14,392 employees, more than 6,000 foreigners were counted on August 31, 1944, including 1,168 prisoners of war, 2,159 Russian civilians, 1,333 Frenchmen and 1,701 women. For the entire duration of the war, the number of foreigners who served in the camp can be estimated at no less than 12,000. These figures are obviously only snapshots...

In September 1943, the surrender of the Italian army had made available a new slave labor force: the 710,000 "IMI", Italian military internees who refused to take up arms to serve the Reich's cause. A contingent of 702 of these prisoners was immediately sent to the Röchling factories. Considered by the German authorities as traitors, they were not entitled to the status of prisoners of war and, therefore, did not benefit from protection under the Geneva Convention. Relegated to the bottom of the social ladder along with deported civilians from Eastern Europe and Soviet prisoners of war, they became forced laborers particularly vulnerable to abuse. If, for all foreigners,

---

228. Christoph M. Frisch, "Ein bißchen geschlagen haben sie alle". Zwangsarbiet im Saarland während des Zweiten Weltkrieges, ("All struck a little". Forced labor in the Saarland during the Second World War), 2011.

the diet was insufficient, for the Soviets and for the "IMI", deprived of aid packages, the situation was even harsher.

Röchling Forges and Steelworks in Völklingen, March 1935
Source : National Archives

How many of these slaves worked and died in the mines and factories of the two Lorraine regions[229]? In Moselle, 8,300 *Fremdarbeiter* were employed in the steel industry, 60% of whom were Soviet women. In the coal mines, out of 27,000 employees, there were 6,800 prisoners of war and an unknown number of foreign civilians[230]. At the Thionville plant alone, 40% of the workers were Soviets, prisoners of war or civilians, 1,660 in total[231]. In Meurthe-et-Moselle, a census

---

229. Pascal Brenneur, "Les prisonniers russes...", *op. cit.* p. 40.

230. AN MM W 1343 bis. Art. 74. Information communicated by the General Secretariat for Economic Affairs in Metz, March 2, 1946.

231. Archives municipales de Thionville, émile Siegemund, ingénieur des mines, Pv de constat. Société lorraine minière et métallurgique, 1940-1944, n.d. See also AN BB 36/107 SEF 548,4: hearing of Louis Zechmann.

of August 1944 indicated that the steel plants employed some 22,000 people, without specifying their nationality. Many of them were prisoners of war, "liberated" from the Stalag camps on Reich territory and repatriated to France to support the German war effort, either at the explicit request of the occupation authorities or as part of the "relief". At the request of Hermann Röchling, in July 1942, 1,600 metal workers and technicians from Belgium and northern France were identified in the Stalags and were eligible for reinstatement at their original post[232].

As far as the mines are concerned, the statistics only cover the period beginning with the reorganization carried out by Speer in 1942: at that time, out of 14,000 miners in the iron basins of non-annexed Lorraine, 4,950 were Soviet prisoners of war; in Moselle, there were approximately 3,000 Soviets out of a total of 6,500 miners. And how many civilians were there in these mines - Poles, Russians or Ukrainians?

As for the French prisoners of war from the African continent, in order to avoid soiling German soil, they were mostly parked in *Frontstalags* in France, forced to work for the Todt organization or on farms[233]. From 1943, they were also put to work in industry. In May 1943, Röchling received a contingent of 130 North African prisoners for the Meurthe-et-Moselle factories, but their performance at these posts seemed so unsatisfactory that he asked that they be sent to load minette at the bottom of the mines. However, according to intelligence information for the French Liberation Committee, in November 1943, Röchling was still operating 800 North African prisoners at the Pompey

---

232. AN AJ 40/328: note from the director of the Belgium and Northern France group to the Commissioner for Iron and Steel, February 22, 1942.

233. For a general overview of the fate of prisoners of war from the colonies and overseas, another little-known chapter of the Second World War, see Armelle Mabon, "Les Prisonniers de guerre coloniaux durant l'Occupation en France", *Hommes & Migrations*, no. 1228, November-December 2000, pp. 15-28. On North African prisoners of war, in particular, see Belkacem Recham, "Les Indigènes nord-africains prisonniers de guerre (1940-1945)", *Guerres mondiales et conflits contemporains*, Paris, PUF, n° 223, 3/2006, pp. 109-125.

steelworks[234] - one of the few sites under his control maintained at maximum production capacity despite increasing restrictions. And in March 1944, he also had a contingent of 150 North African prisoners, Senegalese and Madagascans, at the Micheville factories[235], and 375 for Longwy. In an April 1944 letter to the prefect, the managers of the Longwy steelworks reported "growing indiscipline and laziness" among these African prisoners, who were placed under the sole authority of the Wehrmacht. And they asked the Feldkommandantur to intervene so that the military regime applied in the south of the department could be extended to the north: the discipline would be taken over by French managers who, thanks to their experience with the "natives", would be able to keep them constantly in check[236].

***

(by hand: DCC-MDB-BBH-441)

Völklingen, January 4, 1943
Internal note

"For consultation with Dr. Beck.

Trade Councilor Röchling requests that negotiations be initiated as soon as possible to
obtain Russian youth (about 16 years old) for
employment [*Einsatz*] in the metal industry.
The Southwest has a capacity to absorb about
1,000 of these people. This seems to be the

---

234. AN F/1a/3945: industrial production, note of November 12, 1943.
235. AN F/1a/3945: factories and activity, note of March 20, 1944.
236. AD MM, W 110, art. 12: letter of April 28, 1944.

only way at present to be able to ensure in the necessary and indispensable proportions an adequate succession without the risk of incorporation under arms, *etc.*

Moreover, according to all the information from people well informed about the facts in the East, there must be a good number of skilled workers in the occupied territories. The trade councilor would like to see, as he had previously proposed, negotiations initiated with the appropriate authorities to send a commission to Russia consisting of several specialists from the East who are proficient in the language, with the task of mobilizing this potential skilled labor.

Signed Lutze"

Internal note from the RESW management on the factory work
of Russian miners. Source: AN BB 36/8, SEF n° 736

Under the impetus of Röchling, the project to close the mines in the Nancy iron basin was abandoned, and on October 13, 1942, the General Labor Inspector reported that it was hoped that activity in the Pays-Haut and in the Nancy region would increase by 100,000 tons of steel per month[237]. But, of course, everything depended on the arrival of Soviet prisoners of war, and since the Vichy government turned a blind eye to the policy of the occupier, the French services never drew up official statistics on this subject.

---

237. AD MM W 1342 bis, art. 69.

Nevertheless, the departmental archives contain a few notes on foreign forced laborers.

In August 1942, the services of the *Generalbeauftragter,* headed by Röchling, expected the arrival of 2,500 Soviet military prisoners for the mines of Valleroy, Moutiers, Jœuf, Bouligny, Tucquegnieux, Anderny, Trieux, Amermont, Joudreville, la Mourière and Piennes[238] and, in February 1943, a contingent of 2,572 Russian prisoners and 707 Poles[239]. These Soviets were mostly peasants with no mining experience, and their work was obviously not up to expectations. The performance standards for each mine were established by the German commissioner for iron ore mining in Bouligny, under the orders of Röchling and Raabe. To help these makeshift miners, the French porions would sometimes falsify the yield figures on the daily extraction reports[240] and children would give them food and smoke[241]. The authorities, both French and German, obviously forbade these "manifestations of sympathy" and warned the mine management and the inhabitants of the reprisals that could be taken against them.

In November 1943, a circular was issued to the managers of all the Lorraine mines for another malfunction that was harmful to the war objectives: the Russian prisoners of war were sent back to the accommodation camps, as they were deemed unfit to accomplish the output set for the mines. And since the German officials who ran these camps kept complaining about this, the delegated commissar intervened to enforce the directives:

---

238. AD MM WM art 1142 + bis. These figures are attested to by the notes sent by the sub-prefect of Briey to the Prefect of Nancy on August 6 and 12, 1942.
239. AD MM WM 397, February 1943.
240. AD MM, WM s. 282 (translation of Appendix 8).
241. AD MM, WM art. 1142 + bis.

Chapter 8: "Fortress Europe", prison for the defeated

"I point out for the last time that the Russians who are brought to the mines must work against all odds to load the prescribed tonnage of 12 T.

If the German heads of the camps announce to me again that Russians have been dismissed for any of the above reasons, I will immediately and without delay dismiss the mine employee responsible, a resolution which you will be kind enough to bring to the attention of your bottom employees.

I again call your attention to the following: "Russians who without cause have not reached the prescribed 12 T. must remain in the mine until the set task is reached." Here, too, I will act in the strongest manner against the saboteurs of my instructions[242]."

Speer was concerned about the drop in the performance of prisoners of war, particularly the Soviets, and, following the example of Röchling a few months earlier, he called on Keitel to remedy the situation without further delay, "in the interests of armaments." The productivity of the Soviets would be 50% lower than that of German workers. Not only the lazy or undisciplined, but also the unresponsive personnel of the order services were to be punished. As for the Soviet prisoners who were guilty of assaulting German personnel, the judgment is without appeal: "The execution of the death penalty will certainly be useful to raise discipline at work[243]."

---

242. AD MM WM art. 282. Circular of November 25, 1943, note in appendix 10. Mine of the Mourière in Bouligny.
243. BA R3/1586, letter from Speer to Keitel, December 21, 1943.

The system of repression

Concrete measures, accompanied by sanctions, were put in place to obtain the desired output from foreign labor. This was nothing new, in fact, since since the introduction of the four-year plan in 1936, German workers, who were almost indifferent to the propaganda effort, did not show great zeal. In 1938, after the Anschluss, the Todt organization sent about 30,000 men to the *Westwall* construction site to complete the construction of the fortification system on the western border, but there were many defections, and productivity did not follow. Then came the occupation of Poland: a troop of young Poles judged "fit for Germanization" (LTI: *eindeutschungsfähig,* "E-Polen") joined the German workforce. But the problems remained the same, because the authorities feared revolts, and the war economy needed these arms, so useful.

It should be remembered that, as early as 1933, the judicial system set up at the same time made it possible to send dissidents to prison or even to a concentration camp without the possibility of appeal. However, the unbureaucratic procedure of these *Sondergerichte* or "emergency courts", which primarily targeted the regime's "political enemies", had two major disadvantages: by punishing behavior that was not prima facie political, companies were deprived of these workers, without being able to guarantee their reintegration at the end of the sentence. The multiple construction sites of the Westwall thus offered the opportunity to experiment *in situ* with a new type of confinement, simple and profitable.

In the summer of 1939, the first "re-education through labor camp" was opened under SS control near one of these construction sites, in Hinzert in the Hunsrück, about 60 kilometers north of Völklingen. Hinzert was not created by a ministerial order, but by an initiative led "from below" by the stakeholders of the Westwall project - the DAF, the Gestapo, the Todt organization, municipalities and private companies[244] - and was the prototype for the "AELs" (LTI: *Arbeitserziehungslager*, or "education through work camps") that the Gestapo was to extend little by little throughout the Reich and the occupied territories. It was on the basis of the "economic model" of these camps, the precursor of the *Außenkommandos* set up in the administrative dependence of the concentration camps, that Hermann Röchling attached a "re-education" camp to the Völklingen factories, reserved for foreign forced laborers and conceived according to their immediate economic usefulness, unlike the Lager and other penitentiary institutions.

Under orders from the Gestapo, uncooperative workers, qualified as "in breach of contract" (*vertragsbrüchig*), and not as "delinquents" (*straffällig*), could be interned in these AELs for "educational" purposes, without going to court, and therefore without trial and without the possibility of appeal[245]. With the massive arrival of a foreign work force, cases of refusal, escape, laziness, and sabotage multiplied, and the industrialists increasingly turned to the political police. Thus, during detention, the Gestapo rented out internees to industrialists with a commitment to return them to their employers at the end of the sentence, which allowed it to establish offices within the companies themselves. After Hinzert, in March 1940, the Gestapo set up "Lager 21" in Salzgitter-Hallendorf, on the grounds of the RWHG, for the "re-education" of Polish civilians.

In May 1941, at least eight re-education camps were already open, when Himmler finally decided to intervene to make these camps

---

244. Hermann Röchling was one of them, as evidenced by a letter addressed to him on December 7, 1938 by the head of the Wehrmacht's ordinance service to the Führer. Cf. AN BB 36/30 HR 123.
245. A law enacted on February 10, 1936, stipulated that the Gestapo was not accountable to any administrative or judicial court for decisions made.

official, without trying to regulate them too closely[246]. The "AEL" label was accredited and efforts were made to distinguish between these "re-education" camps and the "punishment" camps (*Straflager*). There was only one restriction in their operation: the maximum duration of internment was set at 56 days; beyond that, preventive detention was required (LTI: *Schutzhaft*, literally "protective custody") before the prisoner was sent to a concentration camp. Many of the existing *Straflager* were quickly reclassified as re-education camps, although the Gestapo interned anyone they wished. From October 28, 1941 to September 21, 1942, an AEL existed in Guénange (Niederganingen), 8 kilometers from Thionville, in the Moselle[247]. The use of these camps varied to such an extent that Himmler supplemented the first order with a second order, dated December 12, 1941, to define its scope of application: incarceration for political acts was formally excluded[248]. In 1945, the AEL network included nearly 200 sites[249]. Living and working conditions, sanitary risks, food - most often this internment was nothing other than a concentration camp, minus the gas chambers. The treatment was just as cruel, and executions were frequent.

---

246. Gabriele Lofti, *KZ der Gestapo. Arbeitserziehungslager im Dritten Reich*, Stuttgart, Munich, DVA, 2002. Himmler's order: *Anweiseng des RfSS und Chef de Deutschen Polizei an alle Staatspolizeistellen zur einrichtung von Arbeitserziehungslagern (May 28, 1941)*. This ordinance left enormous margins of freedom for the contractors; a second provision of December 12, 1941, brought only slight restrictions, so that the LEAs remained lawless zones where the guards exercised arbitrary power with impunity.
247. Thereafter, the convicts served their sentences in the KL of Schirmeck where they worked in a granite quarry.
248. Reprinted in *Quellen zur Geschichte Thüringens. Die Geheime Staatspolizei im NS-Gau Thüringen 1933-1945*. https://www.lzt-thueringen.de/files/uellenb_gestapo-1.pdf (accessed August 19, 2018)
249. This chapter is still poorly explored, and case studies are still scarce. See, for example, the work of the Berliner Geschichtswerkstatt collective: *Das Arbeitserziehungslager Fehrbellin. Zwangsarbeiterinnen im Straflager der Gestapo*, which describes the situation in Fehrbellin, northwest of Berlin. Available on the website of the Brandenburgische Landeszentrale für politische Bildung: https://www.politische-bildung-brandenburg.de/system/files/publikation/pdf/Fehrbellin_1.pdf (accessed on 7.02.2023)

Clearly, "even before the Speer era began, the economy had a major, and by no means moderating, effect on the terror in the camps of the National Socialist regime.[250]"

Rehabilitation through work

The question of discipline never ceased to worry Hermann Röchling, who, since his appointment as head of the RVA, was on the lookout for ways to intervene on a Reich-wide scale and, more immediately, in the factories under his direct control. In December 1942, he asked Colonel Stoffel of the Wehrmacht in Nancy about STO escapees and how to get them back into production at the Völklingen steelworks. What could be the means to overcome these *Vertragsbrüchige* (people in breach of contract)? The success of the war operations depended, in his opinion, on whether they could be taken back and this time not let go[251]. The answer of the military, if any, is not known to us. However, towards the end of the year, the management of the Röchling factories approached the Todt organization to obtain a plot of land in the neighboring town of Etzenhofen to set up a "re-education" camp for foreigners who were unwilling to do forced labor.

At the beginning of the investigations for the Röchling trial in 1948, the executives of the Röchling factories were questioned about this camp. They claimed to be unaware of everything, alleging that the facility was under the complete control of the Gestapo. Although many incriminating documents were destroyed at the end of the war,

---

250. Cord Pagenstecher, "Arbeitserziehungslager", in: Wolfgang Benz, Barbara Distel, *Der Ort des Terrors*, Munich, C.H. Beck Verlag, vol. 9, pp. 75-99, here p. 82.
251. AN BB 36/7 HR 155, TG n° 340: letter from Röchling to Colonel Stoffel in Nancy of December 14, 1942.

the cover-up ended with the discovery of accounting documents: the management of Etzenhofen had been the sole responsibility of the company. However, the investigators were unable to re-establish the precise history of the camp, nor the formal link between Hermann Röchling and the decision to open it. Nevertheless, it is reasonable to assume that the Saarland steel king was able to use his relationship with Speer to obtain the approval of the head of the RSHA. For the duration of the sentence, the company did not have to pay anything for the employment of its slave labor, from which it continued to profit. The Etzenhofen *Straflager* (punishment camp) or *Vergeltungslager* (retaliation camp) was thus the optimal solution to the goal of maximum productivity and minimum costs for accommodation and supervisory staff[252]. According to the testimony of Anton Eisenlauer, head of the Röchling employment department, the creation of an independent retaliation camp was a real convenience for the Röchling firm. To his knowledge, no other Saarland industry had such freedom[253].

The camp, surrounded by reeds several meters high to hide the barbed wire fence, was set up on a plot of land near the Etzenhofen train station, a short distance from Völklingen. The wooden huts were built for an average of 40 people, about one third of them women; four armed *Werkschutz* guards with police dogs were responsible for surveillance. The Röchling factories paid the Reichsbahn an annual rent for the land and the barracks. The Gestapo had, of course, the right to inspect the *Straflager*, which was made available to all local firms, subcontractors and subsidiaries of the Röchling factories, in order to intern their own work-refugitives[254].

---

252. AN BB 36/36 SEF 1067: report by Inspector Marcel Hindenoch of the mobile brigade of the Saarland Judicial Police, October 3, 1947.
253. AN BB 36/8, TG n° 329: pv of March 30, 1947.
254. AN BB 36/7 TG n° 328: Circular of April 30, 1943.

The management of the Völklingen steelworks reinforced its repressive measures with a *Schnellgericht,* an emergency court or expedited court, an authority similar to the *Sondergerichte of* the Reich. The aim was to inspire terror in the staff through its "pedagogical" impact. The defendants were deprived of any right to appeal or legal assistance. The five members of the tribunal - a delegate of the Reich Labor Commissioner, the plant manager and a representative of the Saarbrücken Gestapo, one of the *Werkschutz* and one of the plant management - met behind closed doors every two weeks, but in fact the decisions were taken a few days beforehand by the head of the *Werkschutz,* who was supposed to consult the Gestapo representative before imposing a sentence of more than 15 days[255]. An internal management circular, "Measures to Prevent Loitering by Workers at Work," announced the establishment of the *Schnellgericht* on February 12, 1943: from then on, foreigners who did not make amends were to be sent back to a *Schnellgericht* "without any regard" and could be punished by deportation to the Hinzert concentration camp or to the Schirmeck-Vorbruck concentration camp[256]. Röchling used the effectiveness of this court, and the dissuasive effect of the sentences handed down, to ask the Gestapo to introduce one in Thionville, where a "punishment cell" already existed[257]. The Moselle *Schnellgericht,* with authority over all the factories in the Fensch valley, including the Hermann Göring factories, was to operate from June. Prison sentences of less than 56 days could be served at the *Straflager* in Etzenhofen[258].

---

255. AN BB 36/8 SEF 1028,3: pv of Albert Serf, September 14, 1946.

256. AN BB 36/8, HR 196: report of April 15, 1943.

257. AN BB 36/8 TG 322 and AN BB 36/32 SEF 1057,3/1: testimony of the head of the tour of guards at the Thionville factory, Jacques Wagner, on October 11, 1946.

258. AN BB 36/32 SEF 1057,1: report of October 24, 1946 on the conditions under which deported workers and prisoners of war were treated in the industrial establishments placed under the authority of Hermann Röchling in Moselle during the annexation. August Richter, known for his brutality, gave the order to shoot Russian escapees who had been recaptured.

It was at this time, at the beginning of 1943, that the Saarbrücken Gestapo introduced a new type of detention camp for the region: the extended police prison, the "EPG". It met the requirements of decentralized control and, as with the AELs, was not under the control of the authorities in Berlin, but under the command of the regional SP[259]. The prison structure consisted of two buildings, one for women and one for men, with a bed capacity of about 400 persons. It was intended to alleviate the problem of overcrowding in the main prison "Lerchesflur" in Saarbrücken, through which a large number of political prisoners passed and which was bursting at the seams with convicts[260]. Called the "Neue Bremm", it was set up in barracks at the place called "Golden Bremen" on the main road between Forbach and Saarbrücken, about twelve kilometers from Völklingen. Because of its border location, it was used for the temporary detention of French resistance fighters, Jews, or STO draft dodgers, but also German communists and many relatives of Alsatian-Moselle deserters who had been drafted into the Wehrmacht. And, as one might expect, the management of the Röchling factories sent a number of French or Belgian civilians who had been drafted and Russian deportees who had not been pardoned during their stay in Etzenhofen, not to mention German workers who had been found guilty of "anti-Nazi" activities.

---

259. Elisabeth Thalhofen, *Neue Bremm. Terrorstätte der Gestapo. Ein erweitertes Polizeigefängnis und seine Täter, 1943-1944*. St. Ingbert, Röhrig Universitätsverlag, 2004.
260. At the end of 1942, 30,000 prisoners of war and deportees were used as slaves in the Saarland, and by April 1944 there were at least 70,000, crammed into some 370 camps. Stalag XII, in Forbach in Moselle, alone provided 7,000 prisoners of war - French, Serbian, Russian - for the Saarland mines and factories. See Christoph M. Frisch, *op. cit.* p. 2.

Chapter 9.
The slaves between survival and death

Whether one was in the Saarland or at the other end of the *German Reich*, in the outer commandos of a concentration camp or in a company that employed forced laborers, the structures of exploitation and the mechanisms of repression did not vary much. Sickness, malnutrition, and brutality caused an indeterminable number of deaths and, consequently, a high turnover of workers, and the treatment inflicted on forced laborers varied according to their nationality and according to where they were exploited, in factories or in mines, in the West, in the Reich, or in the East. For Soviet prisoners of war and IMI in German hands, the mortality rate is estimated to be over 50%. In the annexed territories of Upper Silesia, Polish workers liked to repeat this sentence: after the entry of the Wehrmacht, German and Polish horses received the same rations, but for human beings, the standards were different[261]!

---

261. A remark reported by Obersturmführer Brehm in his memoir on the "Polish problem" and the measures to be taken to improve the performance of Polish civilians in the metallurgical industry. *Die Bedeutung des Polen-Problems für die Rüstungswirtschaft Oberschlesiens*, published by the Upper Silesian Institute of Economic Research in 1944, is categorical: the nutrition of the Poles was far too low to be able to "exploit them to the fullest extent". This report was published in 1945 in *Documenta Occupationis Teutonicae*, Posen, p. 212.

The suffering, however, could reach paroxysms. Josif Marcu, sent by the Americans as an official observer at the Röchling trial, was among the American jurists charged with documenting the ordeal of these men and women for the Nuremberg tribunal[262]. During the investigation of the Flick trial in 1947, he drew up a meticulous report based on the account of one of these labor slaves, Vladimir Rittenberg, who was deported from France at the end of February 1944 as a Jew. His story synthesizes the experiences of the deportees, forced labor, during the 14 months of his detention in the service of the arms industry, between Upper Silesia, Austria and Germany. Initially interned at Auschwitz-Monowitz, he soon found himself at the Laurahütte building anti-aircraft guns at the "Oberschlesisches Gerätebau" factory, a subsidiary of Rheinmetall-Borsig. When the Soviet army approached in January 1945, he was transferred to Mauthausen, then to the Gusen II concentration camp in Austria. Ill-treated by the guards, lacking clothes appropriate to the climate, undernourished and living in deplorable hygienic conditions, Rittenberg, although skeletal, was selected by a civilian, director of the Mitteldeutsche Stahlwerke, a subsidiary of the Flick group, to be transferred at the beginning of February to their factory at Gröditz, near Dresden. Here are the exact words, reported by Marcu, of this man who describes his last ordeal before the liberation by the Soviet troops in May 1945:

> "If I said above that the treatment in Gusen was worse than before, life in Gröditz was hellish, day by day the quantity of food was reduced, not to mention the quality. Endless phone calls, blows with the baton and the sadistic treatment

---

262. The U.S. Treasury sent Marcu to Germany in 1946 to work with J. S. Martin to dismantle cartels in industry.

of the camp leader demoralized us more and more, we were weakening visibly, medical care was lacking, no medicine, no bandages, my two frozen feet were getting worse and worse, gangrene was appearing, my feet became huge and I myself was embarrassed by the smell they gave off."

The shortage of medicine in the camps and the lack of hygiene caused lice typhus. Up to 35 people died each day - the number of deaths was posted daily on the front door of the barracks for all to see. Rittenberg and his comrades, although exhausted and ill, worked even on their days off to avoid the bullying of the capos and the camp leader[263]. A French Resistance fighter, André Gernigon, who was also deported to Gröditz in October 1944, confirms this testimony and adds this disastrous detail that is not unlike Etzenhofen: the factory was part of a camp, a *Straflager*, where several of their comrades perished...[264]

Of course, in the occupied territories in the West, the health issue was less dramatic than in Germany and the Eastern countries. But in France too, in the barracks, the beds and clothes of the labor slaves were eaten away by vermin, and a typhus epidemic broke out in January 1942. It was not until the end of the year that Sauckel ordered measures such as proper showers to prevent the spread of communicable diseases. The situation in the Moselle became so dramatic that in March 1943 the health authorities asked the Röchling company to equip the steelworks in Thionville with a delousing station for the entire region. Archival documents show that the application for a building permit was not submitted until a year later, but it is not known whether the plant was ever built.

---

263. AN BB 35/90: pv of Vladimir Rittenberg of March 29, 1947.
264. AN BB 35/90: pv of January 5, 1947 in Rennes.

The cruelest fate awaited those who were sent to the bottom of the Lorraine mines of the Pays-Haut - the Longwy-Briey-Thionville basin - where the mined ore was the most abundant and the labor shortage the most noticeable. In the summer of 1942, a medical investigation revealed that the miners were overworked and undernourished, resulting in weight loss, a drop in blood pressure, muscle weakness and a marked increase in lung diseases and abscesses. The sub-prefect of Briey, who was regularly informed of the living conditions of the Soviets, in violation of the Geneva Convention of 1929, strictly adhered to the regulations issued by the occupying power...[265]

We follow the daily martyrdom of these improvised underground miners in the account of a French worker, a porter at the Mourière mine in Piennes, in the Briey basin. In his diary, entrusted to the purification committee the day after the occupation, this team leader notes the arrival of a first convoy of a hundred Soviet prisoners of war:

> "January 26, 1943. 60 Russians come down to the first post. They seem to be in good health, they come from the culture [agriculture]. It is a disaster for the Krauts: 1 wagon for 2 men [i.e. 2.4 tons. The norm is 12 tons = 5 wagons per miner].
> January 28. Mr. Revenu makes a tour with me and declares that the Russians must give more. I take their defense, alleging that they spend 9 hours at the bottom without eating or drinking. Two hours later, he sends me 4 watering cans for my Russians; with that 1 wagon for 3 men.
> There is not yet a standard of fixed by the Krauts, but it will not be long, as Russian prisoners average about 4 t."

---

265. See various elements of the files AD MM WM art.1142 + bis and AD MM WM art. 282.

Six weeks later, the performance standard was set at seven cars for two men, and anyone who did not load his account remained at the bottom, without food, for a second shift. On April 10, the minimum was raised to nine wagons for every two men, and the Russians who could not keep up were deprived of food and sent "to the cellar in the fleet. In July, the first deaths were recorded among those who, for their masters, were only matricule numbers, n° 182.814, 71.573, 13.661... In November, the chief of operations inaugurated a new control: the porter was obliged to make a list of all the prisoners who had not loaded their wagon count and to hand it over to the German sentries at the time of the ascent:

> "The sanctions are as follows: loss of half the soup ration, 25 to 50 strokes of the stick and the night in prison in the cellar where they are locked up after having undressed them completely and where they have water up to their waist. If they work at the 2nd post, i.e. from 15 to 24 hours, the sentries bring them back to the mine at the 1st post at 6 a.m., where until 3 p.m. they have to load the wagons they lost the day before, then at 3 p.m. without having taken the food, they start their post again until 24 hours[266]."

In Piennes, a German military cemetery perpetuates the memory of 1,138 German soldiers who fell during the Great War; on the other hand, there is nothing in this commune to evoke the memory of the thousands of Soviet prisoners, reduced to the state of nameless slaves before disappearing.

---

266. AD MM WM 282: Bénard file. Report signed Gaspard, October 19, 1944.

***

At Völklingen, the prisoners of war were housed in camps within the perimeter of the factory or in municipal camps [*Stadtlager*] under the authority of German military personnel. The civilian workforce was distributed according to nationality in unbearable and over-crowded barracks around the factory. It is worth noting that after Hermann Röchling was appointed Reich Delegate for Iron and Steel, the supervisory board of his company approved an expenditure of RM 1,150,000 for the construction of barracks for civilian workers in the East on October 6, 1942. "The investment of such a sum shows how profitable the employment of 'cheap' Eastern workers was[267]." This was the largest of the camps belonging to the Völklingen steelworks, called "Am Schulzenfeld", which reached a capacity of 1,500 people at the end of November 1944. After the collapse, Röchling, like all the other employers of forced laborers, made the "DAF", which was in charge of the civilian camps, take full responsibility for this notorious place and for the living conditions of the deportees.

At the Rastatt trial, the prosecution gave some statistics on the "decent treatment" that Hermann Röchling claimed to have offered to the foreigners assigned to his forges and steel mills: a minimum of nine hours of work per day and, very frequently, a daily duration of eighteen hours - two periods of nine consecutive hours - because of the shortage of labor[268]. When questioned during the investigations

---

267. https://stadtarchiv.voelklingen.de/fulcolingas/zwangsarbeit-in-voelklingen/das-la-gernetz-in-voelklingen/ (accessed on 7.02.2023)

268. According to the accounting books of the Röchling factories for July 1944, the French POWs worked an average of 9.6 hours per day, the IMI 10.8 hours and the Soviet POWs 11.1 hours. For civilians, these figures were 10.5 for men and 10 for women. However, when the official working hours were completed, all were mostly still occupied for 2 or 3 hours with work on the spot. In the case of a Soviet prisoner of war, this amounted to nearly 14 hours of work per day. AN BB 36/31 HR 151, TG 289: report of the engineer of the labor service.

for the Röchling trial, one of the French prisoners of war, an engineer by trade, but assigned for five months to the electric furnaces of the RESW, provided some details concerning the weekly rest of the teams:

> "We were not allowed any time off except every third or fourth Sunday, depending on the department. The coke workers worked 16 hours in a row every third Sunday as a result of the rotation. Two shifts had to work 16 hours to give the third shift a day off[269]."

Similarly, Vincent Nicolato, an Italian doctor employed at Röchling between October 1, 1943 and December 2, 1944, revealed that the workers presented themselves to him for the morning medical examination physically and morally exhausted, despite the nightly rest. Their diet was totally inadequate for the overwhelming workload.

A young Frenchman, 21 years old, was taken in June 1943 in a raid at the Gare du Nord in Paris and immediately transferred to Völklingen. He was forced to do the hard work of cleaning the boilers of the Wehrden power plant, which supplied the steelworks. He had to work up to ten hours a day to clean the inside of the still-burning boilers, a task especially reserved for the deportees who were also fed with leftovers: one soup a day, six boiled potatoes, four or five of which were rotten, an eight-centimeter piece of bread, a nine-centimeter piece of butter, and a piece of sausage, which was usually spoiled. Twice a week the deportees were allowed a tiny piece of meat[270]. Another employee at the Röchling factories, French POW Edouard Berck, confirmed that he and his compatriots were only able to survive thanks to parcels from their families and the Red

---

269. AN BB 36/9 SEF 1032: pv of the pg Maurice Algret, Valenciennes, April 14, 1947.
270. AN BB 36/9 SEF 1045,7: pv of Jean Burlot, February 14, 1946.

Cross, an indulgence denied to the Russians and IMIs. Berck gave some details on the work stations to which they were assigned, all nationalities included:

> "The prisoners of war were used for very arduous work, in particular in the rolling mills, where they had to work for 8 hours without stopping; in the coke department, where they had to load 20 one-ton skips in 8 hours; in the blast furnaces, where they had to break up pig iron with a 20-kilogram sledgehammer and load it into the cars; The hammer-drums, as well as the Martin and electric ovens which gave off heat varying between 900 and 1,800 degrees; the transport of bags of cement; and finally, the pitch, a by-product of coal, which came out of the recuperators in a liquid state, a particularly toxic and corrosive material, which the men could only handle when covered with a thick layer of Vaseline. Other prisoners were employed in less strenuous work, but they worked an average of 10 hours a day. Sunday rest was granted only every third Sunday, but this was compensated for by working extra shifts that worked 12 hours instead of eight on Sundays[271]."

During the "Röchling" trial, the public prosecutor pointed out that the mortality rate at RESW was much higher than at other large German companies and that the figures that were to be used as evidence were probably far lower than the reality: many deportees

---

271. AN BB 36/9 SEF 745, TG 253: pv of Edouard Berck, April 10, 1947. This French soldier, taken prisoner in June 1940, worked at Völklingen from March 19, 1941. In September 1942, he was appointed by his comrades as a trustworthy man and it was in this capacity that he protested against their insufficient food, which led to his being sent to Saarbrücken prison in March 1944.

from the East, Soviet prisoners of war and IMI would have died elsewhere than at Völklingen, in hospitals or in camps in the region, where they had been parked once it had become clear that they could no longer be of use[272]. Edouard Berck told the investigators how his seriously ill fellow prisoners were transported to Boulay in Moselle, from where most of them never returned, a statement confirmed by two employees of Boulay: the workers who had become too "defective" to do the work required ended up in Boulay, officially a transit camp, which in fact became their death trap. And the German authorities, who had taken over the Jewish cemetery in front of the Boulay camp, buried there "prisoners and probably also these defective workers who died[273]". To this day, however, little is known about it, because the French army, owner of the site, has never authorized any excavations.

Vladimir Gardner, a Russian who had been in France since 1925, was conscripted in November 1942 and sent to Germany. After spending some time as an unskilled worker at I.G. Farben in Ludwigshafen, he served as an interpreter for the Saarbrücken employment office, accompanying the *Gau* inspector on his visits to factories in the region. During these inspections, which only concerned the camps for foreign civilian workers, he saw the unbearable living conditions of his compatriots and other deportees from Eastern Europe, especially at the Röchling factories in Völklingen. He reported that he had seen three of the camps for civilians who worked for Röchling, in particular in:

---

272. AN BB 36/11: trial in revision, September 20, 1948.
273. AB BB 36/9 SEF 1059, TG 308: judicial information on the death of Russian workers on September 15, 1947 1. pv of Jules Borr of Boulay, employed by the German gendarmerie from November 1940 to November 1942 as a requisite in Boulay; 2. pv of François Fischer, principal secretary of the town hall of Boulay.

"... those of Schützenhausen and Lehock [these are camps III "Am Schulzenfeld" and "Le Hoc"]. I would like to point out that Schützenhausen was the worst. After these inspections I can say that the food served to my compatriots was terrible. The morning drink was dirty unsweetened water, which they called coffee, at noon the food consisted of three quarters of a liter of thin soup and in the evening a piece of bread with a little margarine[274]."

During the four weeks she served in the French camp at Schulzenfeld, Louise Zick, a German cook, witnessed the beatings by the STO *Werkschutz* guards, "always hungry, dirty," when they came to fetch their meager soup: "They were pitiful[275]. According to the testimony of a Yugoslavian civilian deportee, their brutality claimed one or two victims a day, and his own brother died[276]. Following numerous reports to the *Gauarbeitsamt*, notably concerning the state of health of the workers in the East, the violence suffered by Russian women, the numerous cases of tuberculosis and the lack of means to treat them, a particularly lengthy inspection of the RESW took place in 1944. A written report was drawn up, with the threat of prosecution. According to Gardner, Hermann Röchling could have remedied this state of affairs, if he had wanted to... and in fact there was never any sanction: it is true that Hermann Röchling was only carrying out general prescriptions fixing the use of Soviet labor.

In March 1944, the management of the Völklingen plants brought in a German doctor, Paul Grouven, to the medical department with

---

274. AN BB 36/8, SEF 105: pv of Vladimir Gardner, stateless, born in Moscow, commercial employee residing in France from 1925 to 1942.
275. AN BB 36/8 SEF 1031: pv of March 18, 1946.
276. AN BB 36/8 TG 297, SEF 1057: pv of Jasar Ramadan.

the task of remedying the poor state of health of the workers from the East. Grouven said that when he arrived, all the patients, who were being cared for by a Russian doctor, were grouped together in a single room with a toilet; the bathroom was out of order. The doctor only had a thermometer and no means to detect tuberculosis, which was very frequent. According to a confidential report that Grouven submitted to the management in June, the most elementary hygiene was not ensured, neither in the barracks nor in the infirmary: the toilets were unsanitary, the showers defective; there was no laundry and the soap to wash oneself was lacking; the wool blankets, a real rarity, were swarming with lice; and impossible for the deported workers to mend the rags that they wore day after day

The numerous victims of tuberculosis in the *Ostarbeiter* camps, as well as among the Russian POWs and IMIs, were therefore not surprising[277]. Almost all of these tuberculosis patients were considered *arbeitsfähig*, fit for work, and assigned to jobs above their capacity, without a diet suitable for their condition, while they continued to live among others in the overcrowded barracks. Comparing the situation of the foreigners in the two companies, Dr. Grouven, who had previously worked at the Ford factory in Cologne, found the living conditions of those assigned to Röchling to be particularly deplorable, and the indifferent or even hostile attitude of the management to be disgusting, in an atmosphere that did not encourage the medical staff to make any complaints. On the contrary, the person who sought to alleviate the distress of the workers in the East was considered - and the term is used in the LTI - a *Feindfreund*, a friend of the enemy. When questioned by the French magistrate in 1947, Grouven, who had become a doctor in the Saarland town of Brebach, provided the public

---

277. AN BB 36/9 SEF 805, TG 300: report of Dr Grouven, June 14, 1944.

Chapter 9. The slaves between survival and death

prosecutor's office with a number of internal documents in support of his claims, but asked to remain anonymous... for fear of reprisals[278].

According to nurse Trauden, who was also employed in the factory's health department, the many deaths among the workers in the East were the result not only of the brutality suffered, but also of the working conditions themselves and the lack of food:

> "I have had the opportunity to help foreigners who, in the middle of their work, had become so exhausted that they had to be taken to hospital immediately. These people were usually very thin. I also treated foreign workers who had purulent wounds. In my opinion, these were not the result of brutality. They were usually Russians or Serbs. I could only shake my head when I saw men coming to work in this condition. In my opinion, they should have been exempted from any work[279]."

They exchanged even the most essential of their personal belongings for food in an attempt to make up for the lack of food rations. Quite often, in the civilian barracks, the camp leaders, DAF personnel, would even divert part of the meagre food intended for them to feed their dogs[280].

Dr. Vincent Nicolato gave a brief account that illustrates the difference in treatment between the Russian workers and those of other

---

278. AN BB 36/9 SEF 806, TG 300: pv of June 13, 1947. Cf. *infra*, annex 4.

279. AN BB 36/8 TG 302: pv of the nurse Wilhelm Trauden from Puttlingen. The diseases from which these *Ostarbeiter* suffered were mainly pulmonary tuberculosis, hypertrophy of the lymph glands, furunculosis caused by malnutrition, digestive tract disorders due to eating poor quality food, foot injuries caused by wearing clogs without the protection of socks.

280. AN BB 36/7 SEF 1056.

nationalities: during the winter of 1943-1944, a very serious epidemic of diphtheria broke out, causing the death of almost all the Russian children taken in by the Russian corps' children's "garden". As they themselves had to work as much as the others, the mothers could not take care of them. These children were not allowed to use the anti-diphtheria serum that doctors were allowed to use for other patients[281].

The punishment of foreign civilians in Völklingen was, in Hermann Röchling's words, "appropriate and just", but it was commensurate with the conditions of life and, above all, death of the internees in the *Straflager* in Etzenhofen. The accounting department of the Völklingen plant recorded a total of 1,604 people interned in this "special camp" from April 1st, 1943 to December 21, 1944[282], including four people sentenced by the *Schnellgericht of the* Thionville plant in June 1943[283]. During the Röchling trial, the public prosecutor produced more than fifty depositions of former internees at Etzenhofen - French, but also Yugoslavs, Russians, Poles, as well as testimonies of external observers, forced laborers who worked alongside the captives, Etzenhofen residents who observed the camp, and railroad workers who witnessed their daily transportation.

A special wagon was chartered morning and evening for the transfer of prisoners between the factory and the camp under the control of two jailers. These convicts with shaved heads had to wear blue and white striped clothes so that they could be distinguished from the other workers. A mechanic driver from Meurthe-et-Moselle,

---

281. AN BB 36/9 TG 301: pv of September 10, 1947.

282. AN BB 36/7 SEF 744.

283. AN BB/36/9 SEF 1067: report by Inspector Marcel Hindenoch, October 3, 1947. An AEL was in operation at Guenange in Moselle from October 28, 1941 to September 21, 1942. Thereafter, deportation to the camp of Schirmeck was preferred, where the prisoners worked in a granite quarry for the *Deutsche Erd- und Steinwerke GmbH* (DEST), an SS mining company that supplied Speer with construction materials. Cf. *infra*, note 302.

deported as an STO, tells us about the day of a prisoner in the reprisal camp: getting up at 3 a.m., doing gymnastics until daybreak, transferring to the factory and then to the railroad cars, where the internees worked in the coke ovens, a particularly hard job because of the temperature. The break at mid-day was half an hour, then work resumed until 8 pm. When they returned to the camp, they were forced to build shelters for civilians, for example, until 11 pm and beyond. And the abuse was commensurate with this daily condition of slavery. The management could not have been unaware of the living conditions of the Etzenhofen internees, because on many occasions the prisoners themselves reported their complaints to the management through Dr. Nicolato.

A 19-year-old French bank employee told how he ended up in Etzenhofen: in 1943, hired as a construction worker to repair buildings in the Blandan military barracks in Nancy, he bought food for North African prisoners of war in Frontstalag 161 and was discovered. The occupying authorities threatened him with imprisonment to force him to sign an STO commitment and sent him to the RESW. He escaped, was recaptured, and after refusing to return to work, was interned for two months in Etzenhofen, from July to September 1944[284]. A mechanic driver, also a STO at the RESW, spoke out for all those who had suffered the daily brutalities of the guards of this "reprisal camp":

> "The regime in the Etzenhofen camp was as follows: as far as food was concerned, we had tea in the morning with a small piece of bread, at noon we were given a plate of soup without bread, and in the evening the same meal.

---

284. AN BB 36/9 SEF 1071: pv of Raymond Dulot, October 11, 1946.

[...] We were frequently hit by members of the *Werkschutz* who were in charge of our surveillance. These individuals hit us with a piece of rubber that they called "the Koumi" and sometimes even with a stick. Their refinement went so far as to make us play leapfrog and to hit us with the above-mentioned weapons while we were down. For my part, I was hit several times, and as a result of this abuse, I had to be taken to the hospital of the Röchling factory where I underwent an operation on the right side of my stomach as a result of a blow I had received. [...] The management of the Röchling factories was not unaware of the living conditions of their personnel interned at Etzenhofen, because we had repeatedly reported these conditions to them and made complaints through the factory doctor, an Italian named Nicolato[285]."

In Rastatt, the defense attorneys presented a document which showed that the internees at Etzenhofen, although not on the company payroll, were nevertheless paid by the Röchling company: a separate account was kept for each of them, and each hour worked was paid at 0.55 reichspfennig, less social security contributions and the cost of "food", "clothing" and - the most important item! - also "expenses for the maintenance of the re-education camp itself (*die laufenden Ausgaben für das Erziehungslager*[286])"!

Joseph Hernandez was 15 years old in 1942 when he left for Völklingen as a volunteer worker. After a leave, he decided not to go back and hid, but was denounced and sent back to the factory. After

---

285. AN BB 36/336/107 SEF 1038,2, TG 337: pv of Mr. Cund, August 7, 1947.
286. AN BB 36/30 TGD 1564: document prepared by the RESW payroll office, April 22, 1943.

Chapter 9. The slaves between survival and death

refusing to return to work, he found himself, like the young man from Nancy, in Etzenhofen:

> "In this camp, the regime was very hard, poorly fed (only one meal a day and what a meal), ill-treatment (whip blows for no reason), police dogs that bit us at every moment on the orders of the guards, freezing showers, exhausting work, squalid barracks, no infirmary and not the slightest medical care. In the same camp, we were separated from the Russians who were treated even more harshly and depressingly than we were[287]."

According to another young STO, who was sent to Völklingen for a year, the internees in Etzenhofen had to work in the factory in coal tar pitch without any eye protection; after a while they could no longer see clearly and the guards tied them up one behind the other to take them to work[288].

The Etzenhofen prison was even used as a place of detention to serve a common law sentence. After three months of imprisonment in France for theft at the docks of Saint-Ouen, a French coal worker was transferred to Etzenhofen to be employed in the factories as a laborer until the end of his detention. His testimony is also without appeal:

> "[...] Hermann Röchling, his family and his directors could not be unaware of the living conditions imposed on us in the internment camp. We went to work dressed like convicts, shaved, thinned out and watched like animals in the factory and this could not go unnoticed by the

---

287. AN BB 36/9 SEF 1066: pv of Joseph Hernandez, September 27, 1947.
288. AN BB 36/9 SEF 104: Emile Marmagne born in 1924, pv of March 13, 1946.

management. We were strictly forbidden to communicate while working[289]."

The Etzenhofen police often tried to enroll young Frenchmen in the Waffen-SS and if they refused, they shaved their heads; they took from their meager rations enough to feed their police dogs. They woke up at 4 a.m. and took five minutes to report for duty in their work clothes. If the prisoner did not have his shoes laced up, the guard would hit him with as many blows of the bull's eye as there were empty carnations[290]. A man from Nancy, also an STO interned at Etzenhofen, told us that the Russians were the target of special attention from the *Werkschutz* guards who, at the slightest resistance, locked them up naked, without food, in a special barrack. Two of these Russians died after spending six days there starving. During the last 48 hours, they did nothing but shout night and day[291]. Henri Balthazard, another STO who spent two months in Etzenhofen, reported having seen one of the *Werkschutz* policemen kicking a pregnant Russian woman in the stomach[292].

The most damning testimony comes from the local residents who, in the morning and evening, saw the prisoners on their way from the camp to the train station: they always ran the few hundred meters, some so weak that they had to be supported by their comrades. From the Herschenbach hill, the residents could also look into the camp, where a cellar half-filled with water was used to lock up the

---

289. AN BB 36/36/107: investigation of the workforce. SEF 1592: pv of René Ury, police station of Saint-Ouen, September 10, 1947.
290. AN BB 36/8 SEF 1017: pv of Jean Panet, 23 years old, interned several times for a total of eleven months in Etzenhofen; AN BB/36/ SEF 1042: pv of André Eckel, 20 years old.
291. AN BB 36/36/107 SEF 362: pv of Marcel Perrin, October 27, 1947.
292. AN BB 36/32 SEF 1009: pv of August 23, 1947.

Chapter 9. The slaves between survival and death

hostages[293]. The stationmaster of Etzenhofen described the scene of the guards making the prisoners do gymnastics exercises in the morning and evening until they fell down from exhaustion. He also testified that he heard a real clamor from the camp when they hit the pile. Forced to load and unload tar and coke at the factory, the internees often had burns on their hands, faces and, worst of all, their eyes. A Yugoslavian bricklayer, who entered the camp for several days in a row to do some work, saw the guards set fire to the hair of a young Frenchman after spraying it with benzine; his face was also on fire[294]. A German postal worker who took up his post in July 1944 as a guard at a store 100 meters from the camp noticed a covered car coming out of the camp on two occasions. He asked one of the guards why and received this answer: to transport the corpse of a dead prisoner to the camp[295]. The inhabitants of Etzenhofen can attest to the fact that every three months or so the head of the *Werkschutz* came to inspect the camp together with representatives of the factory management!

Several Germans, employed during the war at the rolling mills of "Betrieb 83" at the RESW, confirmed that the work demanded of the foreigners, who were notoriously undernourished and constantly mistreated by camp guards and those of the *Werkschutz*, was beyond their strength[296]. One of these German workers, Jakob Lohrig, an anti-Nazi, was arrested by the Gestapo on December 17, 1943 for lack of discipline and sabotage. At the Röchling trial in 1946, he testified not only to the brutality of the Neue Bremm guards, but also to the

---

293. AN BB 36/36/107 SEF 1049,1: statement by stationmaster Grün; AN BB/36/107 SEF 1050: Josef Wernet, a miner by profession, statement made in Etzenhofen, September 13, 1946.
294. AN BB 36/36/107 SEF 1757: pv no. 13/3, from Johan Merkler, Volklingen, February 26, 1946.
295. AN BB 36/9 SEF 1077: pv of Jacques Meier, September 12, 1947.
296. AN BB 36/36/107: labor survey, testimony of Michael Rischaneck, employee from Völklingen.

beating of civilians and prisoners of war in the laminarium of Betrieb 83, where two "hard-core Nazis", Bruch and Menden, were active[297]. It happened that civilian workers were imprisoned in Etzenhofen or in the Neue Bremm without even being brought before a puppet court. This was the case with the STO Paul Mommer, an electrical fitter, who had been assigned to the Röchling works since the end of May 1943 and who served sentences in both penitentiaries[298]. Nowhere was the treatment as cruel as at the Neue Bremm, as Roger Vanovermeir, a French Resistance fighter, said. He was successively interned in Buchenwald, Lublin, Natzweiler/Struthof, Dachau and the Neue Bremm[299].

***

In the face of these numerous and detailed statements, it is difficult to give any credence to the testimony of Josef Liebling, parish priest of the Catholic parish of St. Eligius in Völklingen since 1929: testifying on behalf of the defense in 1948, he maintained that he had never heard of Etzenhofen, even though he had offered hospitality on Sundays and holidays to many foreign workers, especially the French. It is true that the Röchling family, itself Protestant, had always cultivated the patronage so characteristic of their religion and over the years had never been stingy with donations - land and financing - made to the two churches!

---

297. AN BB 36/36/107: pv of May 25, 1946 in Völklingen.

298. AN BB/36/36/107: interrogation of Paul Mommer, November 2, 1947.

299. Quoted by Jellonek Burkhard, "KZ-Gedenkstätte Neue Bremm in Saarbrücken", *Gedenkstättenrundbrief*, n° 99, pp. 3-12, here. Let us recall, for the record, that the occupying forces established two other places of detention on French soil for those who had resisted the Nazi system: the Vorbruck-Schirmeck camp (*"Sicherungslager"* or security camp) and the Natzweiler-Struthof concentration camp, six kilometers apart, in the Vosges.

Propaganda photos presented by the defense in Rastatt in 1948: canteen of the Thomasmühle camp at the RESW, where more than 8,000 forced laborers from Eastern countries were crammed. Epigraph on the wall of the photo below: "Only one can win, and that is us".

Chapter 10. "Only One Can Conquer, and That's Us!"

The military situation on both fronts left little hope of a German victory, but the Nazi leaders played the loser, deploying the last human and material reserves. The last twenty months of the Third Reich were marked by initiatives, poorly executed, to reorganize the still chaotic civil administration and to "slim down" the military apparatus with its plethoric commissariat structures. At the same time, it was necessary to find manpower for the fighting troops and also for the companies of the war economy, while remedying as quickly as possible the damage caused by sabotage and air raids. As the months went by, the quest for mobilizable men inevitably led to a rethinking of the entire organization of war production and its distribution among several ministries. But the reforms never went as far as untangling this skein, which the Führer insisted on in order to curb the ambitions of his closest followers.

While most of Röchling's personal correspondence with the highest dignitaries of the Reich was deliberately destroyed, the documents seized are sufficient to shed light on the activism of the Saar baron, who was continuously mobilized until the collapse of the regime[300]: letters and memoirs attest to the constant complicity between Speer and Röchling, and to the tenacity of these two men in pursuing a war that had become untenable. Many of the memoirs that Röchling sent to Speer or Hitler during this last period deal with the necessary reorganization of the economy. On September 25, 1943, he had set an example for himself, praising the way in which he had managed to reorganize iron and steel, thanks to his dual role as leader in the Reich and in the occupied territories, in order to make up for the shortcomings of German industry and, better still, to provide it with a "substantial complement" from the countries under military administration. He ordered Speer to abolish the *Rüstungsobmänner*, a bureaucratic body in the occupied territories that generated "unnecessary work overload. He saw this relief as a *prerequisite for* making the steel industry "a coherently managed industry of maximum strength" ("einheitlich gelenkte Industrie von höchster Schlagkraft[301]").

Hitler was reluctant to undo this tangle of competencies that he himself had enacted, even though he was only too aware of this "problem of men for the front" - a million, it was said, if one wanted to keep fighting. Since the von Unruh Commission had produced little or no results, Speer suggested that the Führer call on representatives of big industry to "rationalize" the structures of the Wehrmacht. At the end of November 1943, Hitler agreed: a new commission under the direction of General Ziegler was created and Speer was given the task of choosing the men who would be asked

---

300. AN BB 36/6 TG 72, SEF 1062: pv of Röchling's personal secretary, Mrs. Tona Winckler, wife Hesse, on October 1st, 1947. She attested to having eliminated mainly the correspondence with the main Nazi leaders - Hitler, Todt, Goebbels and Göring - as well as the documents relating to the distribution of the Lorraine factories.
301. AN BB 36/6-22, SEF 1010: letter from Röchling to Albert Speer of September 25, 1943. In handwriting, the names of several recipients of copies, including Hans Kehrl.

to review all military logistics according to the well-tried practices of the private sector[302].

Between January and May 1944, Speer was forced to withdraw from the places of power for health reasons, but he did not give up his prerogatives. In close collaboration with Milch and Pohl of the SS-WHVA, he was involved in the creation, on March 1st, of a "Jägerstab". Its mission: to eliminate the bureaucratic obstacles faced by aircraft manufacturers to enable them to force the production of interceptor aircraft (*Abfangjäger*). In order to produce cheap attack weapons industrially, the system Speer advocated took into account both material resource constraints and the employment of low-skilled slave labor. The *Jägerstab* was the first step in transferring all aeronautical manufacturing to his ministry. Then, on the 15th, he drew up a list of industrialists for the six "sub-commissions" of the Ziegler Commission, limiting himself to those he knew Hitler trusted: Carl Krauch (I.G. Farben), Paul Pleiger (RWHG), Helmuth Röhnert (Rheinmetall-Borsig), Albert Vögler (Vestag) and... Hermann Röchling, who was in charge of the "Nachschub" commission (supply, arms, ammunition, equipment, vehicles). All were urged to send their opinions, comments and recommendations directly to Hitler[303].

And, from April 18, it is done for Röchling who sends him, with copy to Speer, some dithyrambic lines for his birthday, before coming to the subject:

---

302. Gregor Janssen, *Das Ministerium Speer*, Berlin, Frankfurt am Main, Ullstein Verlag, 1968, pp. 267-268.

303. Telegram from Albert Speer to Hellmuth Röhnert, director of the Rheinmetall-Borsig, March 15, 1944, reproduced in: *Anatomie des Krieges*, ed. Dietrich Eichholtz and Wolfgang Schumann, Berlin, Deutscher Verlag der Wissenschaften, 1969, p. 246. Cf. also Wolfgang Bleyer, "Pläne der faschistischen Führung zum totalen Krieg im Sommer 1944", *Zeitschrift für Geschichtswissenschaft*, 10/1969, pp. 1312-1329, here p. 1313.

"You have appointed me as deputy director of Commission IV of the Ziegler Commission. I am concerned that it will be very difficult to achieve significant savings if we cannot thoroughly reorganize to completely eliminate duplication."

Röchling outlines his vision for the reorganization of the commercial management of the Army Arms and Ammunition Office (*Heereswaffenamt*). The work could be handed over to a team of volunteers - he thinks of chambers of commerce - which would free up a huge potential of men for the front. He concludes, however, on a pessimistic note: because the way of posing the problem is not radical enough, the members of the commission will not find the right solution by themselves. And so, Röchling asks for an intervention of the Führer to trigger this transformation on a larger scale[304]!

On the occasion of the national holiday of May 1st, 1944, the Führer awarded the title of "Pioneer of Labor" to nine personalities, including Röchling and Albert Vögler. The event made the front page of the daily newspapers, which reproduced the text that motivated each of them to receive such an award:

"Dr. rer.pol, Dr. Ing. hc Hermann Röchling, Wehrwirtschaftsführer, is a pioneer of rationalization and social progress in the metal industry. He recognized early on the importance of an open exchange of experiences and a real teamwork in the factories as a prerequisite for a general increase in efficiency.

---

304. BArch R3/1596, letter from HR to Adolf Hitler of April 18, 1944.

He was committed to ensuring that the interests of his company were subordinated to
the interests of the nation. In the social
sphere, he has acted in an exemplary manner,
particularly by building workers' housing for
his factories[305]."

May 1st, 1944: Röchling is awarded the title "Pioneer of Work". Source:
Völkischer Beobachter, *April 30-May 1, 1944.*

On May 12, 1944, the hydrogenation plants and oil refineries in
the central and eastern parts of the Reich came under massive and
systematic attack by Allied forces. There was a general stampede
among the regime's top leaders, as the immediate and imperative
need for men to rebuild the damaged sites aggravated the perennial
problem of manpower. A crisis meeting was held at the Führer's home
in Berchtesgaden on 22 and 23 May, during which Speer, who had
just returned from his convalescence, took to the rostrum to castigate
his colleagues: had he not insisted, since Stalingrad, with Göring and
with the support of the industrialists Vögler, Krauch and Röchling,
that the Luftwaffe should launch air raids against the Soviets' energy
production, and, more specifically, against Moscow's electricity
supply[306]? A week later, he obtained from Hitler the nomination of
Edmund Geilenberg as general commissioner for the reconstruction
of the refineries with extended powers. In short: Geilenberg could
have at his disposal all the manpower, specialized or not, that he felt
he needed to carry out his mission.

---

305. See also *infra*, Appendix 3, p. 375.
306. Dietrich Eichholtz, *Geschichte der deutschen Kriegswirtschaft, 1943-1945*. Berlin,
Akademie Verlag, 1996, vol. 1, p. 33.

In a memorandum to Speer dated June 7, copied to Dorsch, Kehrl and Geilenberg, Röchling discussed at length the reconstruction of the refineries and the preventive measures to be taken against the threat of further air attacks. Since the enemy would not fail to attack the plants again as soon as they were rebuilt, and until the damage became unbearable, Röchling proposed a plan of action: to protect the vital parts of the existing plants by pouring concrete slabs inclined at no less than 60° over them; then to install new units underground; and finally, to resolve to use coal tar to increase the production of synthetic gasoline. And while the Battle of Normandy was taking place some 500 kilometers away, Röchling did not hesitate to recommend the installation of refineries on the slopes of the mountains in the Saar-Lorraine-Luxembourg region! Boilers could even be built in disused mines, an operation he considered easy from a technical point of view[307]!

The underground factory of Thil

In December 1943, the *Feldkommandantur* asked the Nancy prefecture for a list of all the underground excavations, natural or dug in Meurthe-et-Moselle, with an indication of the entrances and exits, branches, total surface area and other geophysical data, without giving any details on the purpose of this research[308]. The answer came from the chief mining engineer: apart from a gypsum quarry at Bures, the region had only iron and salt mines. In fact, Röchling, accompanied by General Milch, had already carried out a scouting mission in the spring of 1942 to verify the possibility of

---

307. BArch R3/1633, "Wiederaufbau der Treibstoffindustrie," June 7, 1944.
308. AD MM W 110 art. 12: mail of December 2, 1943.

installing underground arms factories in one of these mines, safe from Allied bombs. An excellent connoisseur of Lorraine's mines, Röchling judged the disused Tiercelet mine in the Pays-Haut to be particularly suitable for such a conversion and, at the beginning of 1944, a visit to the site was organized for a 22-person delegation from the Ministry of Armaments.

With a surface area of 25 hectares, this mine was advantageously sheltered from enemy aerial reconnaissance, on the side of a hill. What's more, it had a convenient entrance on the Moselle side - it was on the border between occupied France, annexed France and Luxembourg - to allow trains to change to the Reich. The project - codenamed "Erz" - took shape in the spring: the Todt organization, assisted by the SS, was asked by Speer to build an underground factory for V-1 and V-2 missiles. Immediately, the spy services of the French resistance noticed that work was in progress in the commune of Thil, on the border between the two Lorraine regions. In a note dated April 1944, an intelligence agent informed London that the occupying forces were employing a thousand Russian deportees or civilians, both men and women, on this construction site, "inflicting on them treatment that revolted all the French people in the region." However, the agent expressed some doubts about the future of this construction site: like so many projects undertaken by the German authorities at this stage of the war, this project seemed to be intended above all to "ambush" a large number of their compatriots[309].

But the operation was much larger than it seemed at first glance. It was planned that the factory would be operated under the name "Minette GmbH" by the engineer Ferdinand Porsche, CEO of the *Volkswagen* factory and one of Hitler's favorites. In this narrow valley

---

309. AN F/1a/3946: press release of April 16, 1944.

outside Thil, the first teams of forced laborers were responsible for setting up wooden huts to house the skilled workers who would be responsible for the production itself. For the construction of the factory, the Todt organization made foreign deportees, mainly Soviets, work day and night on three shifts of about 2,000 people per round. They were housed in two camps in Morfontaine and Errouville and transported to the mine by rail. As the absolute master of the Lorraine metallurgical region, Röchling made office buildings belonging to the Micheville plant available to the "Minette GmbH" and seconded a contingent of some 700 specialized workers to Thil, "taken" from the personnel of "his" steelworks[310].

The maintenance foreman at the Micheville steel mills, which straddled the municipalities of Audun-le-Tiche and Villerupt, observed daily the Russian prisoners of war and deportees who worked on the mine floor unloading material for the factory. Some of these unfortunate starving people, he testified, sometimes managed to deceive the surveillance of their guards to escape to town in search of food for themselves and their comrades. To facilitate the escape of these work deserters, he and the mine manager gave them easy access to a chicken coop where they could steal eggs before going underground[311].

However, in April, Speer received instructions from the Führer that, "for political reasons," only workers from Eastern and Southeastern countries should be employed. By employing people from Western countries on such a sensitive site, there was a risk of information leaks[312]. Speer then set about organizing the transfer

---

310. Eugène Gaspard, *Les Travaux du IIIe Reich entre Alzette et Fensch*. Thionville, Éditions Gérard Klopp, 1992, p. 151 ff.

311. AD MM WM 282: testimony of Marcel Colin in Villerupt, September 8, 1945.

312. Interview in Berlin between Speer and Hitler, April 19-20, 1944. Willi Boelcke, *Deutschlands Rüstung im Zweiten Weltkrieg. Hitlers Konferenzen mit Albert Speer. 1942-1945, op. cit.* p. 353.

of "economically useful" Hungarian Jews to labor camps in the West, including Thil[313]. Technicians "taken" from the underground factory at Peenemünde were transferred to Thil; on May 21, 1944, a first convoy of 300 Hungarian Jewish prisoners arrived, trained for the manufacture of the V1s and placed under the surveillance of the SS of the "Death's Head" division[314], then in June, two other convoys of 500 Hungarian Jews from Auschwitz. Seven convoys of various materials and machine tools were sent from the new external commando of Neuengamme, called KZ Fallersleben[315]. Another convoy of 300 Hungarian Jewish deportees arrived from Fallersleben in July[316]. Thil was officially listed as the external commando of the Natzweiler-Struthof concentration camp, which sent him several dozen internees: 8 Germans, 19 Italians, 8 Luxembourgers, one Belgian, one Czech, two Poles, 8 Russians, three French, two stateless persons, as well as an unknown number of Spaniards.[317]

The "palm of horror goes to the camp of Thil[318]", it was said in Lorraine. When they passed the barbed wire around the camp, the inhabitants of the town were told to look away, but the scenes of torture perpetrated on the prisoners on their way there did not

---

313. See the telegram sent by Speer to Keitel, Appendix 5.

314. Mario Frigoli, "Thil, le camp de concentration oublié", *Le Pays-Haut,* Bulletin de l'Association des amis du vieux Longwy et des Sociétés savantes du Pays-Haut. n° 1-2 et 3-4, 1981, p. 60.

315. The "Fallersleben" camp, located a few kilometers from the factories, opened at the end of May 1944; its slaves were assigned to construction work for Volkswagen. The name "Fallersleben" disappeared from the history of the Volkswagen factories in May 1945: the town, which had been created *ex nihilo* at the end of the 1930s to accommodate Ferdinand Porsche's automobile project, was renamed "Wolfsburg". An estimated 20,000 prisoners of war and deportees from the KZ were forced to work for the car manufacturer.

316. Klaus Riexinger and Detlev Ernst, *Vernichtung durch Arbeit, Die Geschichte des KZ Kochendorf /Aussenkommando des KZ Natzweiler-Struthof,* Bad Friedrichshall, 1996, republished by Silberburg Verlag, 2003, p. 148.

317. "History of the camp of Thil (V)", *Le Républicain Lorrain,* August 18, 1998.

318. Pascal Brenneur, *op.cit,* p. 48.

escape anyone. In the center of the camp, pyres were set up to burn the corpses; the last dead were incinerated in a crematorium that the executioners had installed with material taken from the slaughterhouses in Villerupt. In July, the "Minette GmbH" asked for 10,000 workers to be made available, but the request went unheeded because the site was quickly abandoned due to the advance of American troops. On August 31, 653 internees were transferred to another commando outside Natzweiler, to Kochendorf, where another underground factory dedicated to the production of "miracle weapons" was opened in good time[319]. A few days later, another convoy of about 300 Hungarian Jews was evacuated to Dernau, another underground weapons production site under Buchenwald. From there, they were immediately transferred to KZ-Mittelbau-Dora. How many survived? Archival documents do not allow us to answer this question, nor do we know more about the fate of the thousands of convicts employed in the "Erz" project. In 1946, the municipality of Thil erected a crypt over the crematorium, the only remnant of this hell of forced labor[320].

Röchling and Speer beyond the announced defeat

At the beginning of the summer, raids against refineries and hydrogenation units became almost daily, and the Allies succeeded, as expected, in reaching those that had barely been rehabilitated. On June 9, Speer was in Essen for a speech to an audience of industrialists on the "Wunder der Rüstung" (the miracle of armament, a miracle of which he was obviously the creator). However, Speer was targeting a wider audience and with this intention he had summoned journalists

---

319. "History of the camp of Thil (VIII)", *Le Républicain Lorrain*, August 29, 1998.
320. Mario Frigoli, *op. cit.* p. 65.

to duly report on his words in the newspapers. His intention was clear: to defend the system of autonomous management that he had conceded to private industrialists in 1942, and which was threatened by reorganization projects defended by certain members of his own administration, such as Hans Kehrl. He also used this opportunity to talk behind the scenes and behind closed doors with some of these industrialists who were also his close collaborators and trusted men (above all Vögler, Rohland and Röchling[321]). The meeting was a success: ten days later, Hitler gave him total control over the technical construction and rationalization of small arms and war materials, and the next day Göring handed over to him, *nolens volens*, the supervision of the entire aeronautical and space production. From that moment on, his own activism was constantly spurred on by the initiatives of his most intrepid collaborators, who gave absolute priority to measures for the reconstruction of damaged refineries.

From the end of June 1944 to January 1945, Speer wrote five memoranda for Hitler with figures on the production of the different categories of fuel and a summary of the measures taken to repair and protect the hydrogenation plants and refineries[322]. These memoranda describe the projects carried out under Geilenberg's direction and which are in line with Röchling's recommendations: camouflage of sensitive parts with concrete constructions; installation of small distillation units in caves or caverns, or hidden in quarries; use of alternative fuels from oil shale and coking tar. However, since a number of production units had already been transferred to underground sites, notably the aeronautical factories for the manufacture

---

321. Dietrich Eichholtz, *Anatomy ...*, *op. cit.* p. 42 and n. 173.
322. Fritz Blaich, *Wirtschaft und Rüstung im "Dritten Reich,"* Düsseldorf, Schwann Verlag, 1987. The first of the five memoirs is reproduced in the appendix of the volume, pp. 133-136; the entire set of documents was published in Wolfgang Birkenfeld, *Der synthetische Treibstoff 1933-1945*. Göttingen, Musterschmidt Verlag, 1964, pp. 237-264.

of "miracle weapons", it proved difficult to find protected locations suitable for the manufacture of fuels. Added to this were the problems of transportation, which had become almost insurmountable since the Allied air attacks had paralyzed the main river and rail transportation networks prior to the Normandy landings.

The acts of sabotage that affected the electric transformers and the railroads in the West caused even greater disorder than the bombings, because they disrupted the operation of the metallurgical sector. The supply of coke became difficult and even ore was in short supply where the steelworks did not have adjacent mines. Night work became widespread to compensate for the drop in productivity, and even the activity of the "Röchling factories" had to be slowed down: of the 25 blast furnaces in operation in September 1943, only seven were still in operation in May 1944. The cessation of production in these "protected" factories opened the door to requisitioning for Germany. Röchling was opposed to this, of course, and tried to resume production as soon as possible, regardless of the working conditions[323].

And yet, in a report to the prefect, the divisional inspector for labor in the district of Nancy considers that the relative calm that reigns in the working class environment is somewhat deceptive and...

> "[...] fraught with threatening unknowns, for if the managers and employees remain in a more or less fear-based immobility, it does not seem that the current passivity of the working masses proceeds entirely from the same cause. There is indeed a state of mind whose echoes sometimes reach us in a very discreet way: the working masses, it is said, consider this war as essentially of capitalist origin and

---

323. AN F/1a/5847: information from the secret services, report of the steel commission in Nancy, May 11, 1944.

end, conceived as a revenge and a means of intimidation of the working class which had become too restless before 1939. It is therefore in the collective interest of the workers not to participate and to wait for the time when they can resume their collective action without the risk of exposing themselves to siege measures[324]."

At this point of decay, whether foreigners or *Volksgenossen*, life had no value except as a labor force to achieve the war aims. In his almost monthly reports to Hitler, Speer only briefly indicated an increase in the number of workers employed to repair the damage and to ensure new, more protected production units. After the war, investigators found few figures on the contingents of forced laborers, German or foreign, deported or imprisoned in concentration camps, who were locked up in perilous conditions, often underground or exposed to air attacks, to carry out this rescue plan, which was inevitably doomed to failure.

Speer's second memorandum to Hitler on the subject of fuel reiterated the demand for air intervention against the Soviet power supply, a proposal supported by Röchling, Göring and others: Speer urged the Führer to launch a "Totaleinsatz" of kamikaze attacks on the Soviet power plants by the Luftwaffe and the men of the elite commando around Otto Skorzeny.

As for the use of prisoners to carry out the Geilenberg plan, internees were transferred from Natzweiler to Baden-Württemberg to work in one of the *Aussenkommandos* of the *Wüste* operation, "desert", as these sites were called, where oil shale was extracted for fuel production. In the Baden region alone, more than 12,000 of

---

324. AD MM W 1343 BIS s. 52. Report on the mood of the labor community in the 4th Ward, July 7, 1944.

them were subjected to the living conditions of these camps, "dirty, filthy, stinking", a Tower of Babel with xenophobic conflicts, with hunger, thirst, cold, beatings and exhausting work. During the trials against the executioners of the Natzweiler-Struthof camp in Rastatt in 1947, they reported on the use of prisoners "in order to exploit, in an intensive manner and under particularly difficult and unhealthy conditions, the oil shale deposits of the region and to carry out, under the same conditions, important military work[325]".

In the summer of 1944, the correspondence between Speer and Röchling also dealt with what the regime's notables modestly called the "Menschenproblem". Röchling reported a crying need for German managers in the entire Reich metal industry and, in particular, in the management of production plants in Lorraine. One month after the Allied landing in Normandy, the two strategists aimed to achieve "optimal performance" in the war industry and, to this end, reviewed the avenues of help that they believed were still open: requisitioning managers from factories in other sectors, employing war-disabled people, and repatriating Lorraine residents who had been sent back to the eastern territories at the beginning of the occupation. Speer could not see how to find the 400-500 additional people that Röchling demanded, when there was a lack of manpower, qualified or not, for the reconstruction of the hydrogenation plants and the refineries[326].

On July 12 and 20, 1944, Speer submitted to the Führer his own memoirs on the conduct of "total war" in relation to this "Menschenproblem. It was a simple question of quantity, which he thought he could solve by following the recommendations of the

---

325. Official Journal of the Chief of Command in the French Occupation Zone, April 15, 1947, Year 2, No. 64, p. 654. As with Röchling, this trial took place in Rastatt.
326. BArch R/1596, letters from Röchling to Speer of 7, 17, and 27 June 1944. See Speer's reply of July 12, 1944.

Ziegler Commission, i.e. the industrialists Röchling, Pleiger, Krauch and Vögler. The lack of archival documents prevents us from having an overview of the recommendations made by the members of this commission, but in summary, they recommend a reduction in administrative personnel in all the organizations involved in the war effort - the Wehrmacht, the Todt organization, the compulsory labor service, the Waffen-SS. The "unproductive" sectors of the service sector were also to be combed in order to mobilize the "last reserves" of men and women - students, housekeepers, bank employees. Speer was of the opinion that one should no longer blindly rely on the contribution of the "IMI" and the contingents of foreign workers that Sauckel was trying to raise. After receiving these notes, the Führer instructed his paladins - with the notable exception of Göring - to meet to discuss them. And on July 22, they all agreed on the following recommendations: full powers in the military field, powers granted to the Ziegler commission, were to be transferred to Himmler, and for the civilian field, it was up to Goebbels to take the necessary measures to conduct this "total war[327]".

On the fronts, however, events accelerated. On July 6, 1944, the work at Mimoyecques collapsed following an English bombing raid, causing countless deaths by drowning among the slave laborers[328]. But

---

327. Wolfgang Bleyer, "Pläne der faschistischen Führung zum totalen Krieg im Sommer 1944," in *Zeitschrift für Geschichtswissenschaft*, 10/1969, pp. 1312-1329. Bleyer presents a number of documents that are essential for the understanding of the turning point in the summer of 1944: a letter from Kehrl to Speer of July 10, 1944, the two memoranda from Speer to Hitler of July 12 and 20, and the protocol of the meeting of July 22.

328. The defenders of the V3 did not give in to defeat and, following the aborted attack of July 20, the military, industrialists and even the SS combined their efforts to "save" it by resizing it for use as a mobile intervention battery on the front. On December 30, 1944, the gun fired 78 projectiles at the city of Luxembourg from a position south of Trier. Röchling announced that five other "V3" could be delivered until March. Nevertheless, on February 6, 1945, the advance of the Allied troops forced Kammler, the SS officer responsible for the use of secret weapons, to order the immediate cessation of all work on the V3. See Groehler, "Die Hochdruckpunpe V3...", *op. cit.* p. 743.

the work did not stop until three weeks later, when the Allied troops approached. The occupying forces left the Moselle during the night of August 31 to September 1st, and all the management personnel of the Röchling factory in Thionville were evacuated. Hermann Röchling was embarrassed by the hasty end of his duties as Reich delegate for iron and steel in France: his cousin was arrested before he could inform him about ongoing negotiations with the Vichy government. Did he obtain from Catala and Bichelonne the granting of a percentage on the sale of steel produced by the meurthe-et-mosellanes factories that had just been returned to their owners? *What about the* French government's guarantee to pay him 10 pf per ton of crude steel as a subsidy for the pilot experiments conducted at the Neuves-Maisons plant? In a letter dated mid-September, he wrote to his cousin, who was imprisoned in Berlin, to remind him of these pending matters, which he felt a certain urgency to settle together. He hopes to obtain authorization for a meeting soon.

Regardless of the circumstances, the uncompromising Röchling never allowed himself to be overcome by defeatist thinking. He never ceased to make Speer aware of his knowledge and technical skills and to come up with new projects to meet the urgent needs of the moment. On August 22, ten days before the rout, he wrote to Speer once again about his proposal to reorganize the ammunition depots (the "Munas" or "Munitionsanstalten") of the three branches of the armed forces in order to free up manpower for the front[329]. And he recommended the abolition of one third of the depots and the resumption of the remaining two thirds under a single management. At the same time, he advocated the introduction of night work, to which all foreign workers would necessarily be obliged, and work on

---

329. BArch R3/1622: memorandum dated June 7, 1944; BArch R 3/1617: letter dated August 22, 1944.

Saturday afternoons and every second Sunday. And Röchling thinks it reasonable to expect a clear gain in productivity[330]!

As a response to the series of failures, Röchling wanted to return to the "militaristic principles" of National Socialism by introducing "wartime penal legislation" in the armaments sector: that every worker, every employee, should submit to military laws and, like the army, that the superior should be invested with the right to sanction[331]. From the weakness of authority in Western companies - now lost to the war effort - Röchling concluded that these measures should be introduced as quickly as possible.

```
              "The Red House Report
August 10, 1944.
On the orders of Martin Bormann, head of the
NSDAP  party  chancellery,  German  industry
bosses,  accompanied  by  representatives  of
several  ministries,  met  in  the  greatest
secrecy at the Rotes Haus hotel in Strasbourg.
They all recognized that defeat was inevitable
and that they had to prepare for the post-war
period without delay. The political authori-
ties urged the big industrialists to take imme-
diate steps to secure the trade of the future.
In this case, to enter into partnerships with,
or  stakes  in,  North  American  companies  and
to invest capital abroad via Swiss banks. At
the  end  of  this  meeting,  a  more  restricted
meeting took place in which the modalities for
```

---

330. BArch R3/1617: letter from Röchling to Albert Speer, August 22, 1944.
331. Minutes of the RVE executive committee on January19, 45. Dietrich Eichholtz, *op. cit.* 3/2, p. 643.

securing the hidden financing of the Nazi party were discussed.

An undercover agent working for the French intelligence services in the annexed Moselle territory prepared a detailed report on these meetings, which reached the counterpart services in Great Britain and the USA in November. It lists the participants, including the industrialists Krupp, Messerschmitt, Rheinmetall, Volkswagen, Brown-Boveri, Röchling or their representatives. Representatives of Röchling and Krupp will participate in the second meeting together with a delegate of the Speer Ministry.

This document, called "The Red House Report", has long been the subject of speculation by journalists and historians. However, it was presented on June 26, 1945 before the War Mobilization Subcommittee of the U.S. Senate, the so-called "Kilgore Committee", as part of an investigation into the role of the cartels in the development of the Nazi war machine. It was not until 1996 that the US authorities declassified this report.

During his investigation, Senator Kilgore provided information on the most recent steps taken by industrialists to save their interests from allied control. He underlined the perennial complicity between the state, the army and industrialists and the responsibility of the latter, holding governmental or semi-official positions, in the crimes committed against the peoples of many countries. And Kilgore deplored the fact that until now only the name of Gustav Krupp has appeared on the list of war criminals to be tried at Nuremberg.

"The Red House Report" was communicated to the members of the Interallied War Crimes Commission. The magistrate Charles Gerthoffer, French government commissioner for the economic section, took an interest in it[332]. He asked the head of the territorial surveillance brigade in Strasbourg to conduct investigations to establish legal proof of the facts revealed in this document, which would be introduced into the proceedings in the trial of Röchling and his associates in 1948.

Report on the secret meeting of Nazi notables to prepare for the post-war period. Source: AN BB 35/93, document SEF 623 of October 1945, and AN BB 36/34/104.

However, neither the most expert advice nor miracle weapons programs could reverse the predicted defeat, of which the military, for their part, were only too aware. At the beginning of July, the MBF staff withdrew *nolens volens* to Nancy, and on August 31, all the steelworkers controlling the Moselle steelworks, including Röchling, were forced to abandon the sites in a hurry[333].

When he returned to the Saarland, Röchling made it a point of honor to make daily contact with the generals of the troops on the Lorraine front to organize their nightly supply of arms and ammunition. Speer was inspired by this and, on 9 September, before going to

---

332. AN BB 36/35, document SEF 103.
333. No sooner had Hitler confirmed Röchling and his executive committee to the leadership of the RVE than he was able to do so.

the Western Front himself, ordered all industrialists to assume their "civic responsibility" and to deliver weapons to the fighting units directly from the factories[334]! Speer had to realize that it had become impossible for him to direct this decaying empire from his ministry in Berlin. He therefore decided to appoint regional representatives - eight in all - and to delegate to them all decision-making powers in the field of war production: in December, he gave Albert Vögler of the "Vestag" the direction of the war economy for the Rhine-Ruhr region; at the beginning of February, Heinrich Kelchner, a Röchling man, became the plenipotentiary for the Southwest.

***

The last months of the sinking Third Reich were marked by indiscriminate reprisals against anything that could be interpreted as a gesture of defeatism, and the bloodthirsty reputation of Judge Roland Freisler who reigned at the Volksgerichtshof in Berlin imposed the greatest fear. As the Allied troops advanced through northern France and the Soviets liberated the first concentration camp at Majdanek, the conspirators around Count Claus von Stauffenberg, in fear of a defeat that would be dishonorable for themselves and implacable for the civilian population, finally put into action their plan to eliminate Hitler.

The aborted plot of July 20 in which Caesar von Hofacker, a cousin of Stauffenberg, was involved in Paris also had consequences for the Röchling clan. Ernst Röchling and his friend were arrested together for having welcomed von Hofacker at his home after the failed attempt and not having denounced him. Towards the end of August,

---

334. Dietrich Eichholtz, *op. cit*, vol. 3/1, p. 59.

Hermann Röchling went to Berlin, where his cousin had been transferred to await trial before Freisler. He obtained a meeting with the head of the Gestapo, SS Obergruppenführer Heinrich Müller. The charges against the cousin did not appear to be serious, and Hermann Röchling was allowed to visit him on August 30, the same day that Freisler sentenced Caesar von Hofacker to death by hanging[335].

A tireless defender of his Führer and the Reich, but also of his business interests and his family, Hermann Röchling wrote directly to Hitler on October 26 to plead his cousin's cause. His plea insisted on the "considerable success" that he himself had been able to obtain in the French iron industry thanks to the good relations that his cousin had with the employers, assisted at all times by the minister Bichelonne. Röchling assures the Führer of his deep conviction that Germany will win the final victory, the day when it will succeed in "breaking the air superiority of the Allies", hence the importance of the function that his cousin assures:

> "It is not in our interest to sentence Ernst Röchling in such a way as to defame him. We do not know how we will need him again[336]."

Albert Speer confided to his diary that Röchling's plea had been the subject of a conversation with the Führer on November 28. He noted that Hitler intended to discuss it with Himmler, who had been in command of the internal armed forces since the attack[337]. On December 12, Speer himself intervened directly with Himmler to

---

335. AN BB 36/112 HR 276.
336. AN BB 36/6 TG 185 HR 221: letter from Röchling to Adolf Hitler of October 24, 1944. Cf. *infra*, annex 6, p. 383 ff.
337. Willi Boelcke, *op. cit.* p. 446.

transmit his friend's request. In his accompanying letter, the minister emphasized Röchling's patriotism and unwavering devotion to duty, as he had been active on the Saarland front in the last phase of the war, mobilizing industry and providing material assistance to the troops in combat[338]. In January 1945, the Freisler court sentenced Ernst Röchling to five years' imprisonment. He was then transferred to the Brandenburg-Görden prison, where political prisoners were held. Hermann Röchling immediately requested a meeting with Himmler. His cousin was released in April 1945, when the Red Army surrounded Berlin[339].

***

Hermann Röchling knew from experience that the imminent defeat could lead, in addition to the loss of the occupied or annexed territories, to the at least temporary dispossession of certain border regions, primarily the Saarland. To prepare for any eventuality, he had to return to his "plan B", which revived his interest in the Blumberg site. He first undertook to reopen the mines in Baden and, with the help of the Todt organization, to supply the Saarland factories with Doggererz to replace the Lorraine minette. Speer agreed in November, but with the approach of the American troops, production in the Saarland came to a halt and the project was cut short. The Röchling forges and steelworks in Völklingen were evacuated at the beginning of November in the face of the advance of General Patton's 3rd Army. Hermann Röchling, who withdrew with his private secretary to Heidelberg, instructed those who remained behind to destroy

---

338. BArch R 3/1583.
339. AN BB 36/8 HR 218. The sentence was passed on January 12, 1945; Röchling's letter to Himmler is dated January 15, 1945.

the archives[340]. Questioned after the war for the trial in Rastatt in the context of the investigation against her boss, the secretary declared that she had been charged with the disappearance of a suitcase containing her correspondence with the highest personalities of the Third Reich, exchanges that testified to the personal power of this old hand in politics.

In a second phase, Röchling envisaged a more ambitious project: the construction of a small forge with two blast furnaces in Blumberg, with all the necessary equipment to produce about 60,000 tons of high quality steel. On December 17, he went to Berlin to receive the military award *"Ritterkreuz des Kriegsverdienstordens mit Schwertern"* (Knight's Cross of War Merit with Swords) from his friend the Minister. He used the occasion to talk about his project and when Speer gave him a planning assignment, Röchling deliberately confused it with a promise of financing by the Reich government. The Minister of Finance and the RWM were stunned by his demands for subsidies, which were totally inappropriate at this stage of the war. However, despite their refusal, Röchling and his collaborators continued with the construction. When the French troops occupied Baden on April 23, the mines were definitively closed[341].

With the 3rd American Army at the gates of the Saar, Hitler called for the evacuation of the population to facilitate the defense; the next day, March 19, he issued his "Nero order", demanding the destruction

---

340. On December 27, Karl Theodor Röchling, Hermann's son, and the engineer Heinrich Koch were found murdered in an engine pit at the factory. Two young Russian civilians, forced laborers who had hidden on the site, were arrested and tried for the murders.

341. After the war, the DAG took over the land and facilities and leased them out. The shareholders, the Saarland steelmakers and the state of Baden-Württemberg, the legal successor to the Reich in terms of natural resources, made considerable profits from this activity and from the liquidation of the DAG itself, which took place at the end of the 1970s. See Wolf-Ingo Seidelmann, "Auf Messers Schneide ...", *op. cit.* p. 63 ff.

of any facility that could serve the enemy. Speer, who celebrated his 40th birthday that same day, left Berlin after having submitted a memorandum to the Führer that went against the scorched earth policy. In it, he was asked to think about the post-war period: had he not promised the industrialists around him to keep their factories free of war, whatever the cost?

In his 1969 memoirs, Speer recounts that he then went to the Wehrmacht High Command headquarters at Schloß Ziegenberg in the Taunus. There, in the early afternoon, they were subjected to an American attack of great violence. Once the attack was over, Hermann Röchling joined them. Kesselring, then in charge of the German forces in the West and one of Hitler's loyal followers, informed Röchling of the imminent loss of the Saarland and its factories. Speer reported the words of the Saarland industrialist, who received the news almost with indifference:

> "We have already lost and regained the Saarland once. In spite of my age, it will still be given to me to see it come back to us."

Together, Speer and Röchling drove to Heidelberg to Kelchner's house, who was in charge of the ammunition depots for the southwest. During their journey, according to Speer, they finally spoke "openly", and Röchling, once an admirer of Hitler, was said to have castigated the absurd fanaticism that encouraged Hitler to continue the war! What is surprising, to say the least, is the ease with which Röchling, whom Speer characterizes as a simple "Saarland industrialist" without any other qualification, was introduced into the circle of command at the highest level. Even more surprising is the late date at which these gentlemen realize the folly of the goal

Hermann Röchling: The Factory of the Third Reich

pursued by their revered Führer. This friendly conversation, one can imagine, had certainly not been limited to noting that the debacle was in full swing. Indeed, it is likely that Hitler's two acolytes also agreed, in due course, on a common tactic for the coming battles, this time legal, in order to discharge their respective responsibilities in the work of the Third Reich[342].

---

342. Albert Speer, *Au coeur du Troisième Reich*, Fayard, 2010, p. 613. The German original, under the title *Erinnerungen*, was published by Ullstein in Berlin in 1969.

Part Four:
The aftermath of war and the new war

Chapter 11. From Conviction to Rehabilitation

In February 1942, the American jurist James Stewart Martin was called in by the federal Justice Department to study the conditions for an Allied "economic war" against the Nazi regime. He discovered how German heavy industry had survived the defeat of the Great War and identified the players, including the Röchling family. Then, as he explores this intertwining of agreements and transactions, subsidiaries and holdings in an already globalized market, Martin realizes the extreme difficulty of the problem: how to block the supply of the Nazi war industry and strangle its production without also affecting the economy of the United States?

At the end of the war in April 1945, Martin was sent to Germany as head of the "Decartelization" department of the military occupation government. He and his staff worked for two years to retrieve documents and evidence in support of a program to dismantle cartels and large corporations. They were charged with interviewing German industrialists, collecting and compiling files on their interlocking relationships and multiple complicities in international affairs. However, they were forced to recognize that German industrialists had taken the initiative to avoid sanctions. Support from the highest ranks of the US military administration had made it possible to keep their affairs safe[343].

Reading a New York newspaper in late December 1945, Martin learned that Senator H. M. Kilgore's investigations in Washington into the war potential of the defeated country overlapped with his own observations on the ground[344]. The press release further confirmed his fears about the determination of certain senior officials in the U.S. military government in Germany to thwart the decartelization project. The senator even accused them of being supporters of an industrial organization that bore all the hallmarks of Nazism. And Kilgore names names: first, General William Henry Draper, an investment banker whose role in the stock market capitalization of two major German steel companies is remembered. Appointed head of the economic division of the Allied Control Council, Draper became head of the section in charge of dismantling cartels. To assist him, he appointed Rufus Wysor, president of the third-largest North American steel company, Republic Steel Corporation, and head of the steel sector of the military administration; and Frederick L. Devereux, retired vice-president of a subsidiary of the telecommunications company AT&T. All were delighted to be back in business with the leading German industrialists. And Martin unequivocally referred to them as "termites," busy systematically undermining the work of the commission. "The Nazi industrial organization is not repugnant to them and they have shown themselves perfectly willing to make peace with it[345]."

---

343. J. S. Martin, *All Honorable Men,* Boston, Little, Brown and Company, 1950. In this book, of which there is only one translation, into Russian, Martin tells the story of those men on both sides of the Atlantic who defeated a plan to dismantle the industrial system that was the very foundation of the Nazi policy of enslavement and extermination. The original edition is now available in its entirety on the Internet.http://www.spitfirelist. com/books/honorable01.pdf (accessed on 7.02.2023)
344. *The New York Times,* December 22, 1945, p. 7.
345. J. S. Martin, *op. cit.* pp. 164ff.

Martin resigned in May 1947. General Draper, the inspiration for the new Anglo-American bizone, became Under Secretary of State for the Army. A directive that Draper sent in July to the Governor General of the American zone, Lucius Clay, for whom he was the adviser on economic matters, no longer spoke of decartelization and demilitarization, but outlined the framework of a "productive and stable Germany" for the defence of a prosperous and strong Europe[346]. Thus, Germany will be granted the continuation of a policy - reconstruction, rearmament, amnesties and rehabilitation of Nazi war criminals - which finds its justification in this logic of a bipolar world... and which implies the creation of a community of Western European states to serve as a bulwark against communism.

***

In a report dated March 10, 1945, American intelligence services gave an account of the steps taken by the Nazis to prepare for the post-war period. It was reported that funds from the NSDAP and industrialists had been transferred to neutral countries, reinforcing the fear that guerrilla warfare would be unleashed after the Allied occupation. The writers of the report especially expected that, to serve their own interests, the Nazis would seek to provoke dissension between the Anglo-Saxon and Soviet occupiers. Four pages are dedicated to the career of Hermann Röchling, his role in the political-economic organization of the Nazi system and his entrepreneurial activities. The Saarland's ironmaster is described as "the czar of the German steel industry," a loyal servant of the regime who performed his duties to the complete satisfaction of the Nazis and to

---

346. JCS [Joint Chiefs of Staff] 1770/1 of July 15, 1947.

the benefit of his own family[347]. In August, another document from the American authorities described him, even more accurately, as "Czar in Germany and in all countries under German control[348]". The Soviet leaders were no less well informed of Röchling's effective place in the Nazi domination machine: on June 11, in Berlin, the central committee of the KPD around Walter Ulbricht launched an appeal for the creation of a popular front and demanded sanctions not only against the men of political power and the military, but also against the financiers and heads of the large industrial groups, the "Krupps and Röchlings, Poensgen and Siemens."

Between June and August 1945, the representatives of the four occupying powers met in London and reached an agreement on the creation of an international military tribunal. Since it was feared that mass trials could be seen as "victor's justice" in the eyes of the German population, only the highest-ranking leaders were to be investigated. The tasks of the investigation were divided. At first, Judge Robert Jackson, appointed chief prosecutor for the Americans, was in favor of a trial involving not only the high political and military authorities, but also the notables of the economic and industrial world who had behaved like "ordinary criminals." At the end of July, he was given a provisional list of names of those who should be considered as the main protagonists of the war economy. The list included five

---

347. Online in the Donovan Archives of the Cornell University Library: Office of Strategic Services, Research and Analysis Branch, R & A No. 1113,101, March 10, 1945: http://lawcollections.library.cornell.edu/nuremberg/catalog/nur:01197 (accessed on 7.03.2023)See *below*, the article in Le *Monde*, June 21, 1945, Appendix 7.
348. Secret memorandum prepared on August 17, 1945 by Robert Eisenberg for Lieutenant Commander O'Malley. http://reader.library.cornell.edu/docviewer/digital?id=nur:01194 (accessed on 7.02.2023) In 1943-1944, journalist John Franklin Carter, an unofficial intelligence agent for President Roosevelt, to whom he was close, drew up a "list of 400 key Nazis". Hermann Roechling's name appears on it.https://www.bsb-muenchen.de/mikro/lit200.pdf (accessed on 7.02.2023)

representatives of the business world - the financier von Schroeder for the J.H. Stein Bank, Hermann Schmitz for I.G. Farben and the steelmakers Friedrich Flick, Hermann Röchling and Alfried Krupp - as well as five members of the government - Hjalmar Schacht, Fritz Sauckel, Albert Speer, Paul Koerner and Walther Funk[349].

Throughout the investigations that precede and prepare for the trials, the North American delegation, by far the largest, has an average of 1,700 staff - ten times the British team. Its lawyers dealt primarily with foreign policy issues and charges number 1 and 2, "conspiracy" and "crimes against peace," and relied primarily on the masses of files seized in the ministries and other command posts. The small Soviet and French delegations - the latter numbering only a dozen people - were responsible for supporting charges 3 and 4, "war crimes" and "crimes against humanity," a task that required long and patient searches for witnesses and traces of material facts.

Despite the obvious difficulty of gathering sufficient evidence in the time available, the Americans and the British insisted that the trial begin before the end of the year. The defendants were therefore selected on the basis of the incriminating material already gathered. On August 29, 1945, the official list of 24 people indicted was presented, including four members of the government who had held various positions in the war economy - the economist and financier Hjalmar Schacht, President of the Reich Bank until 1943, Walther Funk, Minister of Economics, Albert Speer and Fritz Sauckel. Only one leading industrialist was charged: the steelmaker Gustav Krupp von Bohlen und Halbach, Alfried's father, whose health had been known for months to prevent him from appearing. The British prosecutor is

---

349. Document prepared by Francis Shea on July 23, 1945 and reproduced in Johannes Bähr, *Der Flick Konzern im Dritten Reich*, Munich, Oldenburg Wissenschaftsverlag, 2008, pp. 880 ff.

hostile to any further modification of this list to include the names of other industrialists[350]. He also said that he was convinced that, in order not to discredit the Tribunal, the proceedings against Schacht *must be* concluded with the acquittal of the accused[351]!

The choice of Schacht and Gustav Krupp to make the link between the economy, the war machine and the crimes committed to ensure Nazi domination in Europe is anything but fortuitous: from the outset, the court will be able to abandon the trial against the bedridden Gustav Krupp. And Schacht, who could boast a good address book and undisputed influence in the world of international business, was effectively acquitted, while his successor, Walther Funk, a man of influence who did not play in the same league as his co-accused, was sentenced to life imprisonment. Before the trial, Schacht reminded his American interrogators that any accusation against German companies was equally valid for their partners across the Atlantic[352]! Often described as "Germany's voice abroad," Schacht had never ceased to maintain close ties with the international financial community in Basel, Switzerland. He was well aware that the peace efforts he had undertaken between 1941 and 1943 would strengthen his reputation as an opponent of war. The proof: at the end of November 1943, two major American dailies, the *Chicago Daily Tribune* and the *New York Herald*, published correspondence announcing that a peace mission to the Holy See had been entrusted to former Chancellor von Papen, who had received credentials from Schacht and Hermann Röchling! Under these circumstances, Hitler's moneyman was convinced that his

---

350. October 3, 1945. See Sidney Alderman, Assistant U.S. Attorney for the Nuremberg Tribunal, "Negotiating on War Crimes Prosecutions 1945," *in*: Raymond Dennett and Joseph Johnson, *Negotiating with the Russians*. World Peace Foundation, 1951, p. 93.
351. Annette Weinke, *Die Nürnberger Prozesse*, Munich, C.H. Beck Verlag, 2006, p. 28.
352. Poltorak, Arkadi, *The Nuremberg Trial*, Moscow, Progressive Publishers, 1969, p. 349.

acquittal was a foregone conclusion, which he would not fail to emphasize later in his autobiography[353]. We will return to the no less confident attitude of Röchling, who could also boast excellent relations with the same world of international finance.

The trials. Acts 1 and 2: Nuremberg

The first trial conducted by the Allied Military Tribunal opened, as the Americans had hoped, on November 20, 1945. Simultaneously, the British and French governments announced their commitment to a subsequent trial of the most influential members of the National Socialist industrial and financial elite, including Alfried Krupp. Given the British reluctance to take legal action against Nazi criminals in general, this declaration was merely a statement of intent. But the issue was of interest to the public, and the press reported on it. An article published in the *Los Angeles Times* on February 17, 1946, even gave the names of a dozen business dignitaries, including Röchling, who were under threat of indictment before this future international tribunal.

However, such a "second trial" will never take place, and this failure sheds light on the action that will be taken against Hermann Röchling and his collaborators. During the first trial, a diplomatic game was played in the background about the possible continuation of the trial. The second international military trial should have been primarily a Soviet and French affair, since it was they who gathered the evidence against the industrialists and financiers in Nuremberg.

---

353. Hjalmar Schacht, *76 Jahre meines Lebens*, Bad Wörishofen, Kindler und Schiermeyer, 1953, pp. 564-574. Obviously, Schacht was to attribute this clemency not to his proximity to Western financial and economic circles, but to his opposition to Hitler's regime!

Chapter 11. From Conviction to Rehabilitation

The American authorities had, however, to fear the bias of these two allied delegations towards the powerful representatives of the capitalist economy! What if they had found it expedient to fuel the criticism of capitalism by insisting on the role of big business, both American and German, in the rise of Nazism?

The Soviets, obviously ideologically in favor of trials against German capitalists, nevertheless remained very much in the background, never providing the names of people to be incriminated. France, which wanted an "international" military tribunal, wanted to see Hermann Röchling in the dock, and the French delegation at Nuremberg devoted the few means at its disposal to searching for evidence. Unlike the British, the Americans never made a formal commitment to a second trial: not wanting to put themselves at odds with an international consensus that was still horrified by the accounts of Nazi crimes, they endorsed, albeit slowly, the work of a "subsequent proceedings division" (SPD) within their delegation. Their logic was simple: if a second Allied trial were to be abandoned, the work of this team could always be used to initiate proceedings against other Nazi notables, industrialists or not, in a move that would strengthen their position as vigilantes of a new world order.

In June 1946, the American authorities gave the go-ahead to draw up a joint list of defendants for a second trial, specifying, however, that their participation would depend on the outcome of the Schacht prosecution - which they were allowed to expect to be acquitted! It was requested that the number of defendants be limited to eight, exclusively industrialists and financiers. The steel industry boss Alfried Krupp was included as a first choice; the American prosecutor then selected the names of two I.G. Farben executives, Hermann Schmitz and Georg von Schnitzler; the British proposed the banker Kurt von

Schroeder; the French designated Hermann Röchling[354]. However, the French authorities knew that they were in a weak position in the face of the inertia of their colleagues, which was skilfully maintained, and they therefore feared that, if this second trial were to take place, the outcome would not be up to their expectations.

With the announcement of Schacht's acquittal in early October 1946, the fiction of a second inter-Allied "trial" was no longer justified. President Truman, on the advice of Prosecutor Jackson, let the project bog down in silence. The French authorities nevertheless wanted clarity and forced the Americans to finally refuse categorically, which happened in January 1947. In the literature devoted to Nuremberg and other proceedings against Nazi criminals, there is rarely any mention of this aborted "second trial"[355]. Instead, the focus is on the provisions of the Allied Control Council Law No. 10, which gave each occupying power the possibility of bringing "lower ranking criminals" before a zonal military tribunal[356].

It is thus within the framework of this Law n° 10 that the American delegation regains its free rein to proceed alone with a series of "successive trials" before its own court. In any case, was it not appropriate to leave the French and the Soviets, whether they were communists or sympathizers, out of the trials against financiers and industrialists? Otherwise, how could one talk about the activities of

---

354. Lord Elwyn Jones, *In My Time*, London, Weidenfeld and Nicolson, 1983, p. 126. The lawyer Elwyn Jones was the assistant to the British Attorney General Shawcross at Nuremberg. Telford Taylor, "Memorandum for the Secretary of War," Final Report on the Nuremberg War Crimes Trials, Washington D.C., 1949, p. 273.
355. Donald Bloxham, "'The Trial That Never Was.' Why there was no second international trial of major war criminals at Nuremberg.' *History*, vol. 87, January 2002, pp. 41-60.
356. The successive trials under American military authority in Nuremberg numbered 12; those conducted by the British in Hamburg and Lüneburg numbered a few hundred, by the French in Rastatt a few thousand, while tens of thousands of Nazi war criminals, both German and of other nationalities, had to answer for their acts before Soviet military tribunals in the Soviet zone of Germany and in Austria.

I.G. Farben in front of the world's media without mentioning their relations with Standard Oil? Or about the car manufacturer Opel Werke without mentioning General Motors, its buyer since 1929, and so on for many other companies, including the aircraft manufacturer Focke-Wulf, whose main shareholder was the telecommunications multinational ITT?

A report sent by an agent of the Ministry of the Economy to the lawyer Michel Habib-Deloncle, a member of the French delegation at Nuremberg, gives us a vivid picture of the preferential treatment that the American and British authorities intended to give to these war criminals who had been the pillars of the war economy and who had thus enabled Nazism to survive for many years. It is a question of the help given by the Americans to the former Konzern Flick. The year is February 1947:

> "Information dating back several months reported that the German subject Flick was, despite the leading role he played in the Nazi war industry, entrusted with important responsibilities by the American military government. Recent information, which has been cross-checked, tells us that the American authorities ordered, in the course of September 1946, the rehabilitation of the Donauworth Maschinenfabrik belonging to Flick Konzern. This work, for which intact buildings of the Hoffmann company (manufacture of aircraft bombs) were used, began in October.
>
> [...] Although Friedrich Flick was thus one of the "heads" of the German war industry, he is currently at large. We know for sure, without knowing the exact name of the job that the Americans have reserved for him, that his deputy in this job is his friend Steinbrinck, who was Führer of the heavy

industry for Holland and Belgium during the occupation. The leniency of the Americans towards these two men may seem strange, but the fact that the Americans formally wish to save the maximum of the Konzern Flick cannot surprise us. [...] It seems that the American and British governments are determined to save German industry for their own benefit, even if it represents a serious war potential. In this regard, it is worth noting that on January 14, 1947, British Radio quoted Prime Minister Attlee as saying on the occasion of President Blum's trip to London: "[...] we hope that the position taken by England with regard to German industry will not alter the good relations we wish to maintain with France. This is a very significant statement[357]."

General Clay, military governor of the American zone, was pressed for time and wanted to finish the "denazification" before the summer of 1948. The American government therefore validated the preparation of a series of "successive trials", but the persons to be charged were chosen according to the evidence already gathered, forcing the investigators to conveniently abandon the opening of files concerning Mannesmann, Bosch, Siemens, etc. The first case against an industrialist was case no. 5, concerning Friedrich Flick and his close associates, which began on March 15; the judgment - seven years in prison, of which the guilty party would serve barely two - was handed down on December 22. The trials against the leaders of the Krupp steel company and the chemical group I.G. Farben then began. And it is then that the French government will be faced with a

---

357. AN BB 35/90, file 238: R. de Frondeville, deputy director of reparations and restitutions at the Ministry of National Economy, report of February 3, 1947, addressed to magistrate Michel Habib-Deloncle, in charge of the Nuremberg military tribunal.

dilemma: should it or should it not let the Americans judge the case against Röchling, a case on which French magistrates have already been working for more than a year to gather evidence?

Act 3: The Röchling trial in Rastatt

Arrested by American soldiers in May 1945, Röchling was imprisoned in Nuremberg. Under the direction of the public prosecutor Jackson, he was interrogated several times between June and August, primarily about his political role, but also about his technical skills and his patents. Under the pretext that a possible indictment for a second international trial at Nuremberg was opposed, the Americans rejected a first extradition request made by the French government and released him provisionally on May 12, 1946[358]. It was not until November 1946 that Röchling was presented to French investigators to answer for his social and economic functions in the service of the Reich. When asked how he viewed the events in retrospect, the steel czar was not distraught. He speaks of his faith in the occult sciences, a fascination he shares with many other Nazi dignitaries, and of predestination:

> "Since I was very young I have been convinced of the inevitability of everything that happens in the world. And today I am more convinced than ever. I myself have had the proofs, quite unshakable proofs, that predicted things have

---

358. Note from Mr. René Lalouette, representative of the Ministry of Foreign Affairs to the French delegation to the International Military Tribunal, to his minister, Mr. Georges Bidault. Nuremberg, July 4, 1946. *Documents diplomatiques français*, vol. 7, tome II. 1944 -1954 (July 1st-December 31, 1946). Bern, Peter Lang, 2003, pp. 14 *ff.*

happened with mathematical certainty, whether we want them or not[359]."

The treatment of the Röchling case will then become confused with that of another Nazi criminal, the engineer and chemist Otto Ambros, former director of I.G. Farben and manager of the Buna factory at Auschwitz, who also worked with Göring and Speer on the research and development of chemical weapons and explosives. Ambros was detained in the French zone, and the French government, no less than the other Allies, sought to exploit the knowledge of German scientists for their own economic interests. The French wanted to hire him as a technical collaborator to restart production at the BASF plant in Ludwigshafen, a branch of I.G. Farben, but the Americans were also interested in Ambros to fill the dock in a trial against the top officials of this industrial empire, I.G. Farben, a powerful competitor in the chemical market. They asked the French to deliver Ambros to them.

At the beginning of 1947, the question of Ambros' extradition against Röchling occupied French diplomacy at the highest level, as shown by the file compiled by the Minister of Justice André Marie[360]. In a note sent for approval to the president of the provisional government of France, Georges Bidault, the minister noted that Ambros seemed to enjoy "strange support in certain French circles[361]" who protected him. Marie, however, was of the opinion that France had no reason to spare Ambros a trial. He attaches a memorandum to his note that summarizes the careers of Röchling and Ambros and highlights how closely the decisions concerning the indictment of

---

359. AN BB 36/32, TG 260: interrogation conducted by Mr. Heuser on January 21, 1947. Röchling evokes in particular the predictions of Nostradamus.
360. AN 445AP/1, n° 1524: Ambros and Röchling case,
361. AN 445AP/1: note of February 8, 1947.

both of them affect the geopolitics of France, and in particular the question of the future of the Saarland. In conclusion, Marie took the measure of what was at stake: "If France has every interest in seeing Röchling convicted by American courts, which would in fact be the arbiters of the situation, an acquittal, on the other hand, would risk placing our country in a delicate condition." He therefore wishes that the Saarlander be handed over to the French authorities.

Röchling was transferred to France, and Ambros was handed over to those responsible for the American zone. A specialist in chemical weapons and designer of a technique for the production of toxic gases (tabun, sarin, soman), Ambros appeared in the "case n° 6" against 23 leaders of I.G. Farben, a trial that began in August 1947. Sentenced in July 1948 to eight years of criminal imprisonment and incarcerated in Landsberg, he was released in February 1951, thanks to the intervention of the American high commissioner in Germany, John McCloy[362]. From that moment on, he shared a common destiny with many other Nazi technicians and scientists and began an international career as a technical director in several companies in the chemical industry, including a large North American group. The trial against Röchling and his colleagues did not start until February 1948...

> "At the end of 1947, a few months before the
> opening of the Röchling trial, the Metz daily
> newspaper *Le Lorrain* began publishing a series
> of articles entitled 'Vultures on Lorraine'.
> The author, Father Jules Annéser of Boulange,
> reproduced and commented on archive documents

---

362. His intervention followed the initiatives of the defense lawyers, financed by the I.G. Farben group, who used the Evangelical Church in Germany as a spokesperson to obtain amnesty or a reduction in sentences for their clients. The part of I.G. Farben that was located in the western zones of Germany was not dismantled until 1952.

that testified in particular to the ambitions of two notables of the Nazi regime, Josef Bürckel, Gauleiter of the NSDAP in Saarland-Palatinate and future governor of the Gau Westmark, and his 'smaller but no less greedy accomplice, Hermann Röchling, the Scarred One, the great magnate of the Saarland steel industry'. Annéser's articles, which were published regularly until February 1948, were then collected in a raging pamphlet, which is a remarkable reference for the 'Röchling affair' because of its numerous excerpts from archive documents. This pamphlet has never been republished."

1947: Vautours sur la Lorraine *appeared in the Lorraine press.*
Source: Jules Annéser, Vautours sur la Lorraine, *Metz,*
Éditions Le Lorrain, 1948.

It should be remembered that the French Military Tribunal, established in Rastatt, had the task of judging persons considered responsible for war crimes, the occupation and the spoliation for facts concerning France and the French. Since the Saarland was part of the French administration zone, the facts relating to the Neue Bremm camp in Saarbrücken came under its authority. In this infamous Gestapo camp, the French - resistance fighters, Jews, forced laborers and "Malgré-nous" - had formed the largest group of internees. In the summer of 1946, the Rastatt court sentenced 14 of its guards to death, but most of those responsible for this "collective murder enterprise" escaped this verdict[363]. In October 1947, the guards of the Kochendorf

---

363. "The death penalty is requested for 16 of the 36 torturers of the Neue-Bremme camp," *Le Monde*, June 4, 1946.

camp in Württemberg were tried, and between 1949 and 1950, the court also tried a commandant and the head of forced labor at the Ravensbrück camp.

At the same time, however, the North American and British allies had already moved on to preparing a monetary reform for their areas. They considered that the search for the culprits was slowing down the reconstruction process, which they were trying to promote by improving the monetary situation. Moreover, the French desire to prevent Germany's economic domination of Europe in the future was clearly an obstacle to the resumption of production in heavy industry, which was essential to counter the "communist danger[364]".

The Röchling trial began on February 16, 1948[365]. It was on the eve of the opening of the London Conference, which sealed the East-West division of Germany and the continent, and the proceedings against the "Steel Czar" would seem decidedly anachronistic in the context of the new Europe in the making. The magistrates had taken almost two years to prepare the indictment; they had insisted on being able to conduct the hearings in accordance with the principles of French law. The small team around Charles Gerthoffer was concerned with presenting a fully written case, unlike the Nuremberg trials, which were conducted according to the Anglo-Saxon procedure, which relied on the hearing of witnesses. The defense attorneys were able

---

364. If post-war German historians will evoke with a certain disdain the "Deutschland-Psychosis" of France (cf. Hermann Graml, *Die Allierten und die Teilung Deutschlands.* Frankfurt/Main, Fischer Verlag, 1985, p. 199), such an attitude will remain without any real impact, in contrast to the "communist obsession" that will animate the policy of the new Federal Republic following the example of the United States government.

365. The text of the indictment presented by the prosecutor Gerthoffer, the judgment of the first trial and the one rendered on appeal have been translated into English and published as an appendix (Appendix B) of volume XIV of the green series of *Trials of War Criminals before the Nurenberg Military Tribunals*, pp. 1061-1143.

to read the case in advance - 10 volumes of the indictment, together with all the evidence documents and their translations by sworn collaborators. Since Röchling's actions did not only concern France, it was decided to set up an international tribunal with seven judges in all - five French, one Belgian and one Dutch. The two French prosecutors, Charles Gerthoffer and Paul-Julien Doll, were assisted by Belgian and Polish judges. Hermann Röchling hired several defenders, including the Frenchman Pierre Leroy, and Otto von Kranzbühler, the successful Nuremberg lawyer of Admiral Martin von Dönitz, as well as industrialists Alfried Krupp, Friedrich Flick and Odilo Burkart, Flick's attorney. Ernst Röchling entrusted his defense to Charles Lévy, a lawyer from Strasbourg.

What are the charges against Hermann Röchling, his cousin Ernst and their closest collaborators? Crimes against peace for having favored the conduct of wars of aggression; war crimes for having exploited the occupied countries to serve the war effort of the Reich; crimes against humanity for having exploited under duress, in the factories under their management, the nationals of the occupied countries and the prisoners of war, and for having incited them to undergo inhuman treatment The indictment highlights the role that Röchling played in increasing the German war potential and Germanizing occupied territories, while at the same time managing to enrich himself personally. Gerthoffer argues the charges of "crimes against peace", plunder and looting, while Doll is charged with crimes against humanity.

*1948: Hermann Röchling in the dock at the International
Military Tribunal in Rastatt*
Source: Fonds Paul-Julien Doll, Coll. La Contemporaire/BDIC

The prosecution presented a study on the state of the Moselle factories following the flight of the German directors in September 1944. This report, drawn up in August 1946 by the mining engineer Legendre, covered the whole of annexed Lorraine and covered not only the situation at the Carlshütte in Thionville, but also the state of the blast furnaces and steelworks in Rombas, which had been operated by Flick, the installations under the control of the RWHG, the Vereinigte Stahlwerke (ex-Thyssen) and those managed by the steelmakers in Neunkirchen (ex-Stumm)[366]. This document confirms and completes another unpublished study by the engineer Émile Siegemund, concerning the Thionville plant alone as of October 1944[367]. The examinations conducted by the two experts concur and allow one to speak of an "intensive exploitation" of the installations during the occupation: the principle of "production above all" had relegated to the background all other considerations, including that of maintenance. Some of the immediate causes of this neglect were: the employment of a large number of unskilled workers, primarily Russian and Ukrainian peasants and women, who were tired and overworked; a lack of qualified maintenance personnel; and the use of poor quality materials for repairs, with insufficient downtime for the machines to perform them properly. Engineer Siegemund also inspected the adjoining Angevillers mine where he noted the same practice of forced mining to the extreme, without regard for the future, which had left the site in a deplorable state by the time the Germans left the Moselle. Wasn't this overexploitation of the facilities by the slaves of labor the simplest expression of a defeat foretold? Experts agree that even Röchling, an experienced technician and member of the ruling elite, never had the means at his disposal that would have allowed him to live up to the plans of the "Great Reich."

The prosecution insists that in order to obtain more and more forced labor, Röchling had incited the political leaders to take measures to deport men and women, and even minors, in the occupied territories; that he had very broad powers, including the

---

366. AN BB 36/8, document 2, Metz, August 22, 1946.
367. Emile Siegemund, *op. cit. See supra* note 232.

requisitioning of concentration camp inmates; that, to achieve his ends, he even harassed his interlocutors at the highest level of the Reich government and advocated in his numerous memoirs servitude far beyond the provisions required by the political authorities. In his indictment, the magistrate Doll summarizes how the treatment in Etzenhofen was very similar to that in the concentration camps: there was no lack of truncheons, police dogs, or cellars filled with water, and if the brutality extended to murder, only the crematorium was missing...

For the prosecution, these crimes deserved the death penalty. However, as it was recognized that Röchling, albeit for reasons other than humanitarian ones, had intervened in the Auboué hostage affair, the prosecution decided to demand life imprisonment for him. For the defense, the late date of the trial and its political context gave the skilful Otto von Kranzbühler convenient arguments: since the sentences against Speer - 20 years' imprisonment - and Sauckel - death by hanging - had already been passed in early October 1946, Kranzbühler was able to make them bear the full responsibility for the relentless exploitation of forced labor. He was also able to take advantage of the Cold War, not to make people forget the role of his client, but, on the contrary, to justify his actions as president of the RVE and Reich Commissioner in the occupied territories: did not Röchling lead a salvific fight against communism, as this threat had become "disturbingly topical" for the West? As for the Etzenhofen camp, Kranzbühler elevated it to the status of a "state institution" and argued that the responsibility for both the *Straflager* and the "Summary Tribunal" could not be laid at the feet of the directors of a private company. At the end of the day, he was indignant, the inmates of Etzenhofen were only "ordinary criminals" who had committed crimes or violated the labor laws of the Third Reich! Kranzbühler ended his argument by contrasting their well-deserved fate with the treatment of "hundreds of thousands" of Germans held by the Allies since the end of the war in internment camps for "political or police reasons[368]", "innocent people" under criminal law. Of course, in putting forward such arguments, Kranzbühler was not speaking to the judges of the Tribunal, but to a certain German public, reluctant to acknowledge its responsibility for the crimes of the Nazi regime, and in particular that of the great industrialists for whom this brilliant jurist was to quickly intercede until he obtained their release[369]!

At the beginning of 1948, Telford Taylor, who had become public prosecutor at Nuremberg and was in charge of the successive trials for the American zone, sent his collaborator, the jurist Josif Marcu, to Rastatt to follow the progress of the Röchling case. Taylor himself was present at times, to witness with Marcu the skill and persuasive eloquence that Kranzbühler displayed in the Anglo-Saxon art of the adversarial trial. However, in Rastatt, this technique failed in every respect, because the French magistrates had wanted to make the Röchling case a trial that was the antithesis of the soap opera that continued to take place in Nuremberg. The absence of cameras in the Rastatt courtroom no doubt minimized the attention paid to the case by journalists. In fact, the major Nuremberg trials, which were exploited by both the prosecution and the defense to gain public attention through the media, had done little to enlighten the German population. The memory of the "Fall 5" against Flick, in particular, will live on in German society as a symbol of the victors' vengeance against its major industrialists. Flick, like Röchling, pleaded "not

---

368. AN BB 36/10, Plea for the commercial counselor Hermann Röchling by Otto von Kranzbühler, p. 173.

369. It is estimated that there were approximately 120,000 internees in the American camps, 90,000 in the British, 21,500 in the French zone and 189,000 in the Soviet.

guilty" and, in order to claim the status of victim, neither of them ever acknowledged any wrongdoing.

Marcu wrote a report for the American delegation on the Röchling case and its place in international jurisprudence. He emphasized the attitude of the judges in Rastatt, who showed "a far greater understanding of the political and historical considerations of each issue than one is accustomed to in an Anglo-Saxon court of law[370]." In his account, which has not been published to date, the American jurist points out the moral responsibility of the heads of industry in the crimes against humanity committed by the National Socialist regime, a dimension that was automatically dismissed by the Nuremberg Tribunal. In the eyes of this jurist, the conviction of the Saarland tycoon and his relatives for using slave labor is based on a very different ethic than that underlying the judgment in the Flick case. Moreover, in the Röchling case, the Tribunal would have had the courage to be simple and concrete, placing the responsibility on a man who, because of his position in the Nazi hierarchy, could be either a force for good or a force for evil. And Marcu summarizes his assessment of the main defendant:

> "Although less important economically than Flick, Hermann Röchling was one of the leading German industrialists and one of the earliest and most ardent supporters of Hitler and the Nazi Party[371]."

During this first trial in Rastatt, Kranzbühler was also present at the successive trials in Nuremberg, where he was responsible for

---

370. "The Judges [...] show a far greater insight into the political and historical implications of each problem than one is wont to find in a traditional Anglo-Saxon court." AN BB 36/11, folder 30: Josif Marcu, "The Röchling Trial", (Rastatt, February 1948, Nuremberg, July 1948), p. 7.
371. Josif Marcu, *op. cit.* p. 2.

the defense of Alfried Krupp and Hermann Schmitz, the managing director of I.G. Farben. As a result, the defense of Hermann Röchling was continued by Me Pierre Leroy of the Paris Bar. Both lawyers portrayed their client as a deeply human man, loved by the entire Saarland population and its employees for his generosity and social spirit. The people of Völklingen and the employees of his company provided them with numerous testimonials. There is even a petition signed by the members of the works council who praise the extreme benevolence of their boss, "who has always been kind and helpful to his subordinates". The numerous social actions carried out by Röchling over many years are described: family benefits for his employees, Christmas parties for pensioners, widows and orphans, a housing cooperative open to all inhabitants of the city, and finally a substantial financial contribution for the construction of places of worship, both Catholic and Protestant. As for the accusation that Röchling had used slave labor for the Reich and for his own enrichment, his employees objected:

> "By his attitude in general, Commercial Counselor Röchling was opposed to the mistreatment of foreign workers and, in conferences with directors and operational managers, he was always committed to the proper treatment of foreign workers[372]."

In total, the defense attorneys submitted six petitions with 657 signatures from employees and pensioners of the Völklingen works, some of which even denied that Hermann Röchling had been a Hitler supporter. The public prosecutor's response was limited to pointing

---

372. AN BB 36/30 TGD 922: affidavit of six members of the works council of the Röchling works on 19 March 1948.

out that it was not up to the supporters of Hermann Röchling to judge him, but to the court.

In June, at the end of the hearings, the role was given to Mr. Leroy to deliver the final plea for the defense. He built his argument around the thesis that Röchling, like so many others, had only acted under duress and as a subordinate of the National Socialist regime. And the Parisian lawyer ends his presentation by depicting his client in an unexpected light, to say the least:

> "A great industrialist, a man of the home, a lover of action for action's sake, always worried about research, a technician passionate about his job, a pangermanist obedient to the boss, in whose hands he is only a tool like any other, a 100% German, such is Röchling. I ask you not to forget him, as well as never to forget the fundamental difference between the Germans and the French.

> What we consider final is provisional for them. You think that your judgment will end the Röchling trial. For them, it will start it. For if, like elephants, they are heavy, like them, they have a memory. They will not forget anything about these proceedings. While all these papers, all these documents will soon be used in our country to wrap prunes or new potatoes, they will be preciously preserved by them, as materials for the construction of the 'becoming' towards which they always tend. Ah, how wise it would have been not to make this trial. It will perhaps put in value certain Frenchmen. It risks to do a lot of harm to France[373]."

---

373. AN BB 36/10: plea of the defense, Me Leroy, lawyer at the Court of Appeal of Paris.

As for Ernst Röchling's defense, his lawyers constructed around him the image of a resistant, deeply anti-Nazi and Francophile, a courageous man who would have supported the attack of June 20, 1945. He was portrayed as a simple liaison between his cousin and the German services on the one hand, and the French industrial services on the other. Ernst Röchling always tried to mitigate the rigors of the occupation regime and to come to the aid of the French people around him. The witnesses for the defense did not hesitate to compare them - Ernst, the "good German," and Hermann, the "convinced Nazi.

The verdict was rendered on June 30: Hermann Röchling was found guilty of crimes against peace, crimes against humanity and war crimes and received a sentence of seven years in prison; Ernst was acquitted. But the case did not end there: between November 15 and December 20, 1948, a retrial took place, but without the presence of a representative of the Nuremberg Tribunal. Of its own accord, the French Tribunal dropped the charge of "crimes against peace" against Röchling in order to comply with the judgments that had just been handed down in Nuremberg concerning Krupp and I.G. Farben. At the end of the deliberations, Hermann Röchling's sentence was increased to ten years; Ernst Röchling was found guilty and sentenced to five years in prison. These sentences were accompanied by the confiscation of their property and the loss of their civil rights.

Almost thirty years later, Walter Rohland, Röchling's deputy at the head of the RVE and one of the witnesses for the defense, recalls the final court hearing: as the sentences of both Röchlings fell, "Hermann the cherub," as he called him, ostentatiously turned his back to the court, and then, while hanging a rose in his buttonhole, manifested "by his personal attitude his willingness to defend the honor of the German steel industry and entrepreneurship[374]."

To win the cold war

The trials of the "Saar Krupp" went almost unnoticed by the French press, except for the daily newspapers *L'Est républicain* in Nancy, *Le Lorrain*[375] and *Le Républicain lorrain* in Moselle. *Le Figaro* and *Le Monde*[376] closely followed the diplomatic game surrounding the division of Germany and Europe through the communist takeover in Czechoslovakia on February 25 and the general strikes in Bavaria, then in the Ruhr, events that gave rise to fears that the capitalist relations of production would be called into question. Only occasional agency reports mentioned the progress of the first trial, which was coming to an end at a time when the Deutschmark had just been introduced in the three western zones of Germany and the Soviet response - the blockade of the West Berlin sectors - was not long in coming. The appeal process was ignored. Behind the scenes, the Americans and the British were negotiating the conditions for the

---

374. Walter Rohland, *Bewegte Zeiten*, Stuttgart, Seewald Verlag, 1978, p. 142: "Hermann the Cheruscan" is a mythical reference in Germany, who liberated Germania from the yoke of the Roman troops during the battle of Teutoburg (*Varusschlacht*). In 2009, an exhibition was dedicated to this "Mythos" and its two centuries of history. It is worth noting that Chancellor Angela Merkel opened the exhibition by reciting Adenauer's credo: European unification and attachment to the German nation are no longer antagonisms, but "two sides of the same coin". https://www.bundesregierung.de/Content/DE/Bulletin/2009/05/58-4-bkin-ausstellung.html (accessed on 7.02.2023)
375. Taken over by *L'Est Républicain* in 1949, *Le Lorrain* continued to appear for some time under its original title.
376. A notice of about fifteen lines appeared in *Le Monde* of February 18, 1948, on page 2. Röchling's importance is reduced to his functions in the annexed Moselle, without mentioning his functions as head of the RVE, as Reich delegate in the occupied territories, or his hold on the metallurgy industry in Meurthe-et-Moselle.

birth of the Federal Republic of Germany. The National Socialist past was forgotten.

In Germany, the weekly *Der Spiegel* devoted a single article to the first trial, right at the beginning of the hearings. It is as much about the star lawyers, Kranzbühler and Leroy, as it is about the defendant himself. Entitled "Not enough profit. War criminal for a second time", this falsely reproving article insists that industrialists of the calibre of Röchling had entered the service of the Nazi regime because they were motivated by the lure of profit. Now, depending on the enemy to be fought, in this case the Soviet Union, these economic aims, which can be criticized for their excess, could prove to be very useful. The topicality of this motivation is illustrated by the story in *Spiegel*, which recounts how lawyer Leroy, upon his arrival at the court, handed Röchling an article that had appeared on the front page of the *New York Times the* day before: an appeal from General Eisenhower to heavy industry to develop its capabilities in preparation for future war efforts[377]! This was certainly a guarantee for the future of the steelmaker Röchling, a temporary "war criminal".

In general, the historiographical literature will pay little attention to the events that contributed to the rapid postwar recovery of large German companies. The key issue of the destruction of industry across the Rhine, for example, has been overlooked, as has the fact that the Anglo-American air attacks deliberately spared many of the major centers of the Nazi economy, especially the high-tech companies. Certainly, seasoned field investigators like Martin and

---

377. *Der Spiegel*, February 21, 1948 (No. 8/1948). The article is entitled "Eisenhower sees war's end remote, advises readiness", *New York Times*, February 16, 1948. The major New York daily devoted more lines to this "Nazi chief" Röchling than did the Parisian press and, in a small item published after the retrial, it was even reported that Röchling was the first industrialist to be convicted of crimes against peace.

Kilgore had brought to light the "United States Strategic Bombing Survey" which, with figures to back it up, reported that only transportation and coal supplies had been seriously affected by the bombing. Nevertheless, the image of a devastated Germany, whose industry had been seriously damaged, still persists. In the end, less than 12% of the productive capacity was affected, in contrast to the residential buildings in the urban centers. To give just a few examples: in Berlin, one third of the houses were reduced to ashes, a percentage that rose to 70% for Frankfurt am Main, where the imposing building of I.G. Farben remained standing in the middle of the ruins. It would become General Eisenhower's headquarters in 1945. In Saarland, where the devastation was very great, the Röchling factories escaped almost unscathed; at Krupp in Essen, a city whose geographical position made it particularly vulnerable to Anglo-American air raids, almost all the residential buildings were hit, but the Wiedia factory, at the cutting edge of steel technology, was spared, and this prodigy escaped the attention of historians.

The same applies to the history of the currency reform of 1948. The introduction of the deutschmark with variable conversion rates greatly favoured the owners of real property at the expense of savers and rentiers. Those, like the industrialists, who came out of the war with debts were relieved of a huge burden (conversion at a rate of 10:1) and were allowed, moreover, to convert their business assets into DM according to a self-assessment procedure and their equity capital at a rate of around 96 per cent. On the other hand, rents and salaries were converted at parity, while bank investments melted like snow in the sun at an exchange rate of 10:1 or even 10:0.65 for various savings contracts! The situation was such that, in order to obtain cash in DM, industrialists had no choice but to exploit their facilities to the maximum - but by "slimming down" the workforce to reduce costs. The production quotas imposed on steelmakers in January 1946 were tacitly abandoned as the months passed. Unemployment tripled in one year, but that was no problem: the economic recovery was underway!

From amnesia to amnesty

In August 1948, shortly after the completion of the first Röchling trial and the trials against the leaders of I.G. Farben in Nuremberg, Otto von Kranzbühler made contact with Konrad Adenauer; the issue at stake was a possible amnesty for his clients. The Federal Republic was not proclaimed until May 1949, Adenauer was not elected Chancellor until September, and the question of a new German army seemed to be a long way off, but Kranzbühler expected that the emerging East-West conflict would soon provide an opportunity to rehabilitate the steelworkers in detention. And he knew that Adenauer had the ear of the Americans. Later, he said that he felt that once the war was over, there would be an "immediate restoration of the order that had prevailed in 1939, or even in 1933[378]". He was not entirely wrong and his efforts on behalf of the barons of German industry were not in vain.

Initially, von Kranzbühler and the law professor Eduard Wahl, a former SA and legal counsel in the trial of the I.G. Farben executives, made it their mission to obtain a reduction in the sentences of these high-profile convicts. Together with other lawyers, they set up the "Heidelberg Legal Circle", which was joined by

---

378. Otto Kranzbühler in *De Paul Law Review* (1965, p. 347), quoted by Telford Taylor, *Procureur à Nuremberg*, Paris, Éditions du Seuil, 1995, p. 643.

churchmen[379]. Theophil Wurm, a former bishop of the Evangelical Church in Württemberg, played an important role in the propagation of a narrative that was designed to make his church a real pole of resistance to Nazism. Kranzbühler, his colleagues and the clergy therefore conducted relentless lobbying campaigns on behalf of the internees. How could they influence the Americans to release them and return their wealth and businesses[380]? The clergymen, both Catholic and Protestant, proved to be particularly effective in promoting the initiatives of the jurists: it was up to them to put forward the moral aspect of these petitions in the context of a "fight against atheistic communism".

In fact, for the authorities of the American military government in Germany, the rehabilitation of the former steel magnates, supported by a strong political will, was only a matter of time. It was simply a matter of being able to overturn the convictions of this industrial elite without prejudice. Germany, not France, was destined to become the keystone of Western European defense against the Soviet system. Washington gave top priority to getting the steel industry back on its feet - in the Ruhr, first of all - and was hardly prepared to accept developments that would run counter to its own interests. While waiting

---

379. A manuscript entitled *Memorandum of the Evangelical Church in Germany on the Question of War Crimes Trials before American Military Courts* (160 pages) was written by Hansjürg Ranke and Rudolf Weeber, members of the Supreme Church Council (*Oberkirchenräte*) of the Evangelical Churches and financed by I.G. Farben. This text in English, never made public, was presented to the American High Commissioner John McCloy in March 1950. His criticism of the Nuremberg trials is largely based on the position of the defense lawyers, especially the arguments of Otto von Kranzbühler in the Röchling trial. Cf. Norbert Frei, *Adenauer's Germany and the Nazi Past. The Politics of Amnesty and Reintegration.* New York, Columbia University Press, 2002, p. 121. German edition: *Vergangenheitspoltik. Die Anfänge der BRD und die NS Vergangenheit.* Munich, C.H. Beck Verlag, 1997, pp. *164ff.*
380. Thomas Alan Schwartz, "Die Begnadigung deutscher Kriegsverbrecher. John J. McCloy und die Häftlinge von Landsberg," *Vierteljahreshefte für Zeitgeschtchte.* 38th year (1990), notebook no. 3, pp. 375-414, here p. 383.

for the right moment to restore the rights of the former owners, everything will be done to keep the trade union movement in check, prevent the "socialization" of the metal industry and thwart the project of public management of the coal industry in Rhineland-Westphalia[381].

For conservative German circles, as for the Americans, the presence of Communists in the unions was a powerful argument, supported by the media, which made it possible to shift the question of the responsibility of the big industrialists and to substitute the struggle between the two systems for class opposition. The American authorities decided to leave the decision on the status of ownership of the means of production in the steel industry and the mining sector to a future German government[382]. But they were confident that the outcome of this arbitration would go the way they wanted it to, if it were led by the Christian Democrat Konrad Adenauer. And it was Adenauer who was elected president of the parliamentary council in September 1948 to lead the work of the constituent assembly.

Adenauer understood early on the objective of American policy towards Germany: to complete the project of a German state of the three Western zones and to integrate it into the market economy and into a defense system under U.S. command. "European integration" was seen as a framework that promised West Germany the protection of its interests, its borders and its companies. For Adenauer, the way to this Europe was through the membership of the nostalgic National Socialists in his Christian Democratic Party. During his entire career, he imposed upon himself an absolute silence with regard to Nazi barbarism, as can be seen in his memoirs[383]. And it was this desire to

---

381. Eberhard Schmidt, *Die verhinderte Neuordnung 1945-1952*. Frankfurt am Main, Europäische Verlagsanstalt, 1970, pp. 150-165.
382. Law no. 75 of November 10, 1948.
383. Konrad Adenauer, *Erinnerungen*. 4 vols. Stuttgart, Deutsche Verlags-Anstalt, 1965, 1966, 1967, 1968.

Chapter 11. From Conviction to Rehabilitation

spare the former Nazis, and even to integrate them into his government, that led him to the policy of amnesty from which the major industrialists benefited.

To negotiate the conditions of their release, Adenauer took centre stage with the new American High Commissioner, John McCloy[384]. McCloy, a lawyer and banker who had been Under-Secretary of War from 1942 to 1945, left his post at the head of the World Bank to join the Allied High Commission at the end of July 1949. As soon as he was elected Chancellor - it was September 1949 - Adenauer was visited by representatives of the "Heidelberg Circle" who presented him with requests for clemency for his protégés. And, initially, it was through the intermediary of the president of the federal government, Theodor Heuss, that these same jurists and ecclesiastics tried to obtain from the French high commissioner in Germany a remission of sentence for Hermann Röchling[385]. However, it was not until the events of May-June 1950 - the announcement of the Schuman Plan and the outbreak of the Korean War - that the authorities finally felt that the time had come to set this coal and steel industrial elite free and to return the sequestered assets. Wasn't the West in urgent need of a powerful metal industry so that this new German state could take its place in a prosperous and peaceful Europe, able to face the Soviet powers? At the end of January 1951, McCloy signed a pardon for 29 of

---

384. His predecessor, High Commissioner Lucien Clay, had already overturned many of the judgments handed down by American courts in Dachau, lightened the sentences or commuted the death sentences of dozens of *Lager* war criminals. Cf. Thomas Alan Schwartz, "Die Begnadigung ...", *op. cit.*

385. André François-Poncet was then High Commissioner for France. Theodor Heuss, *Briefe 1949-1954*, Stuttgart edition edited by Ernst Wolfgang Becker, Martin Vogt, and Wolfram Werner (Berlin: De Gruyter, 2012), p. 160. In a letter to Otto von Kranzbühler on June 17, 1950, Heuss states that he only undertook actions for Röchling, von Weizsäcker, and Ewald Loeser, one of the members of the Krupp Group management. BArch B 122-644.

Hermann Röchling: The Factory of the Third Reich

the war criminals imprisoned in Landshut, including the industrialists Flick and Alfried Krupp.

Faced with the detachment, not to say the indifference of the media and public opinion, it is not surprising that, following Krupp's release in January 1951, the magistrate Telford Taylor took to the pen to denounce, admittedly in vain, but in no uncertain terms, the "political opportunism" of this clemency[386].

In May 1951, Theophil Wurm, acting on behalf of the Heidelberg Circle, sent a request for a pardon for Röchling to the French President Vincent Auriol. Here is an excerpt from his request:

> "As a non-lawyer, I refrain from commenting on the judgment itself. In the different countries, there are widely differing views on the degree of culpability (*das Maß von Verschuldung*) of German industrialists who made efforts in response to their government's wartime economic orders. I do not doubt for a moment that the military court in Rastatt had its reasons for this decision. But I also have no doubt that Mr. Röchling never committed any morally reprehensible acts, since this man is known to all as a faithful and convinced member of the Evangelical Church[387]."

Hermann and Ernst Röchling were released in August 1951. The media chose to treat the release of the steel magnates as a news item rather than an event, as their actions under National Socialism were already far from the public's concern. The context was such that even

---

386. Telford Taylor, "The Nazis Go Free. Justice and Money or Misguided Expediency," *The Nation*, February 24, 1951, pp. 170-172.
387. Landesarchiv Baden-Württemberg, Abt. Staatsarchiv Freiburg: C 5/1 document 728-742.

Chapter 11. From Conviction to Rehabilitation

the news of a pardon granted to Hermann and Ernst Röchling did not give rise to any criticism from the French media. The news items that did mention it - whether good or bad - were placed far from the front page, proving that it was basically a closed case. And who could be surprised that the following year the Siemens Foundation for Science and Technology honored the Saarland Krupp with the prestigious "Werner-von-Siemens-Ring" in recognition of its "pioneering achievements" in the field of metallurgy!

However, for the two Röchlings, unlike Flick and Krupp, their newfound freedom did not mean the return of their sequestered property, since both the Völklingen plant and the Saarland region were under French mandate. In their case, this gesture was the responsibility of the French authorities and presupposed a "Franco-German reconciliation" which would put an end to the age-old conflicts, one of the issues of which was precisely the ownership of the coal mines and steel industries in the Ruhr, Alsace, Lorraine and the Saarland. The Allied Control Council had awarded France all the dismantled equipment of the forges and steelworks as reparations, but Paris chose to abandon the dismantling and continue production with a view to a later takeover under the aegis of a Franco-Sarrian consortium. This was without taking into account Adenauer's patriotic feelings, skilfully concealed behind a certain idea of European construction, which played into the hands of the industrialist Röchling.

Rearmament, a promise for the future

The Saarland question was then intertwined with the question of rearmament, but the first project for a "European Defence

Community" and a genuine European army failed in August 1954 and delayed the solution of both. Although the Anglo-American Allies could hardly doubt that the Saarland belonged to Germany, a European status for the Saarland appeared to be a compromise and a precondition for revoking the occupation status and paving the way for the remilitarization of the Federal Republic. Under the pretext of giving democratic legitimacy to this European mask, Chancellor Adenauer obtained the organization of a referendum for October 1955. He obviously did not suspect for a moment that the Saarlanders, doped up by the rhetoric of the nationalists, to which his own party lent a hand, would respond by an overwhelming majority with a "no" vote[388]! This was indeed the case, and once again the regional parliament took up the Röchling case to demand the return of the Völklingen ironworks and steelworks to this family of Saarland and German patriots!

At the request of the Röchling family, von Kranzbühler entered the scene once again. It was he who negotiated an interest-free loan of 36 million DM with the Federal Ministry of Economics, which allowed the Saarland steel magnates to liquidate the French government's stake in the Völklingen works in 1956. *Le Monde*, which for two years had devoted no less than a hundred articles to this other "Röchling affair", bitterly observed that the return of the Röchlings to the Saarland "marks a starting point for a reduction in our economic

---

388. The Saarland was integrated into the Federal Republic on January 1st, 1957. For the occasion, Adenauer - no more pretending! - held a speech in which he praised the "invincible Germanness of the Saarlanders", despite the eleven years of "distress and suffering" spent under French administration!This speech from Saarbrücken is only available on the Internet on the Luxembourg platform for European knowledge, C.V.C.E. : https://www.cvce.eu/obj/discours_de_konrad_adenauer_sur_le_retour_de_la_sarre_a_la_rfa_sarrebruck_1er_janvier_1957-fr-26fcda98-3c34-4e37-b3d7-155c02874123.htmlHe is absent from the numerous documents put online by the Konrad Adenauer Foundation on the website https://www.konrad-adenauer.de/ (accessed on 7.02.2023)

influence in Europe[389] ". Hermann Röchling, who died on August 24, 1955, had his posthumous revenge. Ernst Röchling took over the management of the Völklingen works after his release in 1951. Despite the trial in Rastatt, he always enjoyed the image of a Francophile who opposed Hitler's regime. In 1963, he invested part of his immense fortune in the creation of a foundation that bears his name with the mission of Franco-German rapprochement. As a result of this work, he received the honorary title of University Senator and his name will be remembered for posterity as a committed European. In Saarland, where the whitewashing of the Nazi past is still the order of the day, an initiative will be launched in 2021 to remove his title of senator. The Röchling family should not be held accountable for its past!

Hermann Röchling with his close family
Source : National Archives

---

389. Gilbert Mathieu, "Les Roechling rentrent chez eux," *Le Monde*, November 29, 1956.

Chapter 12. The Röchling legacy: a heritage without memory?

Since the war, the Röchling family has cultivated an image of tradition and quasi-aristocratic discretion. A discreet veil was drawn over their recent past in the service of the Third Reich, and this discretion, especially in the media, served as a tactical advantage in order to increase their business assets. And in 1956, Ernst Röchling, who is now considered to have been hostile to Hitler's regime, acquired for his own benefit, and with the support of Chancellor Adenauer, a majority share in the holding company *Rheinmetall-Borsig AG*, an important arms manufacturer, formerly dependent on the *Reichswerke Hermann Göring*[390].

Let us look at the question of German rearmament. Even before the birth of the new Federal Republic, the European framework had been desired and designed by the US Department of Defense to resolve the issue of NATO membership and, consequently, the remilitarization of the three Western zones, which was seen not only as inevitable, but also, and above all, as indispensable for the survival of the West[391]. Once the question of the status of the Saarland had been settled, the

---

390. The Röchlings immediately sold the mechanical engineering company Borsig.
391. Annie Lacroix-Riz, "Towards the Schuman Plan: the decisive milestones of French acceptance of German rearmament (1947-1950)", *Guerres mondiales et conflits contemporains*, Part 1: No. 155 (July 1989), pp. 25-41 and Part 2: No. 156 (October 1989), pp. 73-87.

construction of a West German armed force would offer a profitable arms market to all domestic steel producers - including Röchling. The Bundeswehr came into being in November 1955. Seven months later, on June 23, 1956, the *Röchlingsche Eisen- und Stahlwerke* became the majority shareholders of Rheinmetall-Borsig AG, which had become part of the Federal Republic after the war. The company still had a bright future ahead of it, and at the Rheinmetall sites in Berlin and Düsseldorf, arms and ammunition production resumed at an auspicious pace, and the Röchlings made considerable profits from this[392]. Throughout the second half of the 20th century, the German arms industry remained the shared privilege of three family clans: the Bode, the Diehl and the Röchling[393].

The restraint of the Röchling clan was somewhat disturbed, however, in 1966, when Rheinmetall received an order from the Bonn government for the U.S. Department of Defense: 2,500 HS 820 automatic guns, a piece of equipment touted as a "miracle weapon" of the new generation. Immediately, a wave of protests arose across the Atlantic against the purchase of products manufactured by Rheinmetall, and former forced laborers and Jewish organizations demanded reparations from the company's owners. The German courts, however, rejected their claims.

This affair, which was widely covered by the American press, had the unexpected effect of erasing the Röchling's heavy past with a few more strokes of the pen. The weekly newspaper *Der Spiegel*

---

392. The timely acquisition of Rheinmetall guaranteed them a place on the list of the country's largest fortunes after 1945. The loyal Otto von Kranzbühler was rewarded for his services with a position on the supervisory board at Rheinmetall. See Hans Otto Eglau, "Zweifel an der Treue", *Die Zeit*, No. 2, January 3, 1986.

393. The Bode family are the majority shareholders of Kraus-Maffei-Wegmann and the Diehl family is the sole owner of the Diehl Gruppe in Nuremberg. See Dinah Deckstein, "Schwere Geschütze" *Der Spiegel*, no. 49/2004, p. 122.

(circulation: over 750,000) even claimed that the accusation of having made money from slave labor was a real offence against the Röchling family: not only did it have nothing to do with Rheinmetall's activities under Nazism, but one of their own, Ernst Röchling, was "himself a victim of Nazi justice after July 20, 1944[394]"! Over the years, Rheinmetall has been involved in several arms trafficking trials, and although its executives have received suspended prison sentences for their role in these cases, the recent history of the Röchling company does not surface[395].

In the aftermath of the war, the continent's steel industry had begun to feel the effects of global competition, despite the organization of the "Economic Community of Coal and Steel" (ECSC), the precursor of the European Union. Soon, huge investments were needed to restructure and emerge from the crisis in the sector and in 1976 the Röchling heirs decided to withdraw from the coal and steel industry. The Völklingen plants were sold to Arbed, an international consortium of steel companies[396]. The Röchling Group relocates its headquarters to Mannheim on the right bank of the Rhine and invests in the production of technically high performance composites. The Völklingen ironworks and steelworks, a relic of a bygone era, were taken over by the Saarland and closed in 1986. Given the

---

394. *Der Spiegel*, no. 11/1966, p. 54.

395. *The Economist*, August 8, 1980; *Sozialdemokratischer Pressedienst*, 41st year, No. 100, May 30, 1986, p. 5; "Saudis bestellten deutsche Maschinengewehre in..." General-Anzeiger, Bonn, January 22, 1986, p. 3; "Auf Nummer Sicher," *Der Spiegel*, No. 20/87, May 11, 1987; *Spiegel-online*, November 6, 2003.

396. The Saarland region also took a stake in the Arbed consortium. In 1986, 15,000 people were still working on the 250 hectares that remained in operation. The company, which had meanwhile become Saarstahl AG, one of the most important employers in the region, could no longer withstand the vicissitudes of the steel market, which forced it to file for bankruptcy in 1993. In 2001, the company was taken over by a private foundation, but a drastic reduction in personnel could not be avoided in order to save the production site in Völklingen.

Chapter 12. The Röchling legacy: a heritage without memory?

high unemployment rate of 12% in Saarland and the importance of this industry for the inhabitants of Völklingen and its surroundings, it is easy to understand how a "citizens' initiative" could be launched to ensure that this abandoned site would be granted the status of a regional "cultural monument" and thus, with the promise of a new life, escape dismantling or decay. In 1992, a multi-year restoration program supported by the "Deutsche Stiftung Denkmalschutz[397]" ensured its conversion with a grant of 1.1 million euros. The German federal government, the only body authorized to submit a list of sites eligible for Unesco certification, subsequently included the Völklingen factories in the list. In 1994, an event of such magnitude occurred that the Röchling clan could now believe that the stigma of their past would be erased: UNESCO included the oldest part of the Völklingen factory in the World Heritage List!

The designation of Völklingen as a World Heritage Site came barely eight years after its closure, and this choice opens a new page in what heritage itself represents. Völklingen is not the first industrial site to be designated a World Heritage Site by UNESCO. In 1986, it listed the remains of the very beginning of modern industry: the bridge and the remains of the industrial facilities in the Ironbridge valley in England, witnesses of the first industrial revolution (1750-1830). To justify the choice of Ironbridge, the argument put forward by the heritage experts is based on the very broad notion of "landscape", which would allow the various objects and sites to be considered as a whole, both from a social and technical point of view. In the case of Völklingen, however, the industrial work and the social aspects of

---

397. The "German Foundation for the Preservation of Historic Monuments" (Deutsche *Stiftung Denkmalschutz*) is a foundation under private law, 40% of which is financed by funds from the *GlücksSpirale*, the German equivalent of the Française des Jeux, which is managed by the regions.

its history are dismissed from the outset, and the focus is only on the "hard" memory - the installations and buildings, and the technical part of the history:

> "The facilities are symbolic of the human achievement that occurred during the first and second industrial revolutions. They are like a cathedral of the industrial age[398]".

The International Council on Monuments and Sites ("Icomos") had recommended that the site be listed on the basis of its "technological integrity", ignoring the social and economic history and, in particular, the events of the Second World War. What would reflect the work of the workers, their demands, their hopes and sufferings will be relegated to oblivion.

One thing that is surprising is the eagerness of the government to sponsor the former Röchling family ironworks and steel mills for listing just eight years after their closure, at a time when - as fate would have it! - the head of the World Heritage Centre was a German civil servant, Bernd von Droste zu Hülshoff, founder of the prestigious organization. It is also true that with the entry into force of the Maastricht Treaty and the enlargement of the European Union, the States have been forced to adapt to the new situation in terms of aid to economically disadvantaged regions. Budgetary and monetary norms tailored to the dimensions of this vast market were imposed on national governments, and in particular influenced their modes of intervention. If Saarland, because of its location on the European border, is well suited to benefit from substantial aid from the European structural funds, in the same way as the regions to the

---

398. World Heritage List: Völklingen No. 687

east of Germany, the Unesco label undoubtedly represents an additional major asset in an economy made up of networks developed on a global scale!

Of course, the Völklinger Hütte's patrimonialization was motivated by real prospects of success in the face of ever-increasing economic competition between cities, both nationally and internationally. One can hardly blame its designers for having created a spectacular monument to the modern cult of the machine: is the proof of this good choice not provided by its excellent attendance figures - more than 5 million visitors since the opening in 1999? But if the economic profitability is not in doubt, the museological treatment of the site is not without its problems, because this tourist reconversion has led its designers to ignore aspects of the past that are, to say the least, debatable.

***

For a long time the people of Völklingen themselves had an idealized image of the Röchling family. Doesn't the town owe its existence to the success and philanthropy of these industrialists? Their legacy honors this municipality by means of the universal heritage status of the old factories. During his lifetime, the patriarch Hermann Röchling had already become the object of a cult: on the occasion of his 70th birthday in 1942, the city council awarded him the title of honorary citizen on the basis of "his exemplary Germanness [*vorbildliche deutsche Haltung*] in a time of great distress[399]." At the same time, the name "Hermann Röchling Siedlung" was given to a housing estate that was built (by the workers themselves and inaugurated as part of the social policy of the Saar baron to mark the Führer's birthday in 1937).

---

399. AN BB/38/108 file 1915: RESW journal, *Völklinger Hüttenmann*, Dec. 1942, 8th year, no. 12, p. 2.

After the war, the district was renamed "Bouser Höhe" (Bouser Heights) until the summer of 1956, shortly after the death of this Nazi dignitary, history repeated itself: the city council decided to rename it *Hermann Röchling Höhe*. There is no evidence of his past as a war criminal and zealous supporter of National Socialism - quite the contrary. In his inaugural speech, one of the local councillors emphasized what was most important to him: honoring a philanthropist who had done so much for the "Germanness" of the Saarland and for the development of their once unknown community into a flourishing town of 40,000 inhabitants.

However, in 2010, a local citizens' initiative "against oblivion and indifference" was launched with the aim of having the name of the district changed. On the other hand, a large majority of the inhabitants of the district in question and some city councilors, including two members of the extreme right-wing party NDP, formed an association to keep the name and to defend the "Hermann-Röchling-Höhe". In doing so, they declared that they wanted to preserve a "piece" of their own identity through the memory of this industrialist. The discussions that arose from this demand are a quintessential symbol of the way in which the whole past has been dealt with since the war: the very fact that it is a problem shows the depth of the unease that this colorful character provokes. The controversy even aroused the interest of the mainstream media: in January 2013, on the eve of a vote on the issue in the city council, the producers of the political program *Kontraste* sent a journalist to Völklingen for a television report. The weekly magazine *Der Spiegel* published a critical and lucid article entitled *Süßer Hermi*[400] ("The nice little Hermann"), and the monthly political magazine *Konkret* another article entitled "Thanks to the

---

400. *Der Spiegel*, no. 48/2012 p. 54.

Nazis, culture is beautifying[401]", which recommends that UNESCO make the denazification of the city of Völklingen a *prerequisite for the retention of the former factories on the World Heritage List.*

Professor Grewenig, the custodian of the "Völklinger Hütte - Cultural Heritage of Humanity", gave his expert opinion to the city council: the name of the district itself would be considered an "intangible monument". At the time, Grewenig was already enjoying great prestige after 14 years at the helm of the "Völklinger Hütte"; he was awarded the title of "honorary professor" by the Saarland government in 2011, and is a member of the religious order of chivalry of the Holy Sepulchre of Jerusalem, founded in 1933 by Franz von Papen, Hitler's vice-chancellor at the time[402]. And what does his expertise say? Any change or alteration in the "buffer zone" around this heritage enterprise would erase the "traces" of its history and endanger its status as a UNESCO-labeled cultural property! While in the past Grewenig, as director of the site, was careful not to shed light on the crimes committed by the Röchling and even to acknowledge the existence of the reprisal camp in Etzenhofen, he finally said he was in favor of "a comprehensive clarification of the dark aspects of the past[403]." And in his own way, Grewenig put his money where his mouth was: in the following year, he designed an exhibition on the history of the Röchling family and the Völklingen factory.

The city council decided on January 31, 2013 for a "compromise": the first name "Hermann" will be removed from the name of the district, which nevertheless retains its hard monument in memory of its benefactor - Hermann Röchling.

---

401. Erich Später, "Kultur wird erst durch Nazis schön," *Konkret*, 8/2012, pp. 30-32.
402. More recently, in 2016, Grewenig was awarded the National Order of Merit by the French government under François Hollande.
403. June 14, 2012 letter: http://www.hermann-roechling.de/

To cut through the awkward questions about the past connected to the historical monument in his care, Professor Grewenig organized an exhibition between 2014 and 2016 in a hall of the former Hütte: "The Röchlings and the Völklingen Ironworks[404]." The tour began in an area equipped with screens and benches; the tourist was invited to sit down to watch a fifteen-minute film that ran on a loop before further discovering the "technical masterpieces" and "revolutionary innovations" that are owed to the Röchlings, without forgetting "history in its deepest darkest aspect, with, for example, the forced laborers employed during the two world wars." The short documentary film answered awkward questions in advance, giving the floor to the parties involved, first the heirs of the family, then Wolfgang von Hippel, the academic from whom the Röchling family commissioned a biography of Hermann Röchling, and Professor Grewenig himself. Did Hermann Röchling drift to the right? This was due to the red flag that was raised on the factory roof during the 1919 revolt and to the "ruthless humiliation" of the Treaty of Versailles! It was the "general climate of the time" that made him a patriot and a supporter of Hitler. Röchling, who was much loved by his workers, only resorted to forced labor because of a mortal shortage of manpower to run his company, which the political dictatorship had brought to "a dead end" ("in einer Zwangslage eingespannt").

The exhibition focused on the two outstanding personalities of the dynasty, father and son, whose stories are in conflict with each other: Carl, the founder, a man of "European dimensions" and a Francophile, and his successor Hermann, a very competent engineer and economist, who studied in the United States and Sweden, but who turned out to be a "great admirer of Hitler". The "dark pages"

---

404. We visited the exhibition in November 2014.

of the family and business history are discussed at the back of the last room of the exhibition and documented by means of interactive desks and film projections. Curious visitors are even allowed to leaf through the pages of the voluminous Rastatt judgments, in first and second instance, and in their German and French versions!

As for the narrative of the Great War, it is of the same style: this conflict would have favored important technical advances despite its "traumatic dimensions", and above all allowed the Röchling, designers of high quality steel, to be among the main suppliers of material for the imperial war effort[405]! The painful chapter of forced labor is closed in a single sequence that spans both world wars. Is the exploitation of thousands, or even millions, of men and women in the most abject conditions an inevitability of any violent conflict and not the consequence of the actions of a Speer or a Röchling who had thus committed their responsibility[406]?

***

Today, the head of the clan is no longer called Röchling, but von Salmuth. Johannes Freiherr von Salmuth is a member of the various supervisory bodies of the family holding company and with him a few other members of the more than 200 descendants of the four "historic" Röchling brothers. The heirs continue to keep the name

---

405. http://www.voelklinger-huette.org/This page accessed on January 31, 2017 has been removed in the interim.

406. For the opening of this exhibition, the daily newspaper *Bild-Zeitung* - circulation: 3 million - trumpets, "Even the dark chapters of the factory's history [*sic*] are brought to light: this includes the use of forced laborers during the two world wars and the proximity of the entrepreneur Hermann Röchling to the National Socialists." "Ausstellung zeigt die Geschichte der Völklinger Hütte," *Bild-Zeitung*, September 12, 2014. Cf. Saarland edition of the *Bild* on-line accessed 4.02.2023 : http://www.bild.de/regional/saarland/ausstellung-ueber-die-gut-100jaehrige-geschichte-37641030.bild.html

of the Röchlings and Völklingen in good standing, even though the economic and business affairs of the Röchling Group, which celebrates its bicentenary in 2022, are in sectors other than the metal and armaments industry. Some 20 years ago, the family, advised by the bankers Goldmann-Sachs, sold its shares in the arms and automotive conglomerate Rheinmetall AG, known worldwide for its production of Leopard tanks, for an estimated 560 million euros. The man who presides over the affairs of the Röchling dynasty concludes seriously: "Military assets should not be in the hands of private interests[407].

---

407. Johannes Freiherr von Salmuth, "Rüstungsgüter sollten [...] nicht in privaten Händen liegen," *Handelsblatt*, No. 208, October 29, 2018.

Epilogue.
Writing history in the Internet age

We owe the discovery of the Röchling family's past and, from there, of the direct witnesses of the events of the Second World War to a reading on the Internet, and thus the study of the archives and documentary sources. To conclude, we return to the Internet to compare the stories that this global network is now conveying. If nothing can bridge the gap between the historical facts and the knowledge we have today, more than 70 years after the end of the war, we can, on the other hand, mark the insufficiencies and gaps of a representation favored, even structured, by the use of electronic media.

Encyclopedias, biographical dictionaries and other online sites that publish historical accounts and chronicles often draw their information from secondary sources. And since the editors of *Wikipedia*, for example, are obliged to use as references "easily verifiable" texts that have already been published elsewhere, either on other virtual sites or in printed literature, it seems essential to us to refer first to the printed works that explicitly deal with this dynasty of Saarland iron barons in general, and with Hermann Röchling in particular.

Paper sources: the apologists

The Bibliothèque nationale de France has four books in French and German on the history of this family; the catalog of the Deutsche Nationalbibliothek contains a few more titles. This literature is apologetic throughout, with the exception of three recent pamphlets by Saarland authors who intended to enlighten the local population in the context of the campaign to have the Hermann-Röchling-Höhe district renamed[408].

We shall confine ourselves to the four writings in the BNF collection, that is to say to the essential part of this bibliography.

The earliest text, a 1920 pamphlet in French entitled simply *L'Affaire Röchling*[409], is none other than the plea of the German jurist Friedrich Grimm, a notorious anti-Semite, in defense of the Röchling brothers during the trial before the French military tribunal in Amiens in 1919. Grimm later perfected this genre and rose to prominence as a propagandist and apologist for National Socialism, a great servant of Joseph Goebbels[410]. The Röchlings, who had pleaded not guilty, thus became "men of perfect propriety and courtesy." At the time of the events, he argued, Germany's flourishing metallurgy was

---

408. These writings are like a response to the servility of Professor Grewenig, then director of the Unesco site, Völklinger Hütte: Dieter Gräbner, *Wer war Hermann Röchling?* St. Ingbert, Conte Verlag, 2014. Bernd Rausch, *100 Jahre Röchling. Ausbeutung, Raub, Kriegsverbrechen.* Saarbrücken, 2017, and *Weltkulturerbe Völklinger Hütte. Das Erbe der Röchlings.* Saarbrücken, October 2018.
409. Friedrich Grimm, *The Röchling Affair*, Essen, 1920.
410. After arriving in France with Otto Abetz and his staff in the aftermath of the Occupation, Grimm exercised his propaganda skills by writing and speaking in French on the radio and at public demonstrations alongside Marshal Pétain and Laval. As a jurist, Grimm wrote an application to the military occupation authorities in Wiesbaden to overturn the conviction in absentia of Hermann Röchling in Amiens. After the war, having himself escaped a trial, he became an influential and staunch advocate of a general amnesty for all Nazi war criminals.

so far superior to France's that Germany had nothing to gain from a war. The Röchlings, moreover, would have maintained only friendly relations, and never competitive ones, with the French industrialists. Nor would they have ever considered taking over the Briey basin!

Thirty years later, Pierre Leroy, the defense attorney for Hermann Röchling at the Rastatt court, followed Grimm's approach: as soon as the case was decided, he published his concluding statement *Plaidoyer pour Hermann Röchling for* the French public, an excerpt of which we have quoted above[411]. To this day, the text of Me Leroy is the only published document concerning the trial against Hermann Röchling.

The third book, *Röchling, Kontinuität im Wandel*, dates from 2001. Written at the request of the heirs, it is a veritable panegyric of the Röchling industrial dynasty[412]. The author, historian Gerhard Seibold, unequivocally defends the point of view of this elite family, and his benevolent view of the most reprehensible acts of their long history is a mystifying fabric, if ever there was one, but one that is not so easy to refute, since works of all kinds on the history of the two World Wars and the Occupation 1940-1944 are singularly secretive on the war economy and its protagonists. Seibold does not deny the participation of the Röchling industrialists, but he emphasizes that their involvement was only possible because of the coercive measures taken against this family, which had always had a deep sense of loyalty and duty to the German state and society. The House of Röchling was not affected by the Great War, nor by a new conflict with France. And once again, it was out of a sense of duty to his family that Hermann Röchling had to accept the use

---

411. Pierre Leroy, *Plaidoyer pour Hermann Röchling*, Mesnil, Firmin-Didot, 1948.
412. Gerhard Seibold, *Kontinuität im Wandel*, Stuttgart, Thorbecke Verlag, 2001, 523 pages.

Epilogue. Writing history in the Internet age

of forced laborers in order not to stop production at the Völklingen ironworks! The portrait is painted of a "relatively independent" Hermann Röchling with a "profoundly political mind" ("ein zutiefst politisch denkender Mensch") who had to "adapt" to the needs of collaboration with the National Socialists, even though this collaboration would have caused him problems[413]. This assertion is based, as the defense did in Rastatt, on the idea that his cousin Ernst had been an opponent of the Nazi regime: was not this Francophile Röchling given a "great proximity" to the circles of "political opposition to the Hitler regime[414]", hence his arrest in July 1944?

The latest biographer of Hermann Röchling, the academic Wolfgang von Hippel, takes his place among the apologists and, like Seibold, his *Hermann Röchling 1872-1955: Ein deutscher Großindustrieller zwischen Wirtschaft und Politik*[415], a commissioned but scholarly work, takes care of the Röchling family as it should. It is more than 1,000 pages long, with a solid set of notes, which are supposed to allow a "more differentiated" appreciation of the Saarland magnate and to do justice to the "complexity of the historical figure" during an "era of heavy crises and political and economic disasters[416]". Nevertheless, the author celebrates the noble virtues of Hermann Röchling: he would have never ceased to obtain "decent treatment for his foreign workforce, not only at the Carlshütte, but also in Völklingen and in the establishments under his control in

---

413. *Ibid*, pp. 239-247.
414. *Ibid*, p. 267.
415. Wolfgang von Hippel, *Hermann Röchling 1872-1955: Ein deutscher Großindustrieller zwischen Wirtschaft und Politik. Facetten eines Lebens in bewegten Zeiten* (Hermann Röchling, 1872-1955: A great German industrialist between economy and politics. Aspects of a life in a time of great upheaval), Göttingen, Vandenhoeck § Ruprecht, 2018.
416. *Ibid*, p. 14.

Meurthe-et-Moselle[417]". In support of this argument, von Hippel refers to the testimony of a certain Rudolf Winkelmann, a relative of the Röchlings and a proxy of the Röchling company in Thionville from 1940 to 1944. It so happens that the lawyer Winkelmann had to respond, along with one of his subordinates, the SS Schladenhaufen, to an investigation by the Moselle judicial police in October 1946 concerning the complaint of the Lorraine workers of the Thionville steelworks who accused them of having been behind the measures taken to provide the plant with a *Werkschutz* and a *Schnellgericht*[418]. This gives meaning to the "commitment" that Wolfgang von Hippel praised at Röchling to make the life and working conditions of Eastern European workers and Russian prisoners of war "as bearable as possible" within the given framework[419]!

The globalized discourse and French historiography

In the face of this hagiography, let us take note of this reality: nothing has yet come to illuminate the shadowy side of this family whose fortune, literally and figuratively, refers to an entire century of Franco-German history and relations: encyclopedias, biographical dictionaries and French reference manuals - printed or online - mention the Röchlings only very exceptionally, and even questions of economics and war industry are only rarely addressed. And when they are, the general orientation that is given tells us something about what historiography can be in the digital age.

---

417. *Ibid,* p. 782.
418. AN BB 36/36, SEF 1057, 1. Metz, October 24, 1946.
419. W. von Hippel, *op. cit.* p. 783.

1. In an article in the encyclopaedia *Universalis* entitled "Brownfields", which is partly freely available at[420], the author mentions the name of the Röchlings for their technical and innovative capacities, who were at the origin of the Völklingen steelworks, which are to be classified "among the largest installations of their kind in Europe, and even in the world[421]", and which therefore deserve to be listed by UNESCO as a historical monument. This is the kind of "industrial culture" that has fueled the heritage project around the old factories in Völklingen and given new life to a town in the process of deindustrialization.

2. The articles devoted to "Alsace-Lorraine" and to Lorraine in this same *Universalis* ignore the history of the Röchlings. Silence also on the question of access to raw resources, which agitated Saarland, Rhine and Westphalian industrialists, and politicians, in the conflicts between France and Germany from 1870 to 1945. The differences of yesteryear are relegated to the rank of "contradictory ideologies[422]", which are nowadays overshadowed by "economic concerns [*sic*]". The reconversion-recomposition of the border regions and the rescue of the industrial basins of yesteryear between Lorraine, Luxembourg, Belgian Wallonia, Saarland and Rhineland-Palatinate are the subject of a resolutely enthusiastic narrative:

---

420. The "economic model" adopted by the press and by the publishers of magazines is called "freemium": it implies, for the Internet user, a free but limited access to certain contents, the entirety - the "premium" access - being reserved for subscribers who must be of sufficient number to finance the cost of the free access.
421. Louis Bergeron, "Brownfields". *Encyclopædia Universalis*, accessed February 24, 2020.
422. Françoise Lévy-Coblentz, E.U., "Question d'Alsace-Lorraine". *Encyclopædia Universalis* [online].http://www.universalis-edu.com.janus.biu.sorbonne.fr/encyclopedie/question-d-alsace-lorraine/ accessed on April 19, 2022.

this free trade area is presented as a past open to the future, with a European vocation[423].

3. The result of more than 30 years of academic work, the voluminous *General History of the Second World War*[424], which has been reprinted several times and is available in digital form, contains an entry in its index entitled "Röchling, Hermann, German businessman". We refer to the page indicated where the author relates how, during the armistice negotiations in 1940, the Saarland industrialist Röchling had, among other things, "unconcealed designs on the mines and steel companies of Lorraine[425]". However, it is unclear what these "aims" were and what they led to.

4. Praised by critics, especially for the "prominent" place given to history "seen from below"[426], a second work by the same author, *La France dans la Deuxième Guerre mondiale, 1939-1945*[427], does not mention Hermann Röchling, nor the Auboué hostage tragedy.

5. Raul Hilberg's *The Destruction of the Jews in Europe*, a major work in this field, unfolds an organizational chart of the highest Nazi dignitaries in the service of the war economy. In the foreground, Hermann Röchling, placed under the immediate authority of the Minister of

<hr>

423. André Humbert, René Taveneaux, E.U., "Lorraine". In Universalis education [online]. http://www.universalis-edu.com.janus.biu.sorbonne.fr/encyclopedie/lorraine/ accessed on April 19, 2022.
424. Yves Durand, *Histoire générale de la Deuxième Guerre mondiale*, Brussels, Éditions Complexe, 1997, 988 pages. Digital edition in two volumes: Book I: *Armies and States at War*; Book II: *Men and Women in War*. Brussels, Éditions Complexe, Numilog, 2000.
425. *Ibid*, p. 342.
426. Review by Claude Lévy in *Vingtième Siècle. Revue d'histoire*, n° 24, October-December 1989, p. 139.
427. Yves Durand, *La France dans la Deuxième Guerre mondiale, 1939-1945*. Paris, Armand Colin, 1989, collection "Cursus". This book is available in digital version.

Armaments Speer[428]. Hilberg, recognized as an authority, shows how the Shoah was the work of a whole society. And yet, the names of the great industrial bosses - Röchling, Krupp, Flick - or groups such as Vereinigte Stahlwerke, Mannesmann, Hoesch, I.G. Farben, Volkswagen, *etc.,* are far from occupying the prominent place they deserve in this history.

6. The *Dictionary of the Great Names of the Second World War*[429], a translation of an original work in English, only mentions the Krupp family.

7. The *Dictionary of the Second World War* - a 973-page sum that can be consulted on the Internet in the "premium digital university package, ebooks in the humanities and social sciences"[430] - lists politicians and military men of all nationalities, including the SS. No industrialists.

8, 9, 10: The same is true of three reference books for France, *the Dictionnaire France sous l'Occupation*[431], published in 2011 by Larousse, the imposing *Dictionnaire historique France sous l'occupation*[432], as well as *France sous l'Occupation 1940-1944*, a work, however very renowned, by the English historian Julian Jackson[433]: There is no

428. Raul Hilberg, *The Destruction of the Jews of Europe*, Paris, Gallimard, 2006, volume 1, table III-3 "The Economy". p. 59.
429. John Keegan, *Dictionary of the Great Names of World War II* (French translation of *Who Was Who in World War II*. We consulted the 1989 French edition; the English edition was published in 1978.
430. It should be noted that this source emphasizes the access given to the works of "eminent scholars on the Second World War, both European and American".
431. Éric Alary, Bénédicte Vergez-Chaignon, *Dictionnaire de la France sous l'Occupation*, Paris, Larousse Présent, 2011.
432. Michèle and Jean-Paul Cointet, *Dictionnaire historique de la France sous l'occupation*, Paris, Tallandier, 2000, 732 pages.
433. Julian Jackson, *La France sous l'Occupation 1940-1944*, Flammarion 2001; English edition, Oxford University Press, 2001, 853 pages.

trace of the actions of the man who was the Reich's delegate for steel and coal in all the territories, including France, occupied by Hitler's troops and who reigned as a real despot in his personal fiefdom of Meurthe-et-Moselle.

11. Albert Speer, who, with Hermann Röchling at his side, occupied a central position in the war economy of the Third Reich, could not have been unaware of this, since he was the master builder. One is therefore surprised by two surprisingly complacent assessments that contribute to perpetuating the legend, which he himself so masterfully built, of a "lucid" and "honest" man. *Universalis*, in a short biography, slips in this judgment that washes away all his past: "Even his most resolute detractors recognized that he had preserved his morality throughout his career in the service of an amoral system[434]." This is echoed in the *Dictionary of World War II*: "The man appears to have maintained his moral integrity while serving an amoral regime[435]." An appearance that takes the place of revealed truth. Demystification

---

434. André Brissaud, "Speer, Albert - (1905-1981)," *Encyclopædia Universalis* accessed online on April 17, 2017. URL: http://www.universalis.fr/encyclopedie/albert-speer/ Certainly, for *Universalis*, "the most important generalist encyclopedia in the French language and one of the most renowned in the world", the "professionalism" of its authors is an asset that guarantees "documentary resources of great quality and extreme reliability"... and therefore justifies the price of the "premium" subscription.

435. Pierre Montagnon, *Dictionnaire de la Seconde Guerre mondiale*, Paris, Flammarion, 2008, (973 pages), here p. 815. This work is available online in the "premium digital" university package, which brings together studies by a "large selection of eminent researchers on the Second World War, both European and American. It is safe to say that most historians have not been very perceptive in their assessment of the former Minister of Armaments. Alan Milward, considered one of the leading authors on Nazism and the Second World War, even believed in the sincere disinterestedness with which Albert Speer helped him in his research. Thus, in his preface to *The New Order and the French Economy*, published in 1970, the English historian thanks him: "The engineer Albert Speer has given me access to a great deal of information that a less scrupulous man would have kept to himself; he has been extremely kind to someone of no importance while engaged in affairs of far greater importance to himself" (p. vii).

has obviously not been able to overcome the lies and duplicity of the former Minister of Armaments, who succeeded for several decades in masking his complicity in the crimes of the Third Reich - and in saving his head at Nuremberg!

The two world wars have been the subject of works of "global history", a globalized historiographic current that extols the "added value" of a so-called "transnational" point of view, going beyond the traditional "national history". The two publications discussed below bring together articles by contributors of various nationalities. However, the transnational paradigm "formats" the field of observation of these authors in such a way as to retain only events and facts that distance themselves from anything that recalls the territorial ambitions of the elites, German in this case, since the beginning of industrialization. As a consequence, this approach does not give any place to the history of the Röchling family, a protagonist whose deeds and actions are so closely linked to national memories, both French and German.

12. The first of these works, the *Encyclopedia of the Great War 1914-1918*[436], published in 2004, is intended to be a history "outside national borders", outside of national, military and event-based history, "now completed". It does not mention Hermann Röchling, nor the Amiens tribunal, nor the fate of the Russian prisoners of war, the first to be deported to serve the German war machine in the mines of occupied Lorraine. And while the focus is on technical progress, the quintessence of the values that Europeans exported to the world, in wartime as in peacetime, the example is given of the German steel helmet, "camouflage model 1917": a glossy color illustration with a caption that describes in detail its innovative design and praises its

---

436. *The Encyclopedia of the Great War 1914-1918*, edited by Stéphane Audoin-Rouzeau and Jean-Jacques Becker, Paris, Fayard, 2004. 1,343 pages.

ability to protect against wounds inflicted by modern weapons. The article cites the names of the two Germans - surgeon August Bier and engineer Friedrich Schwerd - who had contributed to this certainly meritorious advance in the art of warfare. There is no mention, however, of the contribution of the engineers from the Röchling factories, which produced almost all of these helmets for the German soldiers.

13. The second, *La Guerre-monde 1937-1947*[437], is intended to be the account of a "world-event". Instead of "crossing" national histories, it proposes a construction "like a layered structure": the events would be "restored from the inside, at the level where they were experienced and also in the light of the future that gives them meaning[438]". For all that, the "global perspective" does not erase the cultural roots of each person, nor does it supplant the national fact in the history of populations: does not adopting as a theoretical scheme a construction that claims to illuminate and explain the past in the light of a known present, or supposedly such a present, come under a teleological relationship?

"Transnational History" digital version

With the spread of the free culture on the Internet, which was followed by the appearance of *Wikipedia* in 2001, a new editorial

---

437. *The World War 1937-1947*. Edited by Alya Aglan and Robert Frank, 2 vols, Paris, Gallimard, 2015. Faced with the rise of ebooks, in an increasingly competitive book market, its publisher, Gallimard Editions, opted to produce an original paperback edition. Given the financial risks involved, one can assume that the "transnational" conceptual scheme of this book, favorable to translations, will have to serve as a guarantee of commercial success far beyond linguistic borders!
438. *Ibid*, p. 20.

Epilogue. Writing history in the Internet age

model was imposed not only on newspapers and periodicals, but also on the usual ones. From now on, putting a publication online that is accessible to all, with original content, requires the use of advertising, subsidies and volunteers. The strategy adopted by the government of the Federal Republic has been to rescue the publishing world by generously subsidizing the digitization and publication of scientific works in *open access*. And this proactive policy ensures the wide distribution of reference works - commonplace ones - that convey a representation of the past in line with globalization and the interests of the funding country.

13. In October 2014, the first encyclopedia dedicated to the history of the Great War appears on the web, freely accessible. *1914-1918 online. International Encyclopedia of the First World War*, consisting of original articles in English, is the work of German academics from the Freie Universität in Berlin. The editorial project, which reaches the high level of sophistication of a "technical product", tells the story of the First World War from a "transnational" point of view. The criteria of commercial profitability are set aside due to the voluntary work of its external editors and its financing from public funds, including a grant of one million euros from the Deutsche Forschungsgemeinschaft (German Research Agency). As for the satisfaction of the "customers" - the visitors of the website - the contents are subjected to a "quality management" process[439] made by the team of Berlin academics!

With the help of the internal search engine, we searched for the name "Röchling". The answer took us to an article about... "Art", i.e. to a certain Carl Röchling, a painter and artist of the military pictorial genre, renowned for his work on themes of the Franco-Prussian war.

---

439. http://www.1914-1918-online.net/

There is nothing, however, to indicate the existence of the Röchling dynasty of steelworkers and their role in the history of Alsace-Lorraine[440]! A search for "war crimes" leads to an article entitled "Leipzig War Crimes Trials", the story of a series of mock trials held from 1921 onwards in the Saxon city of Leipzig, after the German authorities refused to extradite those accused of war crimes. The Amiens tribunal in 1919 is not even mentioned. The keyword "Steel Helmet" also refers to an article which, as in example 12 above, deals with this innovation in the art of war, but with one notable difference: the writer merely mentions the names of the designers of the British ("Brodie's steel helmet") and French ("Adrian helmet") models, without mentioning the two German inventors of the *Stahlhelm* and the role of the Röchling engineers and factories in its manufacture[441]!

14. In the index, volume XXI, of an online textbook entitled *Neue Deutsche Biographie* ("NDB"), one finds a list of the names of 29 members of the Röchling dynasty with cross-references to three articles - on the Röchling family, on the founder Carl, and on Hermann Röchling[442]! The "NDB" is a reference work in German, covering the entire German-speaking cultural and linguistic area since the Middle Ages, and is financed with public funds... from the Federal Republic alone[443]; the articles, written on the basis of information

---

440. "Art": http://encyclopedia.1914-1918-online.net/article/art?version=1.0

441. "steel helmet": https://encyclopedia.1914-1918-online.net/article/steel_helmet (accessed on 7.02.2023)

442. *Neue Deutsche Biographie*, vol. 21, 2003. http://www.ndb.badw-muenchen.de/ndb_baende.htm

443. *Neue Deutsche Biographie* is published by the Bavarian Academy of Sciences, a non-university research organization, financed by the federal and state governments through the *Deutsche Forschungsgemeinschaft* and by donations from various foundations. To date, twenty-six of the twenty-eight volumes of the publishing project are available online. The first paper volume was published in 1953. The paper edition of the whole was entrusted to the publisher Duncker and Humblot in Berlin.

taken from "scientific literature" - G. Seibold's book is listed in the bibliography - aim to document the lives of deceased personalities from the German-speaking world who appear as "actors of development", among them the Röchling. It is emphasized that in 2000 the Röchling-Konzern, active in trade, industry and services, was one of the largest family businesses in Germany, with 41,000 employees and a turnover of 6.1 million euros!

While the article on Hermann Röchling reviews the most important functions of the industrialist in the Third Reich, it emphasizes the incompleteness of his participation[444]. Röchling "approved" of Hitler "above all" in terms of his economic policy. Röchling's own action in the war economy is downplayed, and the author also suggests that there were serious disagreements between the Saarlander and the Führer in areas other than economics. Appointed General Delegate for Iron and Steel in Lorraine and southern Meurthe-et-Moselle from 1940 onwards, Röchling did not "succeed in imposing his objectives. Further proof of his failures is the report that after the appointment of "German supervisory bodies" for the Moselle metallurgy, Röchling "only held the 'Carlshutte' in Diedenhofen". That he became head of the RVE in 1942 and, upon appointment by Speer, the Reich Commissioner for Iron and Steel in the occupied territories, is true, but the fact remains that this was not what was expected in the ruling circles, "despite significant increases in productivity and the demand for forced laborers by Röchling." And if mention is made of the use of

---

444. Ralf Banken, "Röchling, Hermann" in: *Neue Deutsche Biographie* 21 (2003), S. 705-706 (online version consulted on 7.02.2023) http://www.deutsche-biographie. de/ppn121748626.html In an article published in *Akkumulation*, an academic journal for a critical history of business (No. 20, 2004), the latest issue of which appeared in 2012, Banken takes a critical stance on Röchling's role under National Socialism and expresses reservations about Seibold's book:http://www.kritische-unternehmens-geschichte.de/de/node/30 (accessed on 7.03.2023)

forced laborers in the Völklingen factories, "as elsewhere in the Reich", the editor does not venture to break the silence surrounding the existence of the Etzenhofen camp, which now belongs to the distant past.

Entrepreneurial chronicles

The three heir companies of the former Röchling works - the "Völklinger Hütte, Unesco Heritage Site", *Saarstahl AG*, which has taken over the metallurgical activities of the Völklingen works[445], and the *Röchling Group*, the holding company which manages the activities of the conglomerate which has remained family-owned and independent - have all posted stories or chronicles about the past of the founders.

These pages of history share the same idea, commonly accepted, with the "scientific" textbooks, paper or virtual, that we have seen previously: History values technology and industrialization, the quintessence of what Europe represents in the world. These narratives retrace the development of industrial culture, minimizing the conflicting aspects of a century of Franco-German relations, the weight of the destruction and the crimes of the two world wars and of Nazism. The price paid by forced laborers and the very phenomenon of slave labor are relativized in view of the "progress" made in industry. After all, who could argue with that? Like the Krupps and Thyssen, were not the engineers and masters of the Röchling forges pioneers in modern steelmaking? And their old factories have been recognized for their universal value, with the Unesco mark to boot! The success story thus highlighted makes it possible to forget everything else.

---

445. The most modern part of the steel plant was kept in operation.

Here are the "snapshots" that we have taken on their sites at a given time and that can therefore be modified at any time.

"Röchling Group"

On this site, Röchling celebrates its industrial culture in eight languages, which is also described as a culture of "diversity": diversity of production, which is already two hundred years old, and the company's ability to "keep up with change"[446], which is in line with the development of state-of-the-art technology!

The history of the men involved in this corporate strategy can be summed up by mentioning Friedrich Ludwig Röchling, the ancestor of the iron baron dynasty, who in 1822 founded "a coal trade that gave rise to an international trading network on which the family's industrial activities were to be built. His heirs, Theodor, Ernst, Carl and Fritz Röchling, took over Völklinger Hütte and thus reoriented the company towards the production of industrial steel. After the death of his brothers, Carl became the sole manager of the company and ensured its growth and prosperity through his far-sighted decisions[447]."

And, indeed, it is a certain foresight of its leaders that has guaranteed the success of the house of Röchling.

"Saarstahl AG"

The website is presented in three languages: German, English and Chinese. Under the heading "Historie [*sic*][448]", a chronology of the development of the Völklingen iron and steelworks shows eight key

---

446. The title of the book by G. Seibold, hagiographer of the Röchling family, is "Kontinuität im Wandel". Cf. *supra*, p. 311.
447. https://www.roechling.com/fr/groupe/a-propos-du-groupe/histoire-200-years-roechling (accessed on 19.02.2023)
448. http://www.saarstahl.com/sag/en/group/sag/history/index.shtml (accessed on 19.02.2023)

dates which help to highlight the successes of the Röchling industrialists and emphasize the "worldwide" recognition of their technology. No entry is given for the period of the two world wars.

"Völklinger Hütte - Unesco World Heritage Site"

The message on the website gives the Unesco logo a unique significance. The Völklinger Hütte is now a World Heritage Site and takes its place among the world's most famous monuments, such as the Great Wall of China, Cologne Cathedral, the Zollverein Mine, the Grand Canyon or the Great Barrier Reef in Australia. For the city of Völklingen, for the region, this international visibility promises significant economic benefits - through tourism. And indeed, with 250,000 visitors per year, it is one of the most visited places in Saarland.

The pages of the website, available in three languages - German, French and English - develop a story about "milestones in the history of modern technology" with a section entitled "Chronology" which traces the development of the Saarland metallurgical site and briefly summarizes the history of the Röchling industrialists. At the same time, future visitors are invited to discover exhibitions, festivals and international concerts that take place in the large rooms and oversized halls equipped with video screens, with the backdrop of blowing machines and gigantic wheels at a standstill. The former factories, which have been transformed into a German limited liability company, "European Center for Art and Industrial Culture", have a double museum function: on the one hand, the disused building is a spectacular monument to the modern cult of the machine; on the other hand, it can be said that this "machine-museum" is an extraordinary event stage.

And, to increase its visibility and optimize the referencing, the editors of the website have included this heritage site in a debate, also with global dimensions:

"[...] as a central site of the Anthropocene-the time when humans have massively changed their environment through technology-it is the best place to discuss the positive and negative effects of this societal development culturally and artistically and to put our present and future[449] in perspective."

Indeed, in a 2018 document, Unesco makes an admission: at the time of Völklingen's listing, "the painful history" of forced labor, that negative side of industrial development, had not been mentioned. Today, however, the heritage experts note that due to an "economic desire to promote cultural tourism, all German industrial World Heritage Sites must deal with this reality". In order not to offend the sensitivities of certain audiences and to take into account the "changing perceptions of history[450]", "authorized shared interpretation [*sic*] and the co-creation of historical narratives" should be used. Interpretation must be open to "reconciliation, even forgiveness," and it will be the job of the "professionals" of memory, namely "journalists, communication specialists and marketing experts," to give the sites an "appropriate museological treatment." The use of techniques such as "virtual reality, augmented reality, immersive reality or mixed reality" does not exclude the appeal to contemporary artists, because art has the "capacity to evoke with force the events of the past, to stimulate new perceptions and to establish a link between past and present feelings, while at the same time attracting a new public[451]".

---

449. https://voelklinger-huette.org/fr/weltkulturerbe/unesco-weltkulturerbe (accessed on 19.02.2023)
450. *The Interpretation of Memory Sites*, a January 31, 2018 study commissioned by the Unesco World Heritage Center and funded by the Permanent Delegation of the Republic of Korea. https://whc.unesco.org/document/194927
451. *Ibid*, p. 21.

Thus, in the former Röchling factories, a "place of memory" will be set up where the French artist Christian Boltanski will be invited to create an installation on the theme of forced labor, an artistic vision called to give life and relief to history and to raise a new awareness of the "practice of forced labor"[452]:

> "Visitors find themselves amidst the narrow walls of the memory archive, which consists of countless stacked bins containing files. In places, one can make out a personnel number while black pants and jackets form a mountain of clothing. The whispered names of the forced laborers resound from every corner of the facility, causing dread. Like lightning, Christian Boltanski's installation suddenly transports the visitor into another world."

In the large ore room, the artist has created a second large, temporary installation entitled "Souvenirs", dedicated to the memory of the workers and their daily work. This staging of metal cabinets recovered in the various workshops and services is supposed to "relive" the emotions of the workers of the metallurgical industry to the visitor:

> "Recordings of testimonies about the work at the Völklingen ironworks leak out of the lockers. These lockers are the point where the whole work crystallizes. Their interiors belong to the private sphere, their exteriors to the steelworks,

---

452.   Website: https://voelklinger-huette.org/de/ausstellungen/christian-boltanski-die-zwangsarbeiter-erinnerungsort-in-der-voelklinger-huette/ (accessed on 7.02.2023) as well as the brochure "Forced laborers at the Völklinger Hütte during the First and Second World Wars". Note the small shift in the story that allows the identity of the owners to be erased from the name of the company: "Röchling'sche Eisen- und Stahlwerke" becomes simply "Völklinger Hütte".

and thus they convey in a striking way a particular form of memory and appreciation of the work done there."

The "locker" is that common place, familiar to schoolchildren or library visitors, the locker rooms of sportsmen in stadiums and gyms! Thus the story of crimes that go beyond comprehension is put at a distance to avoid the spectator confronting inhuman situations - the suffering of the workers in the blast furnaces or in the coke department, with the deafening noises and the exposure to the very high heat, the burns, the dust, the night work, *etc.*

Boltanski's two installations, which only highlight the fate of the victim, divert the gaze from the particular role played by the managers of the Röchling factories, and here is forced labor and the war production it was used for, simply brought back to "the darkest chapter of the history of industrial culture", a striking panorama of the "anthropocene"! Carrying the Unesco label thus requires a strategy that passes, if need be, by the role granted to the event and to the work of art. The skilful choice of the emotional puts the emphasis on the feeling to avoid dealing with reason.

***

In 2017, the website of the Völklinger Hütte announced a lecture series on forced labor during the Third Reich. In order to "treat" - we use the strongly connoted German term "Aufarbeitung"! - the general management of the site, which was responsible for the project, secured the participation of numerous experts[453]. The events took place three quarters of a century after the events, at the very place where these acts

---

453. Email received by the author from Judith Jung, assistant to prof. R. M. Grewenig, CEO of the Völklinger Hütte, on November 19, 2017.

of modern slavery took place. With the advent of electronic media, the function of this "memory" has been profoundly modified. It is not so much a question of remembering events against the background of values and representations shared by the specific public to which it is addressed, but rather of widely disseminating a moral sentiment based on the denunciation of crimes against humanity.

In the end, doesn't this "world cultural asset" that served as their backdrop have as its latent content the message of a Europe finally reconciled - the cradle of modern technology and progress?

Memory as a product of globalized exchange

Wikipedia, the world's most consulted textbook, gives a large place to the Röchling dynasty, to their former factories and to the heir companies, and the texts repeat, often word for word, information posted elsewhere on the web, notably in the chronicles and stories of the three new companies, ensuring them a large diffusion[454]. Indeed, the *Wikipedia* system, which forbids original research and reference to unpublished texts, relies on secondary sources, "easily accessible" and "verifiable", and in priority on information available on other websites. The reason for this process is simple: the "wikipedia" editors, all volunteers, "do not always have the time necessary for library research[455]"! As a "participatory and collaborative" encyclopedia,

---

454. To date, there are six biographical entries in German on the most important personalities of the dynasty, including Hermann and Ernst, in English and French on Hermann Röchling only. There are also articles on the Röchling industrial group, the Völklinger Hütte, on Saarstahl AG and articles in 29 languages on Rheinmetall (accessed on 20.02.2023).
455. And it is suggested that editors point out in their articles the existence of "divergent, commonly held views". https://fr.wikipedia.org/wiki/Wikip%C3%A9dia:Citez_vos_sources#Qualit%C3%A9_des_sources (accessed on 20.02.2023)

Epilogue. Writing history in the Internet age

Wikipedia positively values - following the example of Unesco experts - the "co-creation" of narratives, i.e. the use of a multiplicity of authors who remain anonymous in order to reach a "democratic consensus" and guarantee "neutrality of point of view". In this deregulated and ungrounded space that is the Internet, *Wikipedia* is primarily concerned with the admissibility, the "translatability" from one language to another, of content designed for the widest possible audience. In other words, Wikipedia is concerned with ensuring that those who are dominant on the web are able to make the most of their point of view.

Behind its label as an encyclopedia, *Wikipedia* offers a global and free advertising space where it is good to "communicate". The e-reputation experts hired by the Völklinger Hütte - Unesco World Cultural Heritage Site - take advantage of this to "optimize" the image of this client with an exceptional status: by devoting more than 20 articles to it, the Wikipedia contributors copy and paste the promotional texts put online on the Völklinger Hütte site: a description of the place, images of the most imposing installations, an inventory of past and present exhibitions to promote its museum character. The French *Wikipedia* even includes a few delicate words about the forced labor practiced in the factory from 1940 to 1945:

> "During the Second World War, 12,393 men, women and children from 20 different countries, especially from Russia, Poland and Yugoslavia, worked in the forges and steelworks under very harsh conditions. Of these *Zwangarbeiter* (forced laborers), 261, including 60 children, lost their lives[456]."

---

456.   https://fr.wikipedia.org/wiki/Usine_sid%C3%A9rurgique_de_V%C3%B6lklingen (accessed February 20, 2023)

A hyperlink in English, French, German, Dutch, Japanese *Wikipedia* articles to the external marketing platform "ERIH" maximizes their advertising value. Let's hear it: Völklingen is the starting point of this "European Route of Industrial Heritage[457]" (ERIH) and this tourist information network tells what it was like to be in this intertwining of brownfields and museums. It is an initiative for the "marketing of the common history" of the European countries, which has been supported since its foundation in 1999 by its president, Professor Meinrad Maria Grewenig, the same person who directed the activities of the Völklinger Hütte between 1999 and 2020! Thanks to the support of the German federal government, the "ERIH" - an association under German private law - benefits from subsidies from the European Union, and in particular the Council of Europe. Its website, the main means of communication, promotes this tourist "brand" and "label" on the web, compared to the Unesco label. It provides Internet users with a real "virtual library" with background information on "European industrial history". The "quality label" that the ERIH awards, at their request, to disused industrial sites enhances the technical dimension of this "European identity" project that Europhiles are calling for.

The former Völklingen works and forges have a special place in this European myth: they are an "anchor" of the network due to their strategic location on the border with France and Luxembourg. The ERIH website presents a history of the Völklingen works that reflects this importance: a few paragraphs that focus on the technical achievements of the founder Carl Röchling and the production capacities of the installations, with impressive figures and many superlatives to support them... and a blank: the fate of the thousands of workers

---

457. http://www.erih.net/

- Europeans moreover - forced to work in the Röchling metallurgical works for the victory of Nazi Germany and the personal enrichment of this industrial dynasty. Obviously, the web can hardly find a better reference than a site like Völklingen to maintain the belief of Internet users in Progress towards a better future...

This heritage scheme, universalized by Unesco and taken up by ERIH, thus imposes a certain representation of the German past that conforms to the image that must be given of the largest of Europe's democracies, with an unrivaled economy that owes its excellence to its technological mastery. And we note that the German government has constantly intervened with the two institutions to promote tourism of the "European heritage" in general and of its industrial past in particular[458]. The recent history of the peoples of Europe, enclosed in these "encompassing" concepts, is detached from the national context: facts and events are assembled in a veritable teleological relationship in order to construct a narrative of European dimensions. And it is, indeed, this systematic elaboration of a "transnational", even "global" history that our investigation reveals: a narrative that reconciles German history with that of its neighbors and passes over in silence the very name of the Röchling dynasty.

---

458. In 2018, on the initiative of the government of the Federal Republic, the European Commission has validated a project to encourage more people to discover and appreciate the cultural heritage of Europe: "The European Year of Cultural Heritage". In short, heritage tourism is intended to give citizens a sense of belonging to a common European space. The slogan: "Our heritage: when the past meets the future" leaves no doubt. At the beginning of this year of celebration for European heritage, the German government even succeeded in getting the Ministers of Culture of the European Union member states to adopt a declaration in favor of a "quality building culture". Meeting on the sidelines of the Davos Economic Forum, they will all sign a document of international scope, a first in the field, which introduces and validates the German concept of "Baukultur" for the languages of all EU countries! German planners and politicians will be pleased to see the "dissemination of German culture as a reference culture". A success story for heritage culture!

Conclusion

In contrast to the sagas of other German steel industrialists (Flick, Krupp, Thyssen) and despite the abundant literature and filmography devoted to the rise of Nazism and the Second World War, the feats of arms of Hermann Röchling, this fervent admirer of Hitler, anti-Semitic notary and militant pangermanist, have not received the attention they deserve. Only a handful of books or articles in specialized journals speak of the career of this Saarland tycoon since the Great War, of the despotism he exercised in Lorraine, of his implementation of an industrial policy geared to the war of conquest. And even though this historiography has been forgotten, the life and career of his protector and friend, Albert Speer, continue to attract attention.

However, it was as much through their vision as through their fanaticism that certain industrialists and engineers, such as Hermann Röchling, exerted an influence on National Socialist politicians. In the performance of their duties, these men brought the system of exploitation and economic slavery to a climax. For Röchling, the future could only be seen in close connection with the National Socialist cause, once Hitler and his followers had come to power. From his business strategy, as he himself described it, came the necessity to become "the interpreter of National Socialist principles" and to give proof of being "faithful supporters of the Führer's policy[459]". His competitors, and above all the large steel companies in the Rhine and Ruhr regions, were to be seen as unbelievers who were trying to delay in order to accommodate themselves better to the Reich's policy.

Since then, silence surrounds the misdeeds of Hermann Röchling and his family, and the few publications written by his lawyers and official biographers have no other purpose than to hide the guilt of this talented industrialist and paternalistic boss. However, the investigative work accomplished by the two Alsatian judges in Rastatt, Charles Gerthoffer and Paul-Julien Doll - the latter was named Righteous Among the Nations in 1991 - their personal commitment and the decision taken by the minister André Marie, a lawyer and member of the Resistance who was deported to Buchenwald in 1943, in order to bring the "Röchling trial" to a successful conclusion, deserve to be brought out of oblivion. Thanks to them, the archives contain overwhelming documentation that makes Hermann Röchling the protagonist of a conflictual, age-old history between France and Germany. It gives him an importance that, in many ways, eclipses that of other great German industrialists.

It must be recognized, however, that the primacy of politics remains the preferred mode of argumentation in the historiography of the Third Reich. This vision of history denies the permanence, from one political regime to another, of production relationships and ignores the role of certain industrialists, which goes beyond their sole contribution to the National Socialist "arms miracle": if industry did not exert a preponderant influence on Nazi policy, strategic decisions were by no means independent of its needs.

---

459. AN BB/36/6 TG 349: letter of Hermann Röchling to his banker, A. Pastor, Dresdner Bank, Aachen, December 19, 1939.

Of course, this tangle of authorities, which allowed Hitler and his close associates to intervene at all levels of the administration to impose their decisions, makes it all the more difficult to find out who was responsible, especially in the case of major industrialists. Thus, the large German companies largely concealed their activities under National Socialism until the 1990s. In the face of the late demands for compensation from surviving forced laborers, a number of firms have nevertheless agreed to open their archives, and the studies that have emerged from them tend to reinforce a sobering image: the National Socialist war economy subjected companies to such constraints that they had little possibility of escaping. On this basis, it is all the more convenient for contemporary ideologists to put the "two totalitaria-nisms" - the Nazi economy and Soviet planning - on the same level and to present them, usefully, as systems hostile to free enterprise and the democratic regime.

Indeed, with the end of the Second World War, the systemic East-West conflict provided the necessary ideological legitimization for the policies now implemented by the Allies, in particular the return of Germany as a major industrial power. The stakes of the conflict that opposed them to the Soviet regime induced the founding fathers of Europe in formation to relativize the crimes of Nazism, which implied the responsibility of the industrial world.

German historians, journalists and politicians are accustomed to speaking of the year 1945 as a "Neubeginn", a new beginning, which began with the unconditional surrender of the Reich, called the "Stunde Null", the zero hour. These two expressions sum up the illusion, widely held in the West, of having entered a new era of history with the end of the war. To mark this major turning point, one of the first measures taken by the occupying forces in the Western zones was to ban the teaching of history in schools - until the autumn of

1947 for the American and British zones, and until July 1949 for the French zone[460]. And when this ban was lifted, they introduced a legal provision that henceforth the European, not the national, perspective would shape the historical knowledge of German youth.

This periodization of history imposed its criteria, on the one hand, on the perception of events upstream of the "Stunde Null", influencing the choice of facts deemed significant in the war story. On the other hand, it influenced the way in which post-war events were treated, events that were difficult to reconcile with the Manicheanism of the systemic struggle, such as, for example, the past of Hermann Röchling and the search for information on the role of industrialists in the Nazi project, which aimed to enslave, or even annihilate, entire populations in Europe. Only a few historians of the now defunct GDR - for ideological reasons as well, of course - have attempted to uncover documents that attest to the fundamental convergence of interests between the big industrialists and the National Socialist regime.

It was also with the end of the war that the countries of Europe had to recognize the obsolete nature of their formal borders, which had been overtaken by the global, all-embracing electrical technology. The beginning of the new era was then inaugurated by the reorganization in coal and steel on a supranational scale - at the center of this strategy the heavy industry of Lorraine and Saarland, which had been disputed for so long between France and Germany -, followed by the construction of a military structure of the Western countries, which placed Federal Germany at the center of their defense system. The construction of Europe promised to put an end to Franco-German rivalry; its memory was to be wiped clean.

---

460. In July 1946, the Soviet authorities published the first curriculum for the teaching of "History" in their zone 1946-1947.

This is how this new teleological scheme came about, which places the history of the peoples of Europe in the perspective of European unification and a common experience - that of technical progress, global and inexorable. If the evocation of the former factories of Völklingen is an ideal way to celebrate the solid weave of the History of a now globalized world, the conflicting elements of the history of this place, of the national histories, and the personalities who made them, will have no place there, at the risk of disturbing the consensual, soft reading of this past. And today, some authors - and, in the first place, the followers of a "global history" - even manage to reduce the conflicts of the 20th century to the dimensions of a civil war.

The history of the Röchlings recalls a number of themes and hostilities that belie the illusion of the common origins of this Europe and its irresistible evolution towards the Union. Occulting the real developments that have made France and Germany so different does not facilitate mutual understanding between populations, especially since "globalization", far from having erased it, relies on the national fact that is still dominant in the lives of peoples. But the "Internet" effect, which privileges simultaneity to the detriment of the past and imposes the lowest common denominator to reach a public on a planetary scale, does not make it possible to take into account the conflicts and rivalries that have marked the Franco-German past and liabilities.

One can question the respective importance of Hermann Röchling, his cousin Ernst and the other iron barons, but the responsibility of each of them in the war machine of Nazism is not debatable, and it is this in the first place that deserves to be highlighted.

Annexes

1. Revue industrielle de l'Est.

In the fall of 1919, Félix Leprince-Ringuet, a civil mining engineer, had a series of five articles published in the weekly Revue industrielle de l'Est, *reporting on the German occupation during the Great War. From this* Report on the whole of the 1914-1918 service *we have taken extracts which provide information on the activities of Hermann Röchling and his role in the looting and destruction of French factories.*

The Röchling family was the owner of a mine in Lorraine, but the documents consulted by Leprince-Ringuet do not contain any trace of this, since this mine was operated independently. However, since all the other mines under the control of the occupying power benefited the steel industry as a whole, we will give below the information on their development and the use made of slave labor in each of them. As for the factories, we have retained only the reports concerning those for which it was demonstrated during the Amiens trial that the Röchlings had been involved in their exploitation and plundering.

1. ***Revue industrielle de l'Est,*** **No. 1280, 29th year, September 28, 1919, pp. 761-769.**

"Invaded party.

The invaded part of the Meurthe-et-Moselle department is only interesting from the point of view of iron mines and metallurgical plants. While we will deal specifically with the mining situation, we will be led, by necessity, to mix and study both points of view in parallel, due to the fact that the German administration was common for a long time.

§ 1 Situation on the eve of the war

Mining. - On the eve of the war, eighteen concessions were in operation in the Briey basin and one in preparation; fifteen in the Longwy basin, and four mines of some importance.

Of all these holdings, six had fairly strong German holdings, two of which, located in the Longwy basin, were owned exclusively by enemy companies:

1° The Pulventeux mine belonging to Röchling of Völklingen (Saarland);

2° La minière [*A mine is a shallow or open pit mine*] R. Böcking, extension in France of a Luxembourg mine belonging to R. Böcking.

From a technical point of view, the mines of the Briey basin exploited the grey layer, sometimes in conjunction with the yellow and red layers that overlie it. Exceptionally, Errouville exploited the brown layer. Both are excellent calcareous or neutral ores. In the Longwy basin, all the layers were exploited, mainly siliceous, quite rich in iron, or limestone, and poor.

The use of electricity (traction at the bottom, compressors for pneumatic perforation, exhaustion, ventilation, extraction, *etc.*) was very general, but each mine had its own power station for its needs, except for the mines on the hillside of the Longwy basin, which were supplied by the nearby metallurgical plants.

[...]

The steel factories in the Briey-Longwy region were divided among thirteen companies, three in the Orne valley, the others in the Longwy region.

In 1913 they produced 3,686,000 tons of cast iron and 1,779,000 tons of steel, or 52% and 38% of French production, respectively. The consistency of these plants is shown in Table V.

All these factories were in operation on July 31, 1914. *Only one was controlled* by the German industry.

§ 2 General information on the German occupation.

When war was declared, the mines and factories were shut down. During the first months of the war, fighting took place in the district of Briey, resulting in some damage to the mines. The battle of Spincourt caused difficulties in the extraction of the mines of the Landres group; three operations: Amermont-Dommary, Piennes and Murville were drowned at that time (end of August 1914) and still remain so.

But, with this exception, all the mines and factories in the two basins of Briey and Longwy were in perfect condition when, after the stabilization of the front (October 1914), the Germans organized themselves in occupied territory. They immediately thought of using the resources they could get from it and they did so by creating various administrations. But these administrations never took care of what the Germans owned in France, and this is how the Pulventeux mine [owned by the Röchling company] and the R. Böcking mine continued to operate. Böcking mine continued to operate without any control by the German authorities.

Generally speaking, for the mines, the use was done according to two different processes:

1° Mining and shipping of ore;

2° Stop of the mine, but use of all that could be removed (stock of ores, machines, compressors, etc.).

Sometimes, moreover, the two processes were used one after the other, depending on the circumstances.

For the factories, on the contrary, the use was limited to taking away all that could be taken and most often to breaking the rest. No factory was ever restarted. There were only attempts to do so at the end of 1916 for two factories:

1° Gelsenkirchen, which has a 65% interest in Aubrives-Villerupt, requested that the business be restarted. It could not obtain it.

2° At the same time, the Wendel factories in annexed Lorraine were seized by the German authorities in order to intensify production. The Wendel factory and mine in Jœuf were naturally placed under the same authority, and there was talk at the time of setting the Jœuf factory on fire. But this was not achieved either.

After these generalities, we will give a detailed history of the German occupation from October 1914 to November 1918. There are two successive periods to be distinguished.

In the first period, from October 1914 to December 1916, only one administration, the *"Schutzverwaltung der Bergwerke und Hütten"*, was in charge of all the mines and factories in Metz. This administration was located in Metz and was part of the general administration of the invaded countries (*Zivilverwaltung für das Gebiet von Briey und Longwy*).

Period from January 1917 to the armistice.

The intensification of the services and perhaps also certain misadventures that happened to the Zivilverwaltung lead to the specialization of the services, one in charge of the exploitation of the mines in Homécourt, the other in charge of the stocks and the machines in Longwy.

1° Period October 1914 to the end of 1916.

By decree of December 3, 1914, the Chancellor of the Empire created an administration for Briey and Longwy (*Zivilverwaltung für das Gebiet von Briey und Longwy*) in Metz under the direction of Herr von Gemingen [*sic*[461]]. Among other organs, this administration included a part especially in charge of the "Protection of mines and factories" (*Schutzverwaltung der Bergwerke und Hütten*) thus constituted at the beginning:

Technical management (with some independence): Bergrat Kohlmann (Thionville) and Bergmeister Hönig (Metz) both officials already in charge of the iron mines in annexed Lorraine.

Commercial part: Bergassessor Horten (Hagondange), Board of Directors: Kommerzienrat von Oswald (Coblenz); Kommerzienrat Springoroum (Dortmund); Kommerzienrat Kirdorf (Gelsenkirchen);

---

461. Karl Freiherr von Gemmingen-Hornberg was the father of Hermann Röchling's future gender, Hans Lothar von Gemmingen-Hornberg.

Kommerzienrat Klöckner, (Duisburg); Kommerzienrat L. Röchling [*one of Hermann's brothers*, M.M.] (Völklingen); Lieutenant General von Schubert (Berlin); Bergrat Frielinghaus (Essen); the latter, deceased, was replaced by Direktor Förster (Essen).

It was above all the regularization of a de facto situation because, as early as October 1914, the Germans had started to use the available resources. The Pulventeux mine and the R. Böcking mine had resumed their normal operations with their pre-war management personnel and without any control. In all the other mines and factories, they had started to take away what they found useful, but the Schutzverwaltung responded to the need to create a body that could control and distribute the booty. The guidelines of the Schutzverwaltung were as follows:

a) Mines. - Exploitation and supply of ore.

1° To ensure the drainage by supplying either the current or the necessary coal;
2° to remove the existing stocks of ore on the mine floor, stocks estimated at 8,000,000 tons and underestimated, as proven by the shipments;
3° to restart two or three mines to continue, after exhaustion of the stocks, the shipments at the planned quantum of 260,000 tons per month.

b) Plants and mines for any purpose other than the supply of ore.

Utilization and dispatch to Germany of the stockpiles, including according to the enemy's estimates [...].

In addition, the use and removal of machinery and tools as far as possible, both in the mines and in the factories; in particular at the beginning: 250 ovens and a quantity of pneumatic hammers.

The looting was carried out by the Schutzverwaltung according to a similar program for Northern France and Belgium.

These projects were carried out with increasing intensity [...].

[The Schutzverwaltung in Düsseldorf was soon charged with the question which seemed to be of the greatest concern to German industry, namely: the distribution of manganese ores and manganese products from France. [...] the most important role [...] was to ensure the removal of the remaining stocks in the factories of the Longwy basin and the supply of all kinds of material to the troops, in particular sheet metal, rails, iron bars, wire, etc.

2nd Period from January 1917 to November 1918.

The services of the Schutzverwaltung, concentrated at the beginning in Metz, were gradually decentralized, each service under the direction of one of the heads of the Schutzverwaltung.

[...]

a.) Mining

The Germans continued to implement the Hindenburg program, as evidenced by the monthly reports of the Bergverwaltung. The execution of the Zivilverwaltung program of 1916 has been noted. All the mines announced as having to be exploited were indeed more or less actively exploited during the whole period from January 1st, 1917 to the armistice. [...]

b.) Machinery and raw materials.

The "Rohma" (*Rohstoff- und Maschinenverteilungsstelle des Kriegsamts*) will henceforth deal with everything concerning mines and factories, apart from the exploitation of the mines themselves. This body [...] will ensure the looting of mines and factories and will take care of transporting everything that can be dismantled and is of interest to Germany and transforming the rest into scrap metal, supplying the Martin steelworks. [...]

2. *Revue industrielle de l'Est*, n° 1281, October 5, 1019, p. 791-795.

§ 4 - Economic observations. We always put aside the two German mines of Pulventeux and Böcking, to which nothing of what follows is related.

Worker Personnel. - The Germans had an incredible difficulty in recruiting personnel and this seems to be one of the main reasons for the minimal extraction they made. In addition to the workers they forcibly recruited, they tried, at the beginning, to attract to Briey the Italian workers who were there before the war. They met with the refusal of the Italian authorities, a refusal that was soon followed by Italy's entry into the war. In these conditions, they had to fall back on prisoners of war, the vast majority of whom were Russians.

They also sometimes brought French prisoners, sometimes Belgians or English, but without much result. In sum, apart from the civilian element, the Russians always had a majority, except at Hussigny, where there was never any.

Here are some numbers:

	June 1915	Jan. 1916	Sept. 1916	Nov. 1916	July 1917	Jan. 1918	May 1918	Sept. 1918
Russian P.G.	411	557	1863	3952	4322	?	?	?
Total	120	2383	3269	6248	7951	8038	7785	8324

Among these workers, there were few who were professional miners: in this category came some workers from the region, some French prisoners of war and sometimes German overstayers. In this last respect, reports constantly complained about the fact that those who had been overworked were taken back to the front or to the coal mines. This shortage of miners explains the method of work used by the Germans.

The miner had a real team of workers under him and his output was enormous, 20 to 35 tons, although the output for the whole mine was much lower than before the war. The workers had a daily task to perform, which increased from the beginning to the end of the occupation. The worker who had not completed his task remained after the others, without prejudice to penal sanctions against prisoners. [...]

There is nothing in the official reports that would allow us to give details on the number of accidents, nor on their cause. But some people who remained during the occupation told us that the number of accidental deaths, especially among Russian prisoners in the mines, had been so high that the corpses were brought up and buried secretly, and that fake autopsies very often had to attribute the death to an illness.

Workers' housing. - The workers' housing, created in the majority of farms to house the many foreign workers who worked in the region before the war, were the least respected of the mine outbuildings.

Since the majority of the workers had always been prisoners, who were parked in reserved compounds, these cités were mostly uninhabited and available. The Germans made extensive use of them and ransacked them. Fortunately, most of the time, the damage was limited to the interior of the houses, but in some cases, such as in Amermont-Dammary where the housing was used as stables, the structure itself had to be repaired.

Slaughtering. - Method of exploitation. The German administration has always exploited in a barbaric way, aiming above all to increase the extracted tonnage in any way.

Thus, she was content to strip the prepared quarters without making new tracings to prepare the future. [...]

In the neighborhoods, the Germans ransacked the yards, either by overextending them or by cutting them: in the powerful layers, they often left part of the layer unused.

For all these reasons, important quantities of ore are definitively lost, either because it is dangerous or even impossible to consider access to a part of the mine, or because the landslides contain ore that cannot be recovered.

3. *Revue industrielle de l'Est*, No. 1282, October 12, 1919, pp. 817-819.

§ 6 - Removal of equipment.

This removal involved both the mines and the factories. As we have already mentioned, it even preceded the organization of the Schutzverwaltung and, as early as September 1914, Doktor Lilge was in charge of this service in Longwy.

When the Schutzverwaltung was created, it had to deal with these issues centralized in Metz under the authority of Bergassessor Horten, assisted during the last months of 1916 by Rittmeister Hiby [...].

The Rohma (Rohstoff- und Maschininenverwertungstelle in the beginning, later Maschinenverteilungsstelle) was responsible for the removal and use of machines and the supply of raw metals (Rohstoffe) to industry. [...]

[It] included three different technical sections:

M.A., dealing with the machines;
M.B., dealing with electrical equipment;
M.C., dealing with scrap metal and cast iron.

It is said that this organization was created at the request of Thyssen, who placed a large part of his staff there.

The German companies that robbed the region the most were, in decreasing order of guilt, Thyssen, Röchling, Rombas, Knutange.

During the first years of the war, the looting was organized scientifically without destruction by the Schutzverwaltung at first, then by the Rohma much more intensively. The material was inventoried: German industrial missions came to the site to assess the value of the machines and to choose from among what might interest them. If the industrialists could not be bothered, they were sent documents, photographs and drawings to enable them to obtain information.

[...] The industry sent assemblers to fetch the material and very often these, especially those from Thyssen and Rombas, did not limit themselves to taking away what they had been assigned to dismantle.

This way of doing things, keeping the appearance of regularity, was abandoned during the last twelve months of the war and the only concern seemed to be systematic destruction.

Machines were dismantled and sent without notice, sometimes even without the consent of the recipient. Anything that was not of immediate use was broken with a sheep and shipped as scrap metal, and the Germans even boasted, at the steelworks in Longwy for example, that they were *growing fields of oats on the site of the factories*.

We summarize below the disappearances of material, but for more details we refer to the special observations on each mine and factory that we give in paragraph 9 to show the situation of the region at the armistice.

Mines

As far as machines are concerned, the Germans dismantled and took away everything that could be of immediate use to them. [...] In almost all the mines, all the workshop machines, ovens, milling machines, planing machines, hammers, etc. were dismantled and taken away. [...]

Metallurgical plants

The looting went much further: all usable machinery was gone and many workshops were completely razed.

[...] The new rolling mills were dismantled and taken away; this is how part of the Micheville rolling mills went to Carlshütte (Thionville), the Rehon mills were taken by Röchling, and the Mont-Saint-Martin mills, in particular the continuous trains, were directed partly to Rombas, partly to Knutange and partly to Thyssen.

Finally, there is the removal of all the stocks: hematite cast iron, Spiegel cast iron, Thomas cast iron, scrap, ingot moulds, ferrochrome, ferro silicon, ferromanganese, manganese ores, Thomas slag, copper, tin, bronze, brass, aluminium. In addition, all the broken machines were sent to the state of scrap; a large part of the Micheville factory was in this state at the armistice because of the lack of means of transport to be able to move the scrap, and in Jœuf one found near a rolling mill machine the sheep which was used to break it.

§ 7 - Research.

Mining. - Geological research.

During a meeting held in Bingen on August 17, 1917 and composed of geologists, mining officials and various officers, it was decided to recognize the true western limits of the exploitable iron deposit, by new drillings which were to extend from the south of Longwy to Mars-la-Tour. [...]

Plants

Nothing was done in the French factories. However, as a matter of documentation, we report on the research carried out under the authority of the Schutzverwaltung to ensure the proper functioning of German industry.

1° To get rid of the use of Swedish hematite, obtaining hematite cast iron by recarburization of liquid Thomas steel;

2° Tests to replace ferromanganese by calcium carbide as a deoxidizer in the converter, a process patented by Deutsch Luxemburg Bergwerks- und Hütten A.G.;

3° Trials to use spar in the Martin furnace (Union process in Dortmund). [...]

4. *Revue industrielle de l'Est*, n° 1283, October 19, 1919, p. 841-845

§9. - Special observations for each mine.

Briey basin

[...] *Auboué*. - Mr. Goujon, director of the mine, remained in August 1914 to extract the mine and to ensure the exhaustion with the few non-mobilizable French personnel, some Italians and Luxembourgers. [...]

On December 31, 1914, with a view to restarting the operation for the needs of the war, the engineer Joesten arrived. In spite of Mr. Goujon's protests about the resumption of mining, and in spite of his repeated requests to the various levels of the German administration for a requisition order for the mine, nothing was granted, and on March 3, 1916 the first carload of ore was extracted. Mr. Goujon was sent to Germany where he remained until December 1st, 1918.

So the Germans took over the mine completely. They brought in personnel from the occupied countries and a large number of prisoners of war, Russians and Italians, whose numbers varied between 300 and 1,500.

According to eyewitness statements, these prisoners were excessively mistreated and brutalized; a task, very hard for malnourished and debilitated men, was imposed on them. They had to load at least

6 wagons, that is 10 tons, 500 per man per shift, and they received vouchers of 20 pfennigs for this work.

[...] The exploitation was pushed without any method. A whole district of the mine is lost, the galleries have collapsed in many places and the tracings have been almost null. In addition, the workers' housing was damaged. Although the machines were not damaged very much, the result is that the mine is unable to produce more than a third of its pre-war output in the short term.

Homécourt. - Fond de la Noue. -
[...] From March 23, 1916, the Germans took over the exploitation of the mine... About 200 Russian prisoners, some Italian and English prisoners and some French, Italian and Luxembourg civilians were employed.

The working time was nine hours and the task at the bottom was successively 10 11 and 12 wagons of 1,800 kilos.

Haut des Tappes. -
[...] Russian prisoners and German oversees were mainly employed.

At the two mines of Homécourt, the method adopted by the Germans was the same: the work consisted of very wide workings, widening of old workings, little stripping, no tracing. At the beginning, the ventilation doors and masonry partitions had been removed at the Fond de la Noue, but they were reinstated. After a year's delay, an extraction of half of the pre-war level can be envisaged.

Jœuf. -
[...] Russian prisoners (about 200) were employed, and lastly English prisoners. The daily workload was 10 wagons of 1,100 kilos.

In 1915, all the tracks at the bottom were removed and only a part of them were put back in place when the operation resumed.

Moutiers. - Mining was resumed in March 1916. The work in the mine was carried out by Russian prisoners and workers from the country without work; there were about 540 prisoners and 190 civilians (French, Belgian, Luxembourg and Italian) forced to work under penalty of fine or prison.

The task imposed was to load 6, then 8 sedans of 1,350 kilos per 10-hour day. Anyone who failed to do this task was suspended from the post with his arms behind his back and his feet 60 centimeters off the ground. This suffering lasted half an hour, sometimes an hour (...)

La Mourière. - Former postmaster Bolot remained at the mine until October 23, 1916, when he was taken away to return on March 18, 1918. The exhaustion, suspended on August 22, resumed on September 3, 1915.

The delegate for the safety of the miners, Champouret, was shot by the Germans at the beginning of the occupation.

Lunardi, an Italian worker from before the war, with some knowledge of machining, was in charge of the central station until October 1st, 1917, when he was sent to Landres.

Colson, a draughtsman, had also stayed, he had taken a lot of notes, but on May 29, 1915, on a denunciation, he was obliged to make all his work disappear. [...]

We employed 200 Russian prisoners, German salt miners, and some civilians. The remaining peacetime miners were sent to Auboué.

Landres. - Approximately 300 Russian prisoners, 80 German soldiers and 100 civilians of all nationalities were occupied in the operation which lasted from December 1916 to November 10, 1918. (...)

Murville. - The workings were stopped on August 6, 1914, on the orders of Lieutenant-Colonel Esenborn under the assumption that signals were given by means of the smoke coming out of the chimneys. The horses were not even brought up from the bottom, and the mine was completely flooded with all the underground installations. On August 21, 1914, part of the village of Murville was burned.

The mine floor was transformed into an ammunition park. Asphyxiating gases were produced in the mine buildings. It is not possible to give any information about the date of the eventual restart.

Anderny-Chevillon. - The Germans took over the mine in October 1916. Before that date they had removed the tracks and trolley lines at the bottom, requisitioned machines and the benzol locomotives. [...] A hundred Russian prisoners were occupied. [...]

Joudreville. - The mine was operated from December 1916 to October 16, 1918. [...]

The depletion had been stopped in September and October 1914, to avoid the signals that could have been made by the smoke of the chimneys, same pretext as in the other mines; it was resumed at the end of October 1914 with Franck, engineer of the house Siemens in Paris, installed by the Schutzverwaltung which directed La Mourière. (...)

There were 350 Russian prisoners, 50 German soldiers and 50 civilians of all nationalities. The Belgian, French and Italian prisoners were employed in the wheels and the railroad.

The mine and its installations are little damaged and allow to envisage, in the short term, a normal extraction.

5. *Revue industrielle de l'Est*, n° 1284, October 26, 1919 p. 869-871

Basin of Longwy. Mines controlled by the Germans

Hussigny. - In June 1916, a strike at the Godbrange mine spread to Hussigny. Some workers were taken to Longwy and released ten days later. A poster had been put up at that time, which read:

"Whoever ceases work in the factories operated by the Schutzverwaltung without serious cause shall expect to be relegated from his present residence and to be compelled to do hard work, without contribution of any kind, or to be placed under arrest involving at the same time a reduction of food."

Godbrange. - In June 1916, there was a strike of French miners who did not want to work for the Germans anymore. The Germans brought in German surplus soldiers (about 125) and Russian prisoners (about 500).

Mines owned by the Germans and operated by the peacetime directors, without control.

Pulventeux. - This mine was in operation from October 1st, 1914 to September 21, 1918.

At the beginning of the war, on August 18 and 19, 1914, the main gallery was obstructed, 80 meters from the entrance, by a landslide of the marl of the roof, and a ventilation shaft was blocked by the beams and rails, on the order of the French engineer commander.

The old ventilation shaft located about 180 meters from the mine entrance and the ventilation lift established in the Pulventeux valley were also partially destroyed by explosives.

Then, the operation resumed on October 1st, 1914, under the direction of Mr. Suttor, the peacetime director, without the interference of the Germans, because almost all the capital belonged to the Röchling family of Thionville. Suttor, the peacetime manager, without German interference, because almost all the capital belonged to the Röchlings of Thionville.

The mine has been particularly well cared for and a number of improvements, including mechanical traction, have been made.

Böcking mine. - The mine is working normally. Nothing to report.

§10. - Special observations for each plant[462].

Center of the Orne Valley. - Basin of Briey

Homécourt. - (7 blast furnaces, Thomas and Martin steel mills, rolling mills).

Of the 7 blast furnaces and their cowpers, only the carcasses remain: the hoists, pipes, electrical installations, skips have disappeared. The suffering machines have been removed or demolished.

The Martin steel mill (3 x 40 ton furnaces) has been shipped.

The Thomas steel mill (4 converters of 17 tons) has been demolished, the converters are lying on the ground, unusable. The casting hall has disappeared.

---

462. Only data about the factories in which Röchling participated in the sacking and looting.

Of the rolling mills (2 bloomings, 1 train 850, 1 train 635, 1 wide flat mill and 1 plate mill), only the buildings remain, whose foundations have been disturbed.

The power plant now only has a part of the engines with their alternators. The others have been shipped out. Three quarters of the boilers have been removed.

The factory is out of order.

Basin of Longwy.

Société des Aciéries de Micheville. - (6 blast furnaces, 1 of which is being rebuilt, Thomas steel mills, rolling mills).

The blast furnaces in operation on August 1st, 1914 remain, but none of them can be fired, all the accessories and the blowing machines having disappeared.

Of the five converters, one remains without accessories and unusable. The rolling mills have been demolished or removed.

At the armistice, the factory looked particularly bad: all the machines that had not yet been taken away were lying in a state of scrap metal, which the Germans had not had time to move.

The plant is almost completely rebuilt.

Société des Aciéries de Longwy. - (Mont Saint-Martin plant: 7 blast furnaces, Thomas steelworks, Martin steelworks, rolling mills, foundries. Moulaine plant: 2 blast furnaces)

Two blast furnaces have been completely demolished. For the others, the superstructure exists but the refractory masonry, sometimes the blowers, sometimes the gas cleaning installations and the piping are missing.

Some of the casting halls were transformed into prison camps.

The Thomas steel mill (7 converters) has been demolished, the four most recent retorts having been sent to Hayange.

From the brand new Martin steel mill (1 mixer of 350 t., 3 oscillating furnaces of 60 t. and 2 of 20), nothing remains. Everything has been shipped to Dortmund, Düsseldorf and Rombas.

The rolling mills consisted of fourteen trains, the nine continuous small-iron train was moved, the rest was destroyed with dynamite, and only the frameworks of the halls and some cranes remain.

A power station is demolished, in another one a group of 6,000 II P was taken.

The Mont-Saint-Martin factory is almost entirely to be rebuilt, it presents a desolate aspect.

Société des Hauts-Fourneaux de la Chiers. - (4 blast furnaces, Thomas steel mills, rolling mills). Only two complete blast furnaces out of four remain, the other two have been demolished. The power station, the steel mill, all the rolling mills (two trains) have also disappeared.

Société des Forges de la Providence. - (3 blast furnaces, Thomas steel mill, rolling mills). The superstructure of the furnaces is intact, the steel mill has been demolished and the whole new installation of the electric rolling mills has been carefully dismantled by Röchling to be reassembled in its factories.

§ 11. Summary.

What characterizes the action of the Germans in the Briey-Longwy region is, on the one hand, the relative conservation and use of the mines, and on the other hand, the systematic destruction or relocation of the metallurgical plants. There is even a graduation that means that the installations used for less advanced denaturation, such as blast furnaces, were sometimes spared, whereas those intended for the manufacture of finished products have - with one exception - completely disappeared.

In other words, the Germans waged war on industry at the same time as they waged war on the battlefield; they suppressed competition by destroying competitors, but they kept the mines, because they contained non-renewable raw materials that they intended to appropriate.

And the whole campaign which their industrial associations have directed to prove that the ore is indispensable to them in the future is the most convincing proof that this same ore is a very valuable wealth and that we should deliver it abroad only with the utmost caution.

Moreover, if before the war one had to deal with the Germans to obtain coke in exchange for ore, the question today is posed in a very different light: if the ore is lacking, the Germans will not care about their coke.

Nancy, July 5, 1919
Félix Leprince-Ringuet

Hermann Röchling: The Factory of the Third Reich

2. Hermann Röchling's radio interventions at the Reich Radio, Berlin.

Speech of February 4, 1943.

"I have just arrived from Belgium. On the way to the Führer's head-quarters, I was stopped to say a few words here on the radio. I have been given the important task of directing and supporting iron and steel production in Europe. We have already achieved a great deal. We can achieve even more. Our planning could lead to much higher figures than those already achieved. The forces at our disposal are in principle enormous. We only need to mobilize them, everywhere, both in the Reich and in the occupied territories. We can easily supply our army, our people and the whole of Greater Germany with what is necessary for the conduct of the war. This in itself is not very difficult, it is only necessary to want it and to do everything possible to achieve it.

"I don't want to talk about all that our men accomplished in Stalingrad. The entire German people have understood this, they recognize the extraordinary effort that has been made. And they also know that this immense effort commits us and encourages us all to remobilize for the great tasks. We have already done a lot, we have already made an enormous effort and we are going to achieve much more, because we all know what is at stake. From now on, women will work in our companies, also in the companies of the metal industry. We will employ them wherever possible according to their strengths and we will make sure that they are welcomed as well as they deserve. The young women, the daughters of our farm managers, will give up their studies except in the case of medicine or something else that is immediately useful to the war. They are going to work for us. A vast field of activities is opened to all of them. It is a question of multiplying the success already achieved and we will achieve it and see to it. Because we all have an iron will to give our Führer, our Wehrmacht, what they need. Long live the Führer!"

Interview of March 19, 1943.

Journalist: "Berlin, Tempelhof. A few minutes ago a small Messerschmidt Taifun plane landed on the airfield of the Reich capital, carrying a man who is well known far beyond the borders of Europe, even to our enemies, the *Wehrwirtschaftsführer* and president of the Reich Iron and Steel Association, the business consultant Dr. Röchling.

"We are very grateful to you, Mr. Commercial Counselor, for giving us the opportunity to speak briefly with you, especially since we know how hard you work and how you continue, despite being well into your seventies, to take on this monumental task of which, I am sure, the public can hardly get a correct picture."

HR. "So you got me again. I thought I could run ahead of you, but it was not to be. I have just arrived from the Baltic Sea and will continue my flight to Saarbrücken. My duties require me to travel a lot. If you can do it by plane, many things are possible. But we have to make sure that, through intelligent management and wise choices, we can succeed in producing everything we need in iron for our soldiers. This is the greatest task we have and at the same time the most beautiful. There is nothing more wonderful for a man in the metal industry than to know that with his work he can give our soldiers what they need."

Journalist: "Mr. Commercial Adviser, the *Heimat* knows you as the man who committed the power and strength of his forge to the German fatherland during the difficult years of the Saar struggle. Today we know that your field of work, this immense responsibility, has been considerably expanded, that you are not only responsible for German iron, for German steel, but far beyond that you also organize European ore."

HR. "Our land is extraordinarily round. In the past I had to fight with the French and the Belgians to defend our Saarland, my *homeland*, against unjustified claims. These struggles lasted 16 years, and today I have to work together with industrialists from these countries to produce what is necessary for the old Europe. Yesterday's struggle was not in vain, since it made me win the consideration of our former enemies, who know that I never want what is in my personal interest, but that before anything else I always try to reach what is in the general interest. And I think that I have done well in this respect, because I have found many friends in those countries with which we were until recently at war. This makes it easier for both of us to achieve what is in the interest of both sides. Our former enemies have a responsibility to look after their people, to make sure they have bread and work and so the circle closes very well. Overall I am deeply grateful to have been given this assignment for which I feel I bring a number of qualities because of that background."

Journalist: "Mr. Commercial Counselor, some thousands of guns, tanks, vehicles, grenades and bombs, weapons and devices of all kinds are made of iron, of steel. The grateful and confident soldier at the front who takes up these weapons owes it not only to the miners who draw the ore, he owes it not only to the men who work in the blast furnaces and Bessemer converters, and who refine the pig iron, he owes it also to the men whose foresight and experience are charting the course for these immense forces."

HR: "We who are at the helm of the metal industry are at the helm of our times, but we are not the ones who create the forces, we are only like the starter who is going to put in motion an electric motor of great power. We are only the small force that sets everything in motion, the most important forces come from our people, from the mass of our workers, our employees, who give us their support, and all of us together are imbued with one fundamental idea: how to serve our fatherland, how to serve our soldiers, how to serve our Führer. This is our highest goal. And this is what we are working towards. And then our prayer remains: may God protect our soldiers and our Führer."

Hermann Röchling: The Factory of the Third Reich

3. *Die Zeitung*, London newspaper

This newspaper was the voice of German and Austrian exiles who closely followed the news under the Third Reich. Published weekly from 1942 to 1944, it had a circulation of between 15,000 and 20,000 copies. The journalists, among whom we find the names of personalities such as Peter de Mendelssohn, Sebastian Haffner and Dietrich Mende, were particularly well-informed and provide us with an interesting insight into the various activities, and honors, of Hermann Röchling in 1943 and 1944.

Source: *Die Zeitung*, October 29, 1943, p. 10-11.
https://portal.dnb.de/bookviewer/view/1026594405#page/10/mode/1up (accessed on 20.02.2023)

Businessmen in Hitler's Reich: Hermann Röchling

"Hermann Röchling is the only German heavy industry executive who still seems to feel comfortable in the media. Again and again he makes political speeches and writes articles for the business press and the *Völkischer Beobachter*. He not only adheres to the regime but lately also claims to be a radical anti-Semite.

The "Optimist" got stuck

"Shortly after Hitler's seizure of power Hermann Röchling together with Thyssen and Krupp played a role in a foreign policy maneuver of the regime. Hitler had an interest in weakening France with internal difficulties and therefore called for an uprising in Morocco. German heavy industry was to supply the insurgents with weapons. The "Swiss" colonial company *Arksis Aka*, which was in reality a front for

Krupp, Thyssen and Röchling, the latter having Duescher, his representative in Basel, in the administration of the company, chartered a German liner "Optimist" to load the weapons and the corresponding agents in a Dutch port and transport them to Africa. The case was discovered and the "Optimist" seized.

"In the Morocco affair, Hermann Röchling played a secondary role. In the Saarland referendum, on the other hand, he already proved to be an important pillar of the regime. He, who in the Great War had done business on both sides, distinguished himself as a fervent nationalist. He provoked the French authorities whenever he had the opportunity, and received some complaisant sanctions that served to legitimize him under the Third Reich. He received subsidies from the Third Reich and spoke publicly at the time of the vote. On the subject of the *Kulturkampf* [conflict between the Protestant churches and the state], he declared:

"Only an idiot can speak of a *Kulturkampf* in Germany. National Socialism takes the fundamental principles of Christianity very seriously. The National Socialist relief, the National Socialist children's fund are the practice of love of neighbor. In the face of such actions, it is ridiculous to talk about uniforms in youth associations."

Four Year Plan and the War of Revenge

"While Hermann Röchling made himself useful at the time of the Saar referendum, his brother Ernst did the same later in Paris. Ernst Röchling became director of the German Aid Association in the Rue Huysmans opposite the German consulate. The regime thanked Röchling for his help to the Fifth Column by easing some of the exchange regulations for his benefit.

"Hermann Röchling managed to establish good relations with Göring through his son-in-law Hans-Lothar Freiherr von Gemmingen-Hornberg. Gemmingen-Hornberg was an air force captain during the First World War and it is from this time that his relationship with Göring dates. He was a strong supporter of Nazi racist theories and was quick to join the "EDDA" [*Eisernes Buch des deutschen Adels deutscher Art*, Iron Book of the German Aristocracy].

"There were still other points of rapprochement with Göring. In contrast to the heavy industry barons of Rhineland-Westphalia, Röchling was ready from the beginning to participate in the development of low-grade ore in Germany. Under his leadership, the Saarland metallurgy group, *Doggererzbergbau GmbH*, Blumberg, Baden, was founded, whose share capital grew over the years from 2 to 40 million RM. The exploitation of Baden's ores was only economically justified if it was assumed that Germany would one day be cut off from the French ore that was 'on the doorstep' of the Saarland. Röchling had therefore envisaged a conflict with France. He probably also called for this conflict as a prime opportunity to regain his interests in Lorraine."

Göring's support

"That he considered the Blumberg mines only in this light is shown by the fact that he immediately wrote off his participation to its sentimental value. He considered this creation to be a preparation for war and that its value would be nil after the resolution of the 'French question.'

"Röchling's political connections compensate to some extent for its more modest capital strength. Although the Röchling group was ranked far behind the large metallurgical groups in western Germany (pre-war capacity about 750,000 t. steel), Röchling managed, through his relations with Göring, to secure key positions in the economy. He became head of the economic group of the metal industry and head of the Reichsvereinigung Eisen and a man of influence in the Ministry of Production under Speer.

"In the occupied territories, too, Göring's support was useful for Röchling. While Thyssen had to sell Alpine Montan AG to the Göring Group, Röchling was apparently able to retain his stake in the fine steel factory Poldihütte, which was also absorbed by the Göring conglomerate after the occupation of Czechoslovakia. A relative of Röchling, Achim von Mosch, a member of the management of Röchling GmbH in Völklingen, was even appointed managing director of the von Mosch-owned Waffenwerke Brünn. This relationship undoubtedly proved to be very useful for the fine steel orders of the German factories and the Poldihütte. Today Achim von Mosch is director of the economic grouping of the metal industry in the protectorate, so that the Röchlings control the central positions in both the Reich and the protectorate.

"In the Ukraine, too, Röchling moved into the shadow of Göring. While Göring reserved the scrap metal business in Transnistria for his Romanian companies, in the Ukraine a man of Röchling's confidence was in charge of scrap metal processing - on behalf of the entire German metal industry.

"Occasional tensions did not change this close collaboration between Röchling and Göring, as for example in North Silesia, when Röchling returned the König and Laura factories, since the Göring conglomerate appropriated the adjacent coal mines. In the meantime, Röchling has established itself in the iron industry of the Mährisch-Osstrau region."

A simplified balance sheet

"Röchling expanded not only into southeastern Europe but also into the East. The companies in Lorraine, which had belonged to him until 1918, were returned to his group. Its domestic sphere of influence was also expanded. In the chemical and cement industries the group also has a strong position.

"In order to assess the war profits made by Röchling, there are some numerical benchmarks. The Röchling-Buderus AG metallurgical plants in Wetzlar are dominated by the Röchling Group although it only owns 50 percent of the share capital. The share capital and reserves of this company increased from about RM 6 million in 1938 to 26 million in 1942. Even the newspaper *Der Deutsche Volkswirt* could not help but comment on the profits made by the Röchlings. It characterized the Röchling-Buderus AG as a 'textbook case of undercapitalization; the intense activity of recent years has led here to exorbitant profits.' For what is Röchling'schen Eisen- und Stahlwerke GmbH in Völklingen (all shares are still in the possession of the family) things are more opaque, since limited liability companies do not have to publish their balance sheets. After all, in 1940 this company was even able to increase its profits by four and a half million RM compared to 1938, even though its factories were shut down for much of that year because of the war with France. *Der deutsche Volkswirt* explains this 'accounting miracle' by the substantial subsidies that were paid to Röchling 'from outside.' In the meantime, Röchling's profits must have risen considerably. A few months ago its share capital rose from 20 to 36 million."

Hans Heidler

Source: *Die Zeitung*, London, May 5, 1944, page 1.

https://portal.dnb.de/bookviewer/view/1026594677#page/1/mode/1up (accessed on 20.02.2023)

"Röchling sucht Kontakt" Ehrenverleihungen am 1. Mai"
Röching is looking for contacts. Presentation of medals on May 1st.

"The 'highest civilian honor' which the Nazi regime can bestow upon its German servants, the title 'labor pioneer,' was awarded this May 1 to nine men, while last year only one was considered worthy of this high honor. Five of these new labor pioneers, thus more than half, are not members of the working class, but are patent representatives of capitalist business interests. But this is not the only characteristic of these new appointments: even more significant for the current internal division of powers in Germany is the fact that some of these new labor pioneers are known for their international connections. The Nazi regime wanted to give the impression that the type of international industrialist who was presumably moderate and rational in his convictions was currently dominant in the Reich, in anticipation of the military decision and the defeat.

"At the head of this group was the business consultant Dr. rer. pol., Dr. Ing. h.c. Hermann Röchling, master of the Saarland's heavy industry and dictator of the German metal industry. Röchling from the Saarland always had a *'westlich orientiert'*: his main interest was to extend the power of German heavy industry to France, Luxembourg and Belgium. After the invasion of the Nazi troops in these countries, Röchling considerably strengthened his influence there, especially in the steel industry in Lorraine. He was often called 'the foreign minister of German heavy industry.' Röchling himself never tried to conceal his political agenda for the future. On the day of his appointment as 'Labor Pioneer,' he gave a radio interview. On this occasion, he made a point of presenting himself as an angel of peace in Europe: 'The work in the European area in the iron industry is extremely interesting. The cooperation with all these people, with all these men from different nations, always poses new problems and brings new and interesting things. When I work in France, in Belgium, in the Eastern countries, it is always the cooperation with the industrialists in the different fields that is most important to me. The most important thing is to have contact everywhere."

The pillars of the Volkspartei

"It is difficult to argue with Albert Vögler of the Vereinigte Stahlwerke, who received the same award as Röchling, about this 'contact' with international industrialists. Both had been leading members of the 'liberal' Deutsche Volkspartei [German People's Party]. However, Vögler hardly appeared politically after he had handed in his parliamentary mandate in 1928. One can imagine that the Nazi leadership speculated that Vögler could be considered by the Allies as a possible negotiating partner. [...]

"The honors that were bestowed on Röchling, Vögler, etc., were echoed in the press with praise for 'German socialism' in order to mask the bad impression that this had made on the German working class. The newspaper *Rheinisch-Westfälische Zeitung* stated that one must always bear in mind that in Germany the economic leader is no longer a capitalist exploiter, but a 'political entrepreneur'. His dominant position in the economy results not from the principle of profit, but from the political trust placed in him by the German 'socialist' leadership. The *Völkischer Beobachter* commented that it would be futile to try to explain the essence of German socialism to Germany's enemies. Ley cut the Gordian knot in his May Day address when he declared that only in Germany does socialism reign, that elsewhere in the world only profiteering capitalism reigns. Finally, in *Der Reich*, Goebbels devoted his last article entitled 'Our Socialism' to this problem, in which he stated: 'National Socialism was and remains that modern political movement which does not use its program as a flagship product to attract the masses. This war is a war for socialism. Production no longer has the objective of increasing the wealth and power of a small ruling class. Who could claim that so far there have only been beginnings? The party leaders serve the welfare of the people alone, the Reich ministers are loyal administrators of the power entrusted to them. The enemy is fighting to preserve an old world that has outlived its usefulness, we are fighting to build a new, modern world. That is the difference. We are the pioneers of a new era.'

"The last sentence is formulated in such a way that everyone understands the allusion to the new 'pioneers of labor.' It is a rather crude attempt to present Messrs. Röchling, Vögler and comrades to the working population as the 'pioneers of a 'new modern world'" and as the gravediggers of the old one that has run its course. These leaders of heavy industry sponsored the takeover of National Socialism and have since followed without fail their power plans, which are anything but socialist. The principle "one hand washes the other" with which the German people were chained between the barons of heavy industry and the party gangsters and ruined must be applied even today in the search for a way out of the catastrophe.

"The Nazis now need the 'economic leaders' for their 'international relations'; the economic leaders, for their part, have an interest in their real power growing stronger toward the end of the regime and appearing without a veil so that they can impose themselves in negotiation with allies as 'solidly supported partners.' It is unlikely that these new 'pioneers of German labor,' as Goebbels puts it, will be accepted by the world as the 'pioneers of a new era.'"

4. Grouven doctor's report.

Dr. Paul Grouven worked as a doctor at the Röchling works in Völklingen from March 1944 until the end of the war. When questioned in June 1947 by the delegated magistrate Paul-Julien Doll, he testified to the particularly poor sanitary conditions in which the foreigners working at the steelworks lived. A member of the NSDAP since 1933, Grouven had been disbarred from the medical profession and the party in 1939, following a conviction for illegal abortion. Despite this ban, he was hired at Röchling to deal with the numerous complaints to the regional authorities, especially concerning Russian workers. Before Grouven's arrival, a doctor, who was herself Russian, took care of her compatriots alone, without having the means to detect tuberculosis or to ensure the isolation of contagious persons.

Source: Minutes of Dr. Paul Grouven, AN BB 36/9 document SEF 806, TG 300.

"It is certain that the situation of foreign workers at Röchling was not normal. The best proof of this is the fact that in July 1944 the Gauarbeitsamt [Gau employment office] carried out an investigation. Imig, who carried out the investigation, told me that his office never bothered lightly and that he was moved by about 100 complaints from foreign workers.

[...] Before I came to Röchling, I had worked at the Ford plant in Cologne. There, the doctor was listened to much more and he did not hesitate to inform the management of anything that seemed abnormal in the situation of the foreign workers.

In Völklingen it was quite different. My superior, Dr. Ossenbuhl, was afraid to voice complaints. He considered my complaints and suggestions to be embarrassing and I felt that it was unpleasant for him to pass them on to the management.

I was never in the Etzenhofen camp, I have recorded in the above mentioned reports what I knew about it.

The Russian doctor made me understand halfway through that she had already had to deal with several fatal cases and Dr. Ossenbuhl must not be unaware that the stay in the reprisal camp caused the death of some workers. These workers arrived in a pitiful state and were noticeable by their emaciation. In general, they did not speak German, so I could not get any confidences. On the other hand, I had to be careful because of my background.

In September 1944, an alleged conspiracy attempt among Russian workers was discovered. Several, including a medical assistant, were arrested and disappeared without their fate ever being known. I learned that in the Etzenhofen camp there was brutality and that after work the internees were forced to do strenuous physical exercises.

***

Three months after his entry in the service of the Röchling factories, Grouven addresses to his hierarchical superior a long detailed report which he will join in appendix to his testimony of after-war:

"Völklingen, June 14, 1944

To the attention of the company's Chief Medical Officer, Dr. Ossenbühl

With a copy to Directors Rodenhauser and Schuler

Report on hygiene conditions in the barracks under my responsibility, with practical proposals.

The alarming increase of tuberculosis cases in the workers' barracks in the East urgently requires that special attention be paid to the hygienic conditions, especially as these carry the risk of spreading other epidemics. [...]

As for the urgent question of tuberculosis cases, I must say that now, with the completion of the renovation of the infirmary, the most important task, the isolation of the sick, has been completed, and as soon as the construction of a barrack for tuberculosis patients has been completed, we will also be able to correct this disconcerting situation that causes them to die continuously inside the camp without being able to provide them with any effective help.

However, the fact that the number of tuberculosis cases in the barracks of the eastern workers has already exceeded 100 and that this number is obviously still increasing - since June 1st there have been 18 new cases - requires additional measures.

It is therefore necessary to question the causes of the disease, which are to be found on the one hand in the reciprocal contamination and on the other hand in the low resistance of the people living in the camps. This last circumstance explains why latent tuberculosis occurs, but also why able-bodied people are receptive to the contagion.

At present, maximum efficiency in work is demanded, while the food rations established by the Reich, which could be considered sufficient under normal circumstances, cannot be increased; this leaves no possibility of acting to significantly improve the resistance capacity of these people. [...] This imposes narrow limits on the lengthy therapeutic procedures for tuberculosis in which the food situation plays an essential role. This cannot be taken into account at the moment.

[...] The physical stamina of those who are already ill but able to work can be improved by assigning them part-time work that corresponds to their productive capacity, to preserve their strength as long as possible for work. We are already doing this so that despite the large number of tuberculosis patients, only a relatively small percentage of 5% are not able to work.

The best solution would of course be for the labor office to take these people away from us and place them where the working conditions are healthier (gardening or agriculture). This would be in accordance with the official position (see circular of the *Reichsminister der Landwirtschaft* of June 9, 1940) that the economy cannot unnecessarily give up the labor force of tuberculosis patients who are willing to work, and that even the phthisis who does not cough much and behaves in a disciplined way under normal working and environmental conditions is less of a danger to the adult than what everyone is exposed to every day in modern means of transportation.

Several cases of tuberculosis were also found in the barracks of the Italian military internees [IMI], and two cases among the Russian prisoners of war. On the other hand, conditions have improved in the IMI camp, where the situation was very worrying when I arrived at the end of March. In the meantime, many patients who are only a burden and for whom the prerequisites for effective treatment are not yet given have been transferred to the military hospital. It is very difficult to get the products for treatment, and sometimes not possible at all. The work in the infirmary of their camp has been going on for a long time but is finally coming to an end.

Fortunately, the cases of edema and exhaustion among the Italians have greatly decreased. I attribute this also to an improvement in nutrition, for which both the AFA [the labor front] and the Stalag are to be commended for their commitment. A few days ago, additional rations were approved for 50 particularly weak people. What is possible for the IMI should also be possible for the workers in the East, who are especially appreciated as good workers.

In summary, it can be said that the health situation at this time in the barracks of the Eastern workers is poor, in the IMI camp mediocre, among the Russian POWs satisfactory, and that the condition of the French POWs can be estimated good, thanks to additional feeding."

5. Telegram from Albert Speer to Generalfeldmarschall Keitel

This "ciphering" of human life, addressed to the head of the Wehrmacht High Command, illustrates the entire logic of the Nazi war economy. Hungarian Jews judged "valid" - after a first "selection" in Auschwitz - were sent to the Reich and employed initially by the Todt organization in construction projects. The installation of underground factories in Mittelbau-Dora and Thil, among others, was awaited with some alacrity, so that they could be used for arms production.

Source: Telegram from A. Speer to W. Keitel, BArch R3/1586

Geheime Reichssache (Top Secret)
June 7, 1944
In triplicate

Telegram!
Generalfeldmarschall Keitel
Headquarters of the Führer

I contacted the SS about the Hungarian Jews and found out that of all the Jews deported to Germany only 50 or 60,000 are fit for work (*einsatzfähig*). The rest were old people, children, sick people, etc. From these Jews, the armament has not yet received anything. According to the regulations, they are to be used first for the construction of large bunkers. Insofar as these construction projects are sufficiently supplied with such labor, I will engage the substitution of Italian military internees in a proportion yet to be determined.

Heil Hitler! Your Speer

6. Letter from Hermann Röchling to Hitler

Here is the complete text of Hermann Röchling's letter to Hitler concerning his cousin Ernst, who had been imprisoned for three months following the attack of July 20, 1944. At the same time a justifying memoir and a boastful statement, this letter contains no less than its share of truth, notably for what it reveals of the relations that Herman Röchling maintained with the Führer, also by its confirmation of the beautiful complicity that developed between Ernst Röchling and the minister Bichelonne, for the benefit of the German war effort.

Source: Hermann Röchling to Adolf Hitler, AN BB 36/6, document TG 185, HR 221.

October 24, 1944

My Führer,

In spite of all my hesitations, especially because it concerns my cousin, Dr. Ernst Röchling, and therefore a close relative, I dare to address you in this matter, which is also very serious for me. If it were not a relative, I would not hesitate to intervene on his behalf, as I have done on many occasions with all possible authorities.

Here are the facts:

My cousin lives in Paris, but he has much to do for us in Switzerland and Italy. He was returning on July 21 when he found in his apartment Lieutenant Colonel von Hofacker, a direct cousin of Count Stauffenberg. The latter asked him to welcome him to his home under some pretext. My cousin granted him hospitality, as he had known him since 1940, due to their common efforts to obtain the voluntary cooperation of French industry in the realization of our war interests. On 24-7 one of the SD leaders, whom my cousin also knew very well, came to his apartment and asked for Mr. von Hofacker. Although he knew he was there, my cousin replied that he did not know where he was. A few minutes later, Mr. von Hofacker was arrested in the apartment, and my cousin, of course, was arrested as well.

There is no doubt that my cousin committed a serious error, at least in theory. Practically it did not lead to any consequences, because Mr. von Hofacker was arrested hardly fifteen minutes later. I do not know what Mr. von Hofacker did. I only know that he was a personal aide-de-camp to General von Stülpnagel, who had committed suicide because he had had SD men arrested. My cousin certainly had nothing to do with the crime of July 20. No investigation will reveal either his complicity or even his participation in a conspiracy, let alone discover a connection of ideas with the events of July 20.

But these are not the reasons why I address you, my Führer, as I would every man who would find himself in a situation similar to that of my cousin. Since 1940, with a happy hand for the treatment of the French, he has been extraordinarily active in improving Franco-German relations whenever it was needed. I put his abilities to good use, and it was not in the least a merit of my cousin's that I achieved considerable successes in the French iron industry, in part so considerable, that I fear that a large number of the men who followed me have already been liquidated by now, or will be in short order. We complemented each other very well. His fascinating friendliness won over the French, while I involved them in technical problems and thus interested them in our work.

Judge, my Führer, how successful this activity was, when in the first days of September of this year we had practically only Nancy left on the left bank of the Moselle, while the Americans occupied the old fortress of Mont-Saint-Vincent near Neuves-Maisons, the director of the forge located in the valley had benzol distilled for us troops and handed it over to us as fuel. I have seen similar cases in the north of France. Of course, it was not directly the action of my cousin, but continually assisted by the minister Bichelonne, there was such a confidence between a large part of the directors of the French factories and us that, in spite of many difficulties, we were always able to settle matters without having to resort to violence. Our relations with the minister Bichelonne were always excellent, and my cousin was really the guarantor. In the same way, for the restitution of the factories of the South of Meurthe-et-Moselle to the Administration of the French owners in February of this year, he led the negotiations in such a skilful way that we were able to restitute factories without having to fear that we would not obtain what we had before. These negotiations even gave us, with the approval of the French, more extensive possibilities of action in the Longwy district where the situation was not so clear.

There is no doubt that it is not in our interest to sentence Ernst Röchling in a way that would defame him. We do not know how we will need him again. I am firmly convinced that the present situation, in which we are forced to defend only our own lives, will change the day we break the enemy's air superiority and acquire our own. And even if this were not to be achieved very quickly, I am no less firmly convinced of our final victory, now more than ever, since after the gigantic blows we have suffered this summer, the Americans and the British, despite all the attacks, have not succeeded in breaking through the northern Front. And I don't think they will be able to get through to us either. In any case, everything possible is being done here to make it easier for our admirable soldiers to accomplish their task or simply to make it possible for them.

If, in consideration of these facts, I submit the case of Ernst Röchling to a thoughtful and impartial judgment, it appears that he has committed a fault which, according to the letter of the law, can be considered very serious, but that it has not led to any disastrous consequences; that, on the other hand, we are dealing with a personality who, in Franco-German relations, has had considerable merits, since we have achieved many things which would have been impossible without him; that these successes were to be obtained only by this means, given in particular our incapacity to withdraw from the French people sufficient forces and means of power which would have made it possible to dominate them; that my cousin has been incarcerated for three months, that he has thus had time to reflect on the situation in which he has put himself by his ridiculous and incredibly limited way of acting.

If I may therefore express a prayer, please consider, my Führer, whether in this case grace can prevail over formal law.

Heil, my Führer, Your faithful HR

7. *Le Monde* of June 21, 1945

A month and a half after the German surrender, the name of Röchling was put forward in an article in Le Monde. *The press then began to shed light on the machinations of the "steel czars" and followed the investigations conducted by the French delegation, led by Charles Gerthoffer, at the Nuremberg Tribunal.*

The post-war plans of German industrialists

Berchtesgaden, June 20

There is a striking similarity between the big German industrialist and the Prussian soldier. If they had the ability, both would be ready to pass the sponge on this unfortunate business of the Second World War for them.

As General Heinz Guderian said, "It would be elegant if the winner and the loser shook hands like the captains of two soccer teams do after the game."

Based on a great deal of information from different sources gathered over the past several months, it is safe to say that the Allies will be more successful in subduing the leaders of Prussian militarism than in preventing German industry from becoming an arsenal of war again.

Both goals can obviously be achieved, but the Allies will have to keep a close eye on these German industrialists, who are finicky, and whose ability to do wonders with ersatz products is unquestionable, in order to prevent the rebuilding of powerful arms industries under the harmless guise of factories producing a thousand and one objects of everyday use.

From the world-famous czars of heavy industry, such as Krupp von Bohlen or Roechling and Rohland of the United Steelworks, to the engineers or heads of research laboratories, all these Germans prepared plans for the post-war period. Although during the war they worked conscientiously for their Nazi masters, they did not forget their own interests. During the last half of the war they probably foresaw, better than any other class in German society, that defeat was inevitable, and from then on they devoted more and more time and effort to the preparation of a post-war plan.

It is also clear, according to certain well-informed people, that these same members of German industry, whose ramifications extend over the entire economy of the country, were able to quietly sabotage Hitler's work in the final phase of the war. This sabotage was certainly not based on a high idea of opposition to Nazism, but simply on the cold calculation of personal interest. These German tycoons said to themselves: "We would be fools to continue playing the wrong horse. Instead of using up our resources, and especially the latest discoveries of our scientific technology, for this war, which is lost anyway, let's save everything we can for later."

Allied investigators have found thousands of cases that support this theory.

8. File of the French magistrates concerning Hermann and Ernst Röchling

One of the files drawn up by the French delegation at Nuremberg, responsible for economic and financial questions, includes several lists containing the names of industrialists whom the Allies wished to bring to justice. At the top of the very first list drawn up by the British authorities is the name of Hermann Röchling.

This dossier also contains biographical notes, based on biographical reference works and Nazi newspapers, but also thanks to the information presented by Franz Neumann in the expanded edition of Behemoth, published in 1944. In this collection we find a rare, relatively detailed biography of Ernst Röchling, reproduced below in its entirety.

The British delegation drew up by hand an initial list of names of people to be prosecuted by the allied countries:

Source: AN BB 35/89 document SEF of April 17, 1946

Roechlin[g] Hermann

Schmitz Hermann

Schnitzler (von) Georg

Schroeder (von) Kurt

Flick Friedrick

Krupp von Bohlen und Halbach Alfried

Pleiger Paul

Poensgen Ernst

Voegler Albert

Zangen Wilhelm

***

Biography of Ernst Röchling
Source: *AN BB 35/89 Document SEF of May 23, 1945*

The German national RÖCHLING Ernst, born on March 28, 1888 in Ludwigshafen (Germany) of August and LANZ Helene is married to his compatriot KORNIS Wilna, born on June 19, 1889 in Baja (Hungary). He arrived in France on December 9, 1932 with a German passport n° 3070 issued in Mannheim on July 2, 1930. On April 6, 1934, he obtained an identity card n° A.A. 54 190 which was withdrawn in November of the same year following a refusal of residence by ministerial decision of November 8, 1934. However, on December 6, 1934, he was authorized to reside in France by way of a renewable reprieve and on November 15, 1941, he was granted an alien identity card.

Röchling Ernst belongs to a German family, whose members, all of whom are Francophobic, must be considered the leading magnates of German industry. He is the nephew of the co-owner of the Völklingen steel mills, one of the most important industrialists of the Saarland, an avowed enemy of France, who has always pursued with his hatred all that is Francophile. He was the cousin of Roechling Hermann, a Saarland industrialist, who was sentenced in absentia on December 22, 1919 by the Amiens War Council to 10 years imprisonment, 15 years of disqualification and a 10 million fine for robbery and wilful destruction of property. Hermann Röchling was also the head of an espionage organization against France before the Saar plebiscite. The agents handed over their information and documents collected in France to the management of the Völklingen factories, which then sent them to Germany.

RÖCHLING Ernst was also one of Hermann Göring's friends, for whom he served as financial advisor before the 1939-1940 war and for whom he made several trips to South America.

In Paris, RÖCHLING Ernst, who was domiciled at 36, rue Scheffer, had represented for many years the Société française des Forges et Aciéries de la Sarre (S.A.F.F.A.S), of which his uncle [*sic*], Hermann Röchling, was the major director. Three-fifths of the capital in this business was Nazi. He also had interests in the German company "Röchlingsche Eisen- und Stahlwerke A.G." and was in close business relations with the bank Bauer and Marchal.

RÖCHLING Ernst was one of the leaders in Paris of the "Deutscher Hilfsverein", a German relief association whose permanent secretary was a man named Reinert, who seems to have been in charge of spying among German refugees before the war of 1940. This association, whose headquarters were located at 1, rue Huysmans, had been included, since the advent of the Hitler regime, in the "Labor Front", under the immediate dependence of the foreign section of the National Socialist party.

He was also a member of the Board of Directors of the Hitler Association "Deutsche Gemeinschaft" (German Union), located at 3, rue Roquepine, in the premises of the German House, whose aim was to cultivate the National Socialist spirit among Germans in France, in the social and cultural fields, and to establish a close link between all Hitler Germans living in France.

RÖCHLING Ernst's past includes numerous connections in French political circles and at the time of the STAVISKY affair he was mentioned in connection with a search of his home and the stopping of a campaign in the "Voltaire" with funds that he had provided.

During the occupation, dinners were often held at the home of Denise DINTEN, a lawyer at the Court of Appeal in Paris, which she presided over with Ernst ROECHLING. Among the most frequent guests were General OBERGH [*Oberg*] and Colonel BOEMELBURG.

RÖCHLING Ernst was arrested in Paris by the German authorities on July 27, 1944, for reasons that remain unknown.

RÖCHLING was considered in the S.S. circles of the capital as a clever man, having "Göring's ear". He had access at all hours to Colonel KNOCHEN[463], deputy director of the S.S. services in France.

Although no information allows us to affirm that RÖCHLING Ernst was during his stay in France a major spy, everything allows us to believe however that he gave himself over to a curiosity of command in the economic, financial and even political domains, a curiosity that manifested itself in different forms, but always to the detriment of our country.

RÖCHLING was fully committed to the Nazi regime, and in spite of the correctness he always observed, he was always animated by feelings clearly hostile to France.

It results from the procedures followed at the Financial Section of the Court of Justice of the Seine, that the named Ernst Röchling, whose civil status will be specified, principal animator of the Société des Forges et Aciéries de la Sarre and its subsidiaries (companies of French legal character but of German obedience) was able to deal in France through this company, since June 1940, for the benefit of Germany, of numerous and important business deals which have resulted in the French economy being deprived of most of the productive potential of its metallurgical industry.

On the other hand, we note that a man named RÖCHLING, probably Ernst, as Reichsbeauftragter Eisen und Stahl, had been allocated a commission of 0.6% on the invoices of the factories in

---

463. Helmut Knochen: Befehlshaber der Sicherheitspolizei Paris, under the orders of Oberg, responsible directly to von Stülpnagel

Meurthe-et-Moselle, Centre, West and North France by BICHELONNE as of February 29, 1944. This commission was to be paid to RÖCHLING by the Comité d'Organisation des Produits Sidérurgiques, known as Corsid.

In May and July, RÖCHLING claimed through his lawyer (the Miss DINTIN, who committed suicide during a search of his home after the Liberation) the monthly payments for the months of March, April and May 1944, which he does not appear to have received. (The monthly payment for the month of March would have been about 200 million francs).

Sources and selective bibliography

For our subject, the archival documents constitute the essential part; some articles of specialized reviews concerning particular points are quoted in the notes, without being listed below.

I. National Archives

BB/36/1-160 Sub-series of the Ministry of Justice. Trial of Röchling before the General Court of the Military Government of the French Occupation Zone in Rastatt.

BB/35 International Military Tribunals (Nuremberg). Documents of the economic section of the French Public Ministry

BB/30/1785-1831 War Crimes Investigation Service 1941-1949

F/1a 3945-3947, F/1a/5847 Ministry of the Interior. Mission militaire de liaison administrative (MMLA) (1943-1944): files concerning Moselle, Meurthe-et-Moselle and Meuse.

AJ/40 German funds concerning France and Belgium during the occupation

AJ/41 Archives of the organizations resulting from the 1940 armistice

Wendel fonds 189 AQ 143, 145, 146, 148

II. Departmental archives

Meurthe-et-Moselle (Nancy)

W 1094 bis General Inspectorate of the National Economy

W 1343 General Inspection of Industrial Production (1939-1945)

Cab. 184 -188 Labor requisitions (Sauckel actions)

WM 282 - 397 Purification Records

102 W 72 Regional Criminal Investigation Department (case no. 1801:
H. Röchling)

Moselle (Metz)

Archives of the German organizations of the de facto annexation

1W 3

1W 109

1W 462-463

1W 522/523

German National Socialist Party, related organizations, companies

2W 246

III. Archives of the Federal Republic of Germany, Berlin

Archiv des Auswärtigen Amts. Files concerning the activities of the
Röchlings in the Saarland and in France 1920-1935.

Bundesarchiv. In particular, the rich press file "Hermann Röchling"
from the archives of the Reichslandbund (BArch R 8034 /III 377)

Deutsches Rundfunkarchiv, Babelsberg and Frankfurt/Main

Geheimes Preussisches Staatsarchiv, Berlin

IV. Periodicals

Parisian press

Le Figaro

The World

Lorraine press

Le Lorrain

Le Républicain lorrain

Industrial magazine of the East

North American Press

Chicago Tribune

New York Times

Los Angeles Times

German-language press (1933-1945)

Völkischer Beobachter (official organ of the NSDAP, 1920-1945)

*Westdeutscher Beobachter (*NSDAP newspaper, 1925-1945*)*

Deutsche Allgemeine Zeitung (conservative newspaper, organ of the Ruhr industrialists in the 1920s, 1919-1945)

Die Zeitung (newspaper of German exiles in London, 1941-1945)

Neues Wiener Tagblatt (1867-1945)

Volk und Reich (militant National Socialist newspaper for the Germans of the periphery, *Grenzlanddeutschtum,* 1925-1944)

Stahl und Eisen (1880-1944) http://delibra.bg.polsl.pl/dlibra

Der Vierjahresplan (diary of the four-year plan of Minister Göring, 1937-1943)

Völklinger Hüttenmann. Werkzeitung der Röchling'schen Eisen- und Stahlwerke (1935-1966)

(1946 -)

Bild-Zeitung

Konkret

Der Spiegel

Die Zeit

V. On-line manuals

1914-1918 online. International Encyclopedia of the First World War.

Encyclopedia Universalis

Larousse

Neue Deutsche Biographie (http://www.ndb.badw-muenchen.de/)

VI. Articles

ARBOIT, Gérald, "L'Utilisation de prisonniers de guerre russes dans l'industrie ferrifère de la Lorraine allemande pendant la Première Guerre mondiale". *Guerres mondiales et conflits contemporains. Civils et militaires dans les conflits du xxᵉ siècle*, n° 202/203, April-Sept. 2001, pp. 65-79.

BLEYER, Wolfgang, "Pläne der faschistischen Führung zum totalen Krieg im Sommer 1944," *Zeitschrift für Geschichtswissenschaft*, 10/1969, pp. 1312-1329.

BLOXHAM, Donald, "The Trial That Never Was". Why there was no second international trial of major war criminals at Nuremberg. *History*, vol. 87, January 2002, pp. 41-60.

BRENNEUR, Pascal, "Les prisonniers russes dans les mines de fer lorraines (1940-1944)", *Les Cahiers lorrains*, March 1989, n° 1, pp. 39-57.

BRENNEUR, Pascal, "Les nécropoles soviétiques en Lorraine", *Le Pays lorrain*, vol. 70, 1989, pp. 48-59.

FREYMOND, Jean, "Les industriels allemands de l'acier et le bassin lorrain (1940-1944)", *Revue d'histoire moderne et contemporaine*, n° 19, January-March 1972, pp. 27-44.

GÉRARD, Pierre, "Le protectorat industriel allemand en Meurthe-et-Moselle", *Revue d'histoire de la Deuxième Guerre Mondiale*, n° 105, January 1977, p. 9-28.

GILLINGHAM, John, "Zur Vorgeschichte der Montanunion. Westeuropas Kohle und Stahl in Depression und Krieg", *Vierteljahreshefte für Zeitgeschichte*, no. 3 /1986, pp. 381-405.

GROEHLER, Olaf, "Die 'Hochdruckpumpe' (V3) - Entwicklung und Misere einer Wunderwaffe", *Militärgeschichte*, 16 /1977, n° 4, pp. 738- 745.

HERZ, John, "The Fiasco of Denazification in Germany," *Political Science Quarterly*, vol. 63, no. 4, December 1948, pp. 569-594.

KRIER, Émile, "La sidérurgie du Luxembourg pendant la Seconde Guerre mondiale", *Les Cahiers Lorrains*, n° 1, mars 1989, pp. 59-68.

LEPRINCE-RINGUET, Félix, *"Report on the entire 1914-1918 service," Revue industrielle de l'Est, Sept-Oct. 1919, nos. 1280, 1281, 1282, 1283, 1284.*

MANALE, Margaret, "Hermann Röchling : un baron de fer allemand en Lorraine (1914-1944)", *Les Temps Modernes* (n° 679, 3/2014), pp. 214-24

MANALE, Margaret, "War industry and heritage: the Röchling factories facing history," *Les Temps Modernes* (No. 673, 2/2013), pp. 76-106.

MANALE, Margaret, "The Völklingen factories, heritage without memory?" *Man and Society* (No. 192, 2/2014), pp. 31- 48.

Sources and selective bibliography

Mioche, Philippe, "Les entreprises sidérurgiques sous l'Occupation", *Histoire, économie et société*, 1992, 11ᵉ année, n° 3, pp. 397-414.

Montagne, André, "Les mines de fer de Lorraine II. The Lorraine Iron Empire (1914-1939)." *Le Pays lorrain*, vol. 71, 1990, pp. 235-247.

Schwartz, Thomas Alan, "Die Begnadigung deutscher Kriegsverbrecher. John J. McCloy und die Häftlinge von Landsberg", *Vierteljahreshefte für Zeitgeschtchte*. 38th year, 1990, booklet no. 3, pp. 375-414.

Seidelmann, Wolf-Ingo, "Die Eisenerze der Baar im Frühstadium der NS-Autarkiepolitik (Schlattmann-Plan)", *Schriften des Vereins für Geschichte und Naturgeschichte der Baar*, vol. 40, 1997, pp. 61-88.

Seidelmann, Wolf-Ingo, "Die Eisenerze der Baar im Rahmen des Vierjahresplans von 1936", *Schriften des Vereins für Geschichte und Naturgeschichte der Baar in Donaueschingen*, vol. 41/1998, pp. 44-83.

Seidelmann, Wolf-Ingo, "Pläne zum Bau einer Eisenhütte auf der Baar (1938-1940)", *Schriften des Vereins für Geschichte und Naturgeschichte der Baar*, vol. 53, March 2010, pp. 35-58.

Seidelmann, Wolf-Ingo, "Die Baar verliert ihre Montanbetriebe (1940-1942)," *Schriften des Vereins für Geschichte und Naturgeschichte der Baar*, vol. 54 (2011), pp. 37- 60.

Seidelmann, Wolf-Ingo, "Auf Messers Schneide - das Schicksal Blumbergs und seiner Industrie (1941-1945)" *Schriftendes Vereins für Geschichte und Naturegeschichte der Baar*, vol. 55, March 2012, pp. 43-70.

Volkmann, Hans-Erich, "L'importance économie de la Lorraine pour le IIIᵉ Reich", *Revue d'histoire de la Deuxième Guerre mondiale*, n° 120, 1980, pp. 69-93.

Wolter, Heinz, "Das lothringische Erzgebiet als Kriegsziel der deutschen Großbourgeoisie im deutsche-französischen Krieg 1870-1871," *Zeitschrift für Geschichtswissenschaft*, 19th year, 1971, pp. 34-64.

VII. Works

ANNÉSER, Jules, *Vautours sur la Lorraine*. Metz, Éditions Le Lorrain, 1948.

AYÇOBERRY, Pierre, *La Question nazie. Les interprétations du natio-nal-socialisme 1922-1975*, Paris, Éditions du Seuil, 1979.

BOELCKE, Willi, *Deutschlands Rüstung im Zweiten Weltkrieg. Hitlers Konferenzen mit Albert Speer 1942-1945*. Frankfurt am Main, Akademische Verlagsgesellschaft, Athenaion, Bibliothek der Geschichte, 1969.

BONNET, Serge, *L'Homme du fer*, t. 1. 1989-1930, Nancy, Presse Universitaires de Nancy, 1986.

BRECHTKEN, Magnus, *Albert Speer. Eine deutsche Karriere*. Munich, Siedler Verlag, 2017.

EICHHOLTZ, Dietrich, *Geschichte der deutschen Kriegswirtschaft, 1939-1945*. 3 volumes:

> 1. *1939-1941*. Akademieverlag, Berlin (Ost), 1969
> 2. *1941-1943*. Akademieverlag, Berlin (Ost), 1985
> 3. *1943-1945*. Akademieverlag, Berlin, 1996

EICHHOLTZ, Dietrich and Wolfgang Schumann, eds, *Anatomie des Krieges*, Berlin, Deutscher Verlag der Wissenschaften, 1969.

FISCHER, Fritz, *Griff nach der Weltmacht. Die Kriegszielpolitik des kaiserlichen Deutschland 1914/18*. Düsseldorf, Droste Verlag, 1961.

GRIMM, Friedrich, *The Röchling Affair*. Essen, 1920.

HALLGARTEN, George W.F., Radkau, Joachim, *Deutsche Industrie und Politik. Von Bismarck bis heute*. Frankfurt am Main, Cologne, Europäische Verlagsantstalt, 1974.

HARBULOT, Jean-Pierre, *Le Service du travail obligatoire. La région de Nancy face aux exigences allemandes,* Nancy, Presses Universitaires de Nancy, 2003.

HERRMANN, Hans-Christian, *Hermann Röchling in der deutschen Wirtschaftspolitik gegenüber Elsaß-Lothringen 1940-1944.* Unpublished diploma thesis, Saarland University, 1991.

HILBERG, Raul, *The Destruction of the Jews of Europe*, Paris, Gallimard, 2006.

HIPPEL, Wolfgang v., *Hermann Röchling 1872-1955: Ein deutscher Großindustrieller zwischen Wirtschaft une Politik. Facetten eines Lebens in bewegten Zeiten.* Göttingen, Vandenhoeck § Ruprecht, 2018.

HOBAM, Nicolas, *4 years of clandestine struggle in Lorraine*, Nancy, 1946.

KEHRL, Hans, *Krisenmanager im Dritten Reich. 6 Jahre Frieden - 6 Jahre Krieg. Erinnerungen.* Critical notes and afterword by Erwin Viefhaus. Düsseldorf, Droste Verlag, 1973.

KUPFERMANN, Fred, *Pierre Laval* Paris, Tallandier, 2006.

LEROY, Pierre, *Plaidoyer pour Hermann Röchling.* Mesnil, printed by Firmin-Didot, 1948.

LOFTI, Gabriele, *KZ der Gestapo. Arbeitserziehungslager im Dritten Reich*, Stuttgart, Munich, DVA, 2002.

MAGRINELLI, Jean-Claude, Magrinelli, Yves, *Anti-fascism and Communist Party in Meurthe-et-Moselle*, 1920-1945, Jarville, 1985.

MALLMANN, Klaus-Michel, PAUL, Gerhard, *Herrschaft und Alltag. Ein Industrierevier im Dritten Reich.* Verlag J.H.W. Dietz, Bonn, 1991.

MARTIN, J.S., *All Honorable Men.* Boston, Little, Brown and Company, 1950. *http://www.spitfirelist.com/books/honorable01.pdf*

MOINE, Jean-Marie, *Les Barons du fer. Les maîtres de forges en Lorraine.* Nancy, Presses Universitaires de Nancy, Éditions Serpenoise, 1989.

MOLLIN, Gerhard Th., *Montankonzerne und "Drittes Reich".* Gottingen, Vandenhoeck & Ruprecht, 1988.

NEUMANN, Franz, *Behemoth. Structure and Practice of National Socialism, 1933-1944.* Paris, Payot, 1987 (1st American edition, New York, 1942).

RÖCHLING, Hermann, *Wir halten die Saar.* Berlin, Verlag Volk und Reich, 1934.

ROTH, François, *Lorraine, France, Germany.* Metz, Éd. Serpenoise, 2002.

SCHMIDT, Eberhard, *Die verhinderte Neuordnung 1945-1952.* Frankfurt am Main, Europäische Verlagsanstalt, 1970.

SCHMIDT, Matthias, *Albert Speer - Das Ende eines Mythos.* Bern, Scherz Verlag, 1982.

SEIBOLD, Gerhard, *Kontinuität im Wandel.* Stuttgart, Verlag Jan Thorbecke, 2001.

SEIDELMANN, Wolf-Ingo, *"Eisen schaffen für das kämpfende Heer!" Die Doggererz AG - ein Beitrag der Otto-Wolf-Gruppe und der saarläischen Stahlindustrie zur nationalsozialistischen Autarkie- und Rüstungspolitik auf der badischen Baar.* Constance, Munich, UVK Verlagsgesellschaft, 2016.

SPEER, Albert, *In the Heart of the Third Reich.* Paris, Fayard, 1971 (*Erinnerungen*, Berlin, Frankfurt-am-Main, Vienna, Propyläen Verlag, 1969).

SPEER, Albert, *Diary of Spandau.* Paris, R. Laffont, 1975 (*Spandauer Tagebücher*, Berlin, Frankfurt-am-Main, Vienna, Propyläen Verlag, 1975).

THALHOFEN, Elisabeth, *Neue Bremm. Terrorstätte der Gestapo. Ein erweitertes Polizeigefängnis und seine Täter, 1943-1944.* St. Ingbert, Röhrig Universitätsverlag, 2004.

WOLFANGER, Dieter, *Nazification de la Lorraine mosellane.* Sarreguemines, Éditions Pierron, 1982.

Glossary and acronyms

AAA: Archives of the Auswärtiges Amt (Foreign Office), Berlin

AEL: Arbeitserziehungslager (labor education camp)

ADM : Departmental Archives of Moselle (Metz)

ADMM : Departmental Archives of Meurthe-et-Moselle (Nancy)

AN : National Archives, Paris, Pierrefitte site

BArch: Bundesarchiv, Berlin

BDIC : Library of International Contemporary Documentation, Nanterre (La Contemporaine)

Corsid: Comité d'organisation de la sidérurgie, an employers' organization of the Vichy regime, created in 1940

DAF : Deutsche Arbeitsfront (German Labor Front)

EPG: *erweitertes Polizeigefängnis* (extended police prison)

Lorsar: Société anonyme de vente des aciers fins de la Lorraine et de la Sarre

GBA: Generalbeauftragter für den Arbeitseinsatz (General Commissioner for Labour)

IMT: International Military Tribunal Nuremberg

MBF: Militärbefehlshaber in Frankreich (Military High Command in France)

MBVR: Militärbefehlshaber des Vichy-Regimes (Military High Command of the Vichy regime)

OKW: Oberkommando der Wehrmacht (Supreme Command of the Military Forces)

NSDAP: Nationalsozialistische Deutsche Arbeiterpartei (National Socialist German Workers' Party)

RESW: Röchling'sche Eisen- und Stahlwerke, Völklingen (Röchling Forges and Steelworks)

Roges: Rohstoff-Handelsgesellschaft mbH (Ltd. for raw materials)

RoMBA: Rohstoff- und Materialbeschaffungsamt (Office for the Distribution of Machinery and Raw Materials)

RSHA: Reichssicherheitshauptamt (Reich Central Security Office)

RVE: Reichsvereinigung Eisen (Reich Association of Iron Industries)

RVK: Reichsvereinigung Kohle (Reich Association of Coal Manufacturers)

RWHG: Reichswerke Hermann Göring (Reich Works "Hermann Göring")

RWM: Reichswirtschaftsministerium (Reich Ministry of Economics)

Saffas : Société française des Forges et Aciéries de la Sarre

SD: Sicherheitsdienst (Security Service)

SEF: Economic Section of the French delegation to the Nuremberg Tribunal

STO : Obligatory work service

VSt or Vestag: Vereinigte Stahlwerke (conglomerate of the United Steelworks, including the Thyssen plants)

WuMBA: Waffen und Munitionsbeschaffungsamt (Office for the Requisition of Munitions and Armaments at the Prussian War Ministry)

Acknowledgements

The author is grateful to Jean-Charles Gérard and his team, who were of great help in my research. I am also indebted to Frau Dorothee Fischer, Deutsches Rundfunkarchiv, Frankfurt am Main, who allowed me to obtain the radio documents concerning Hermann Röchling, as well as to the staff of the Bibliothèque municipale de Nancy, to whom I owe the scans of the *Revue industrielle de l'Est*, a newspaper that is certainly preserved at the BNF, but which is inaccessible to researchers. Mr. Dominique Laglasse and Mr. Frédéric Gaudinet of the Municipal Archives of Thionville, Mrs. Hélène Say and Mrs. Raymonde Riff of the Departmental Archives of Meurthe-et-Moselle have intelligently guided my first researches in a field that was not then very familiar to me. I have also benefited from the advice of Mr. Jean-Claude Magrinelli, a great connoisseur of the history of Lorraine, and from the unfailing support of Dominique Bouchery, who is in charge of the German language collections at the BDIC. I would also like to thank Jean-Pierre Harbulot and Wolf-Otto Seidelmann for allowing me to consult materials from their own collections. My gratitude also goes to Louis Janover, an attentive reader, who followed my work and gave me valuable suggestions throughout this research.

Table of contents

Best sellers Max Milo Editions

Hitler's banker, Jean-François Bouchard

Confessions of a forger, Éric Piedoie Le Tiec

The Koran and the flesh, Ludovic-Mohamed Zahed

Governing by fake news, Jacques Baud

Governing by chaos, Collectif

A political history of food, Paul Ariès

Mad in U.S.A.: The ravages of the "American model",
Michel Desmurget

Mondial soccer club geopolitics, Kévin Veyssière

Putin: Game master?, Jacques Braud

Treatise on the three impostors: Moses, Jesus, Muhammad,
The Spirit of Spinoza

TV Lobotomy, Michel Desmurget